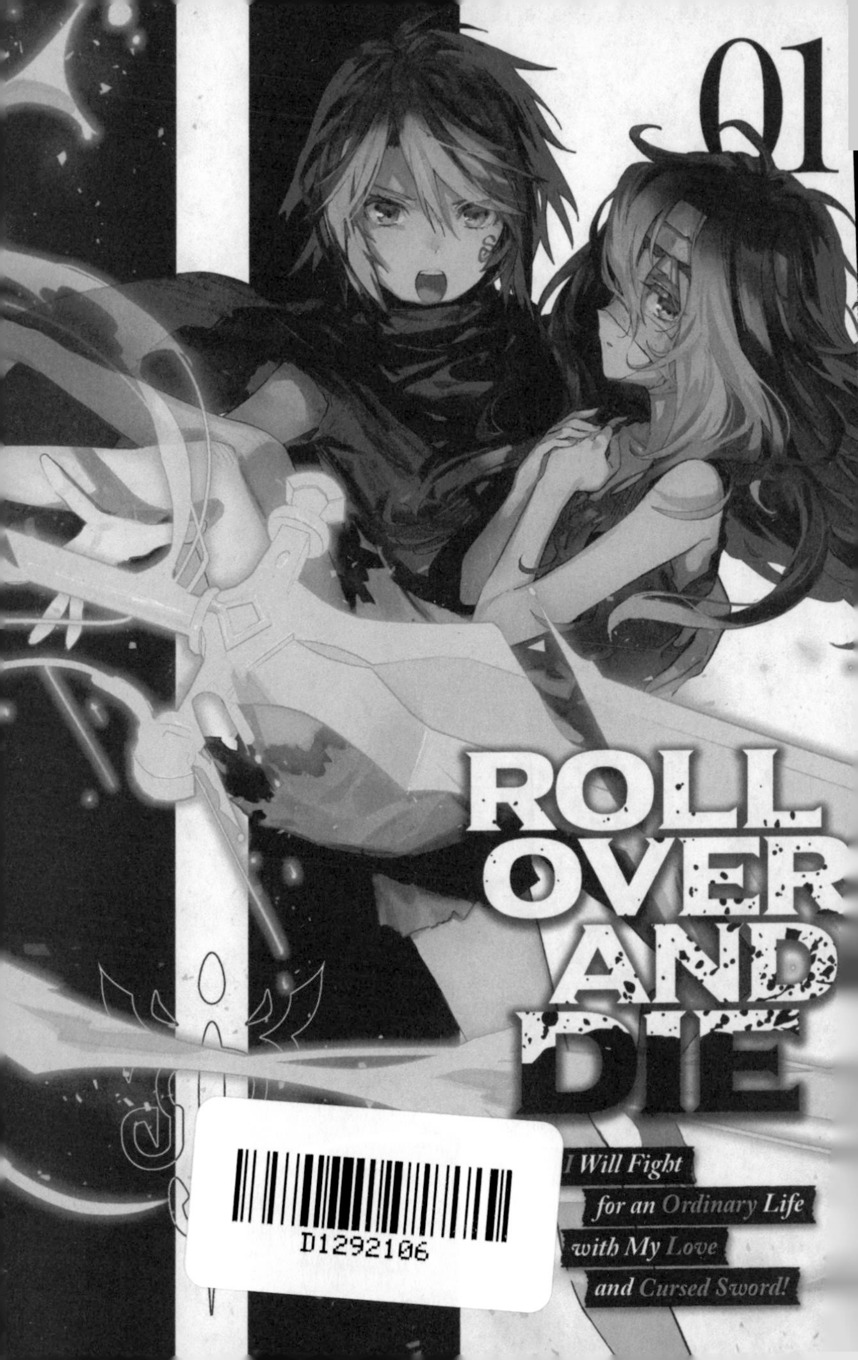
01
ROLL OVER AND DIE
I Will Fight for an Ordinary Life with My Love and Cursed Sword!

CONTENTS

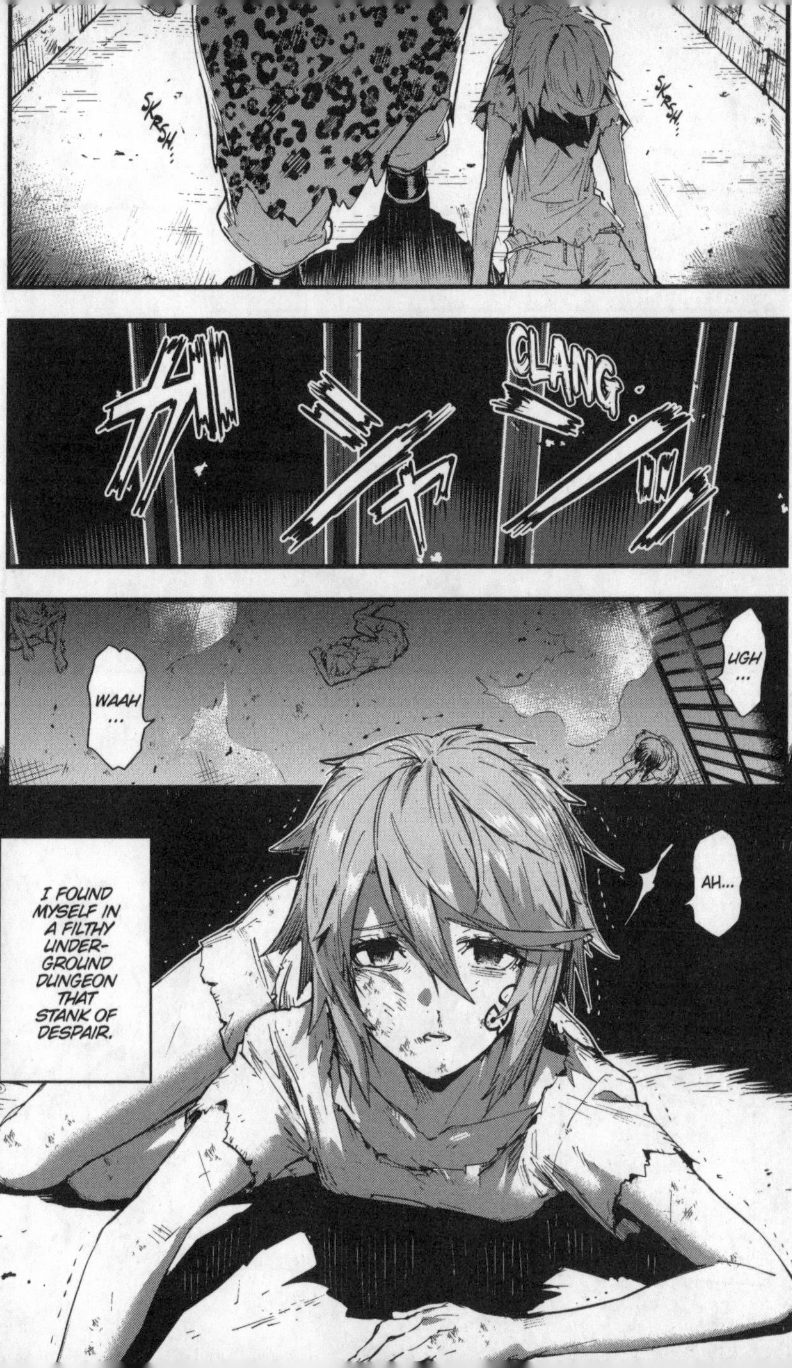
SKRSH...
SKRSH...
CLANG
UGH...
WAAH...
AH...
I FOUND MYSELF IN A FILTHY UNDER-GROUND DUNGEON THAT STANK OF DESPAIR.

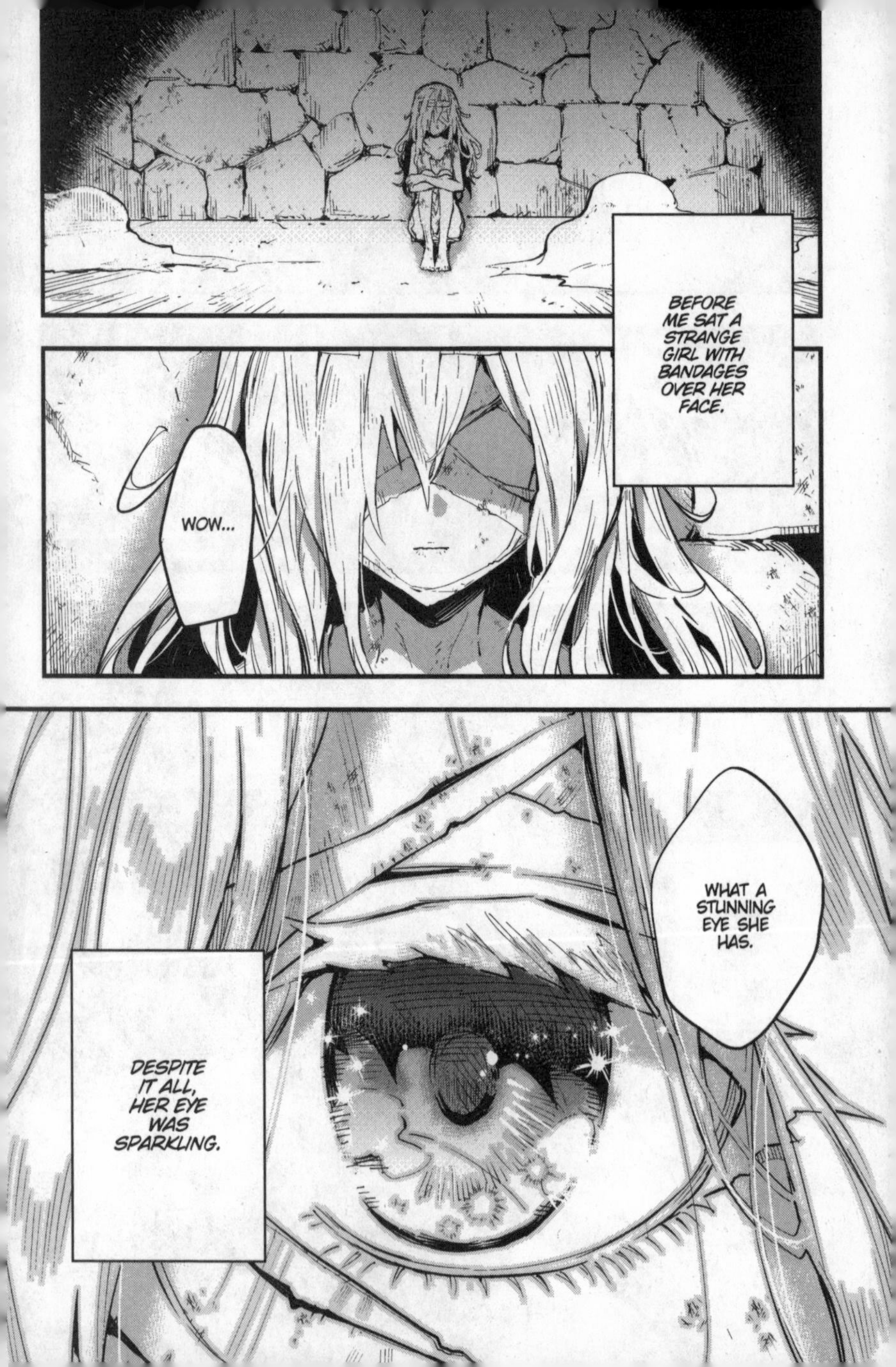
BEFORE ME SAT A STRANGE GIRL WITH BANDAGES OVER HER FACE.
WOW...
WHAT A STUNNING EYE SHE HAS.
DESPITE IT ALL, HER EYE WAS SPARKLING.

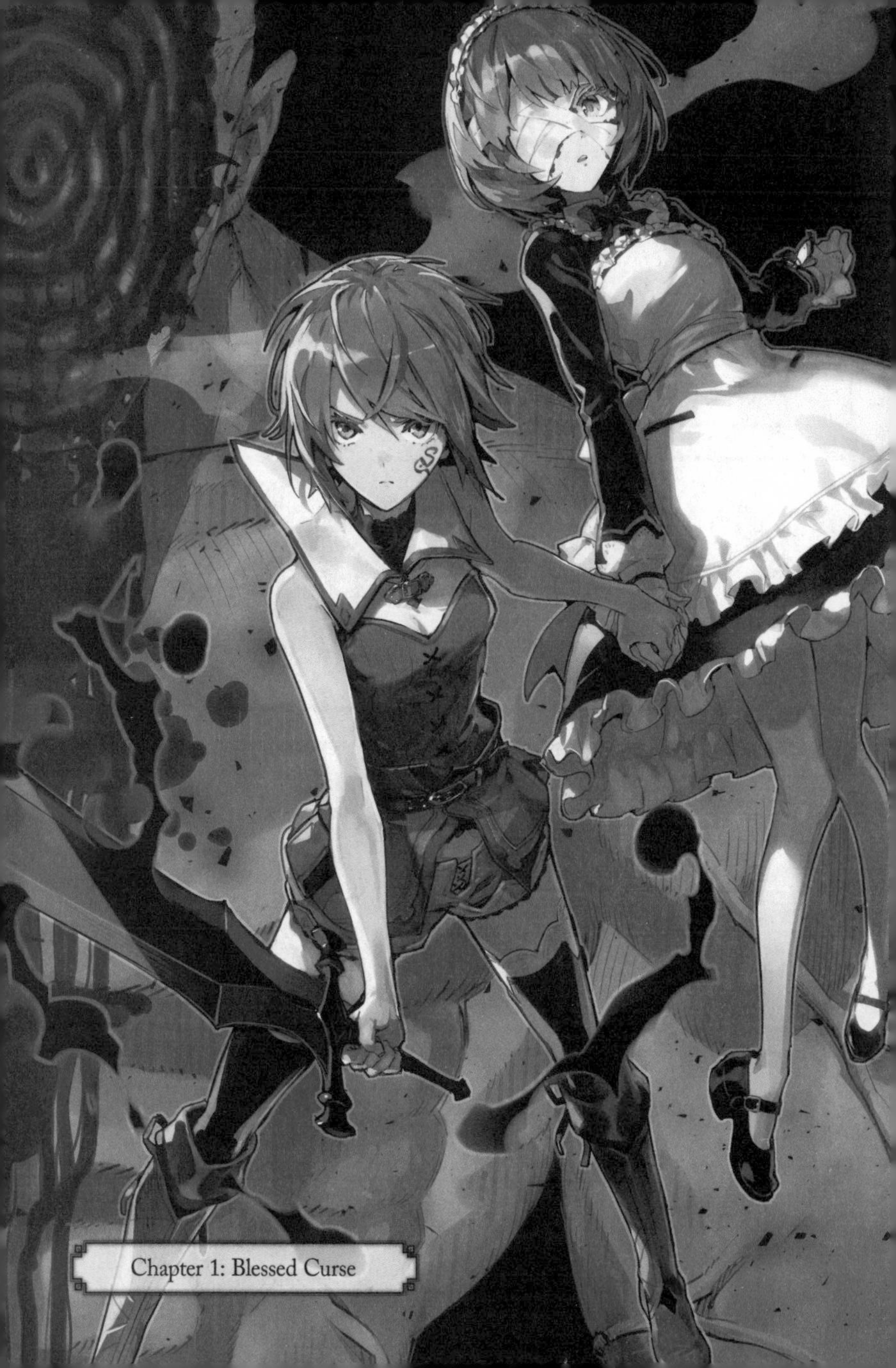
Chapter 1: Blessed Curse

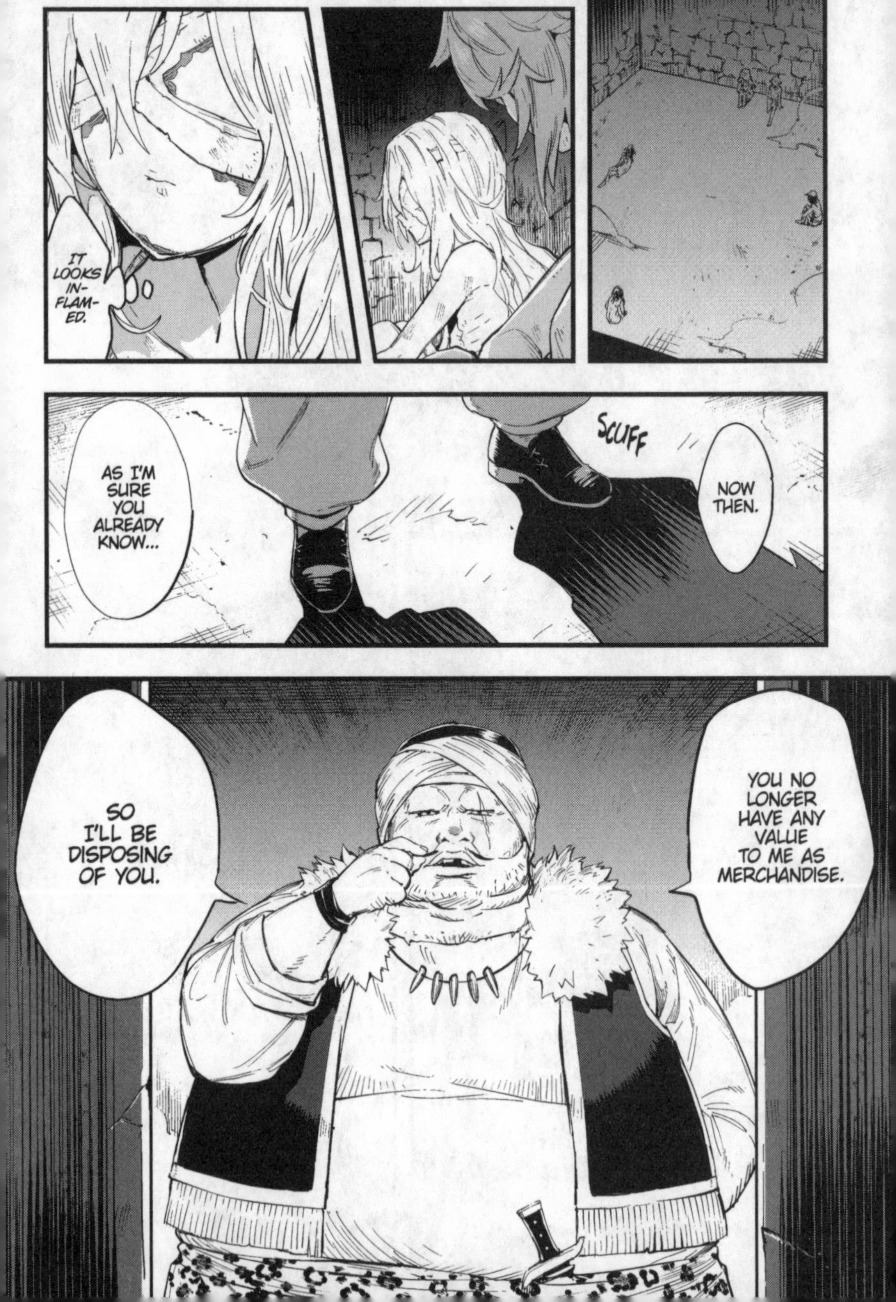
IT LOOKS IN-FLAM-ED.
NOW THEN.
SCUFF
AS I'M SURE YOU ALREADY KNOW...
YOU NO LONGER HAVE ANY VALUE TO ME AS MERCHANDISE.
SO I'LL BE DISPOSING OF YOU.

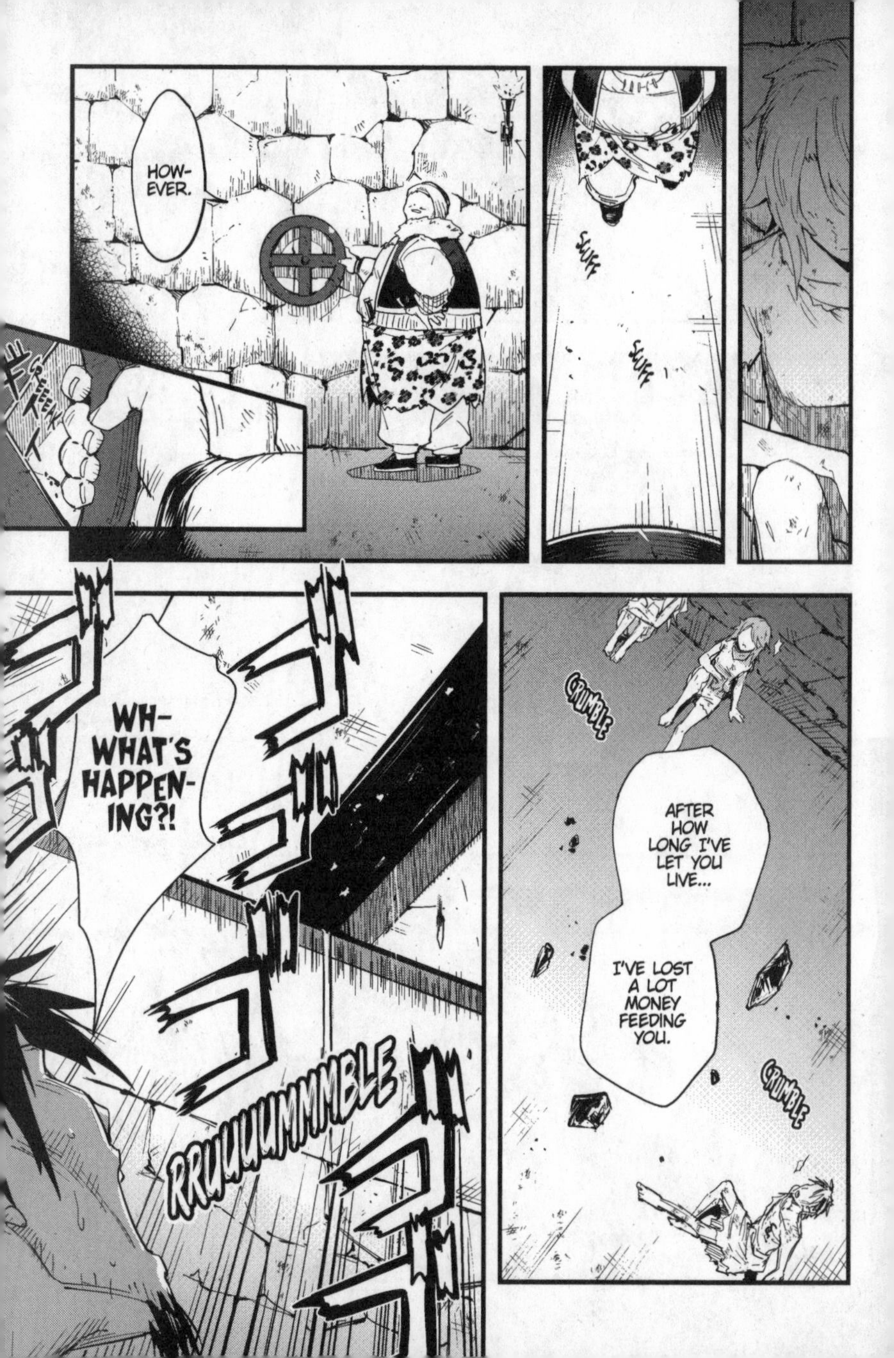
SCUFF
SCUFF
HOW-EVER.
CREEEAK
CRUMBLE
AFTER HOW LONG I'VE LET YOU LIVE...
I'VE LOST A LOT MONEY FEEDING YOU.
CRUMBLE
WH-WHAT'S HAPPEN-ING?!
RRUUUMMMBLE

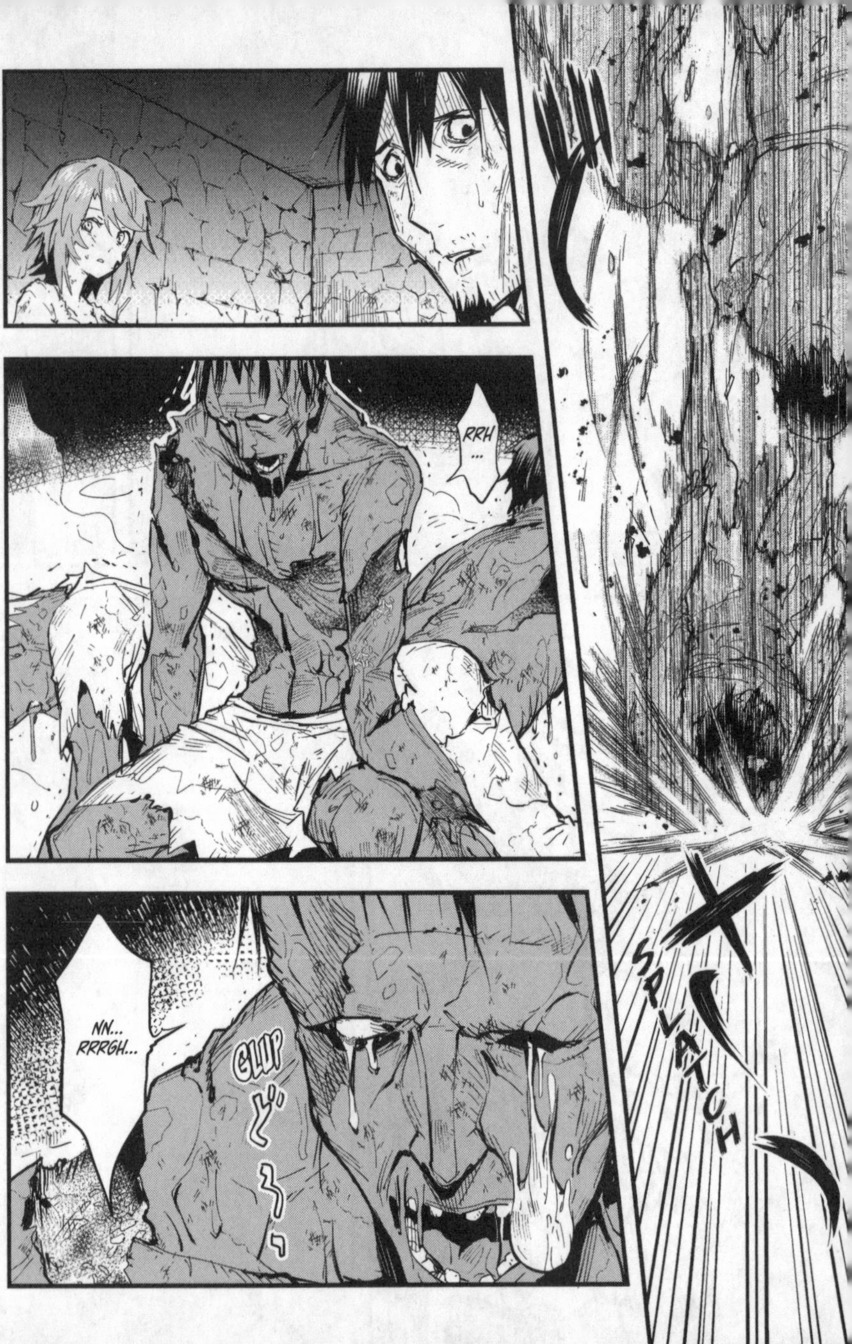
SPLATCH
RRH...
NN... RRRGH...
GLUP

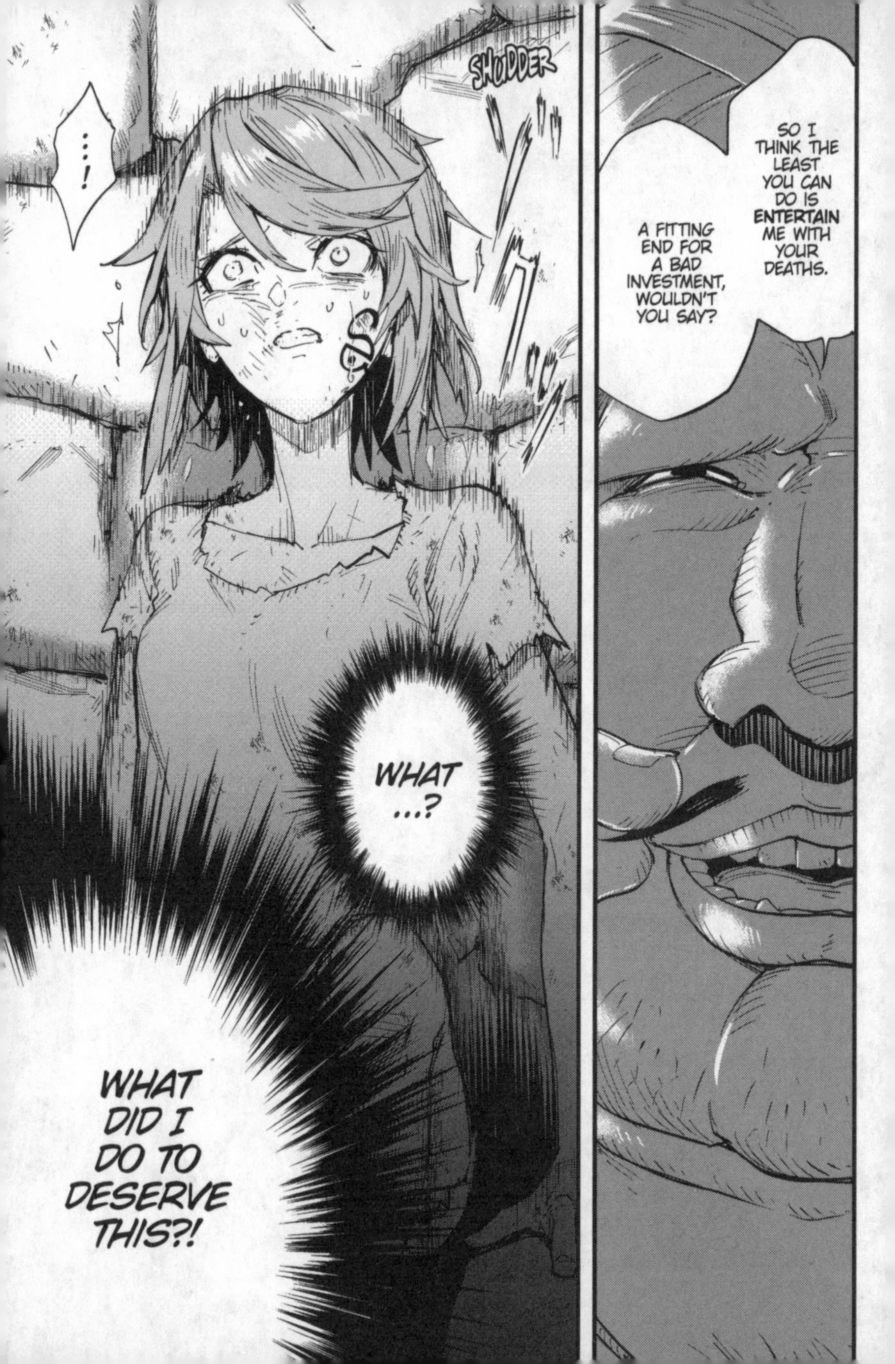
SO I THINK THE LEAST YOU CAN DO IS ENTERTAIN ME WITH YOUR DEATHS.
A FITTING END FOR A BAD INVESTMENT, WOULDN'T YOU SAY?
SHUDDER
...!
WHAT ...?
WHAT DID I DO TO DESERVE THIS?!

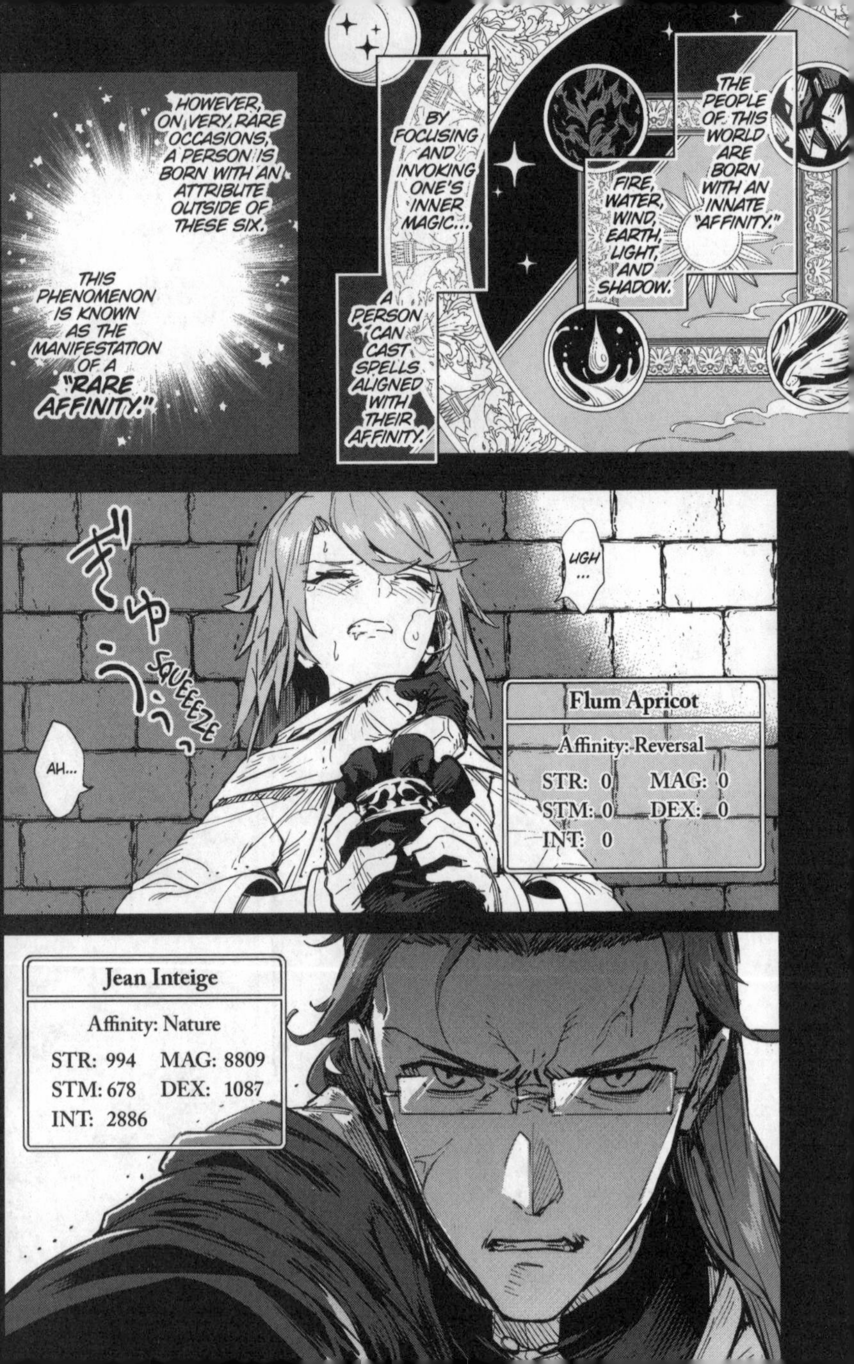
THE PEOPLE OF THIS WORLD ARE BORN WITH AN INNATE "AFFINITY."
FIRE, WATER, WIND, EARTH, LIGHT, AND SHADOW.
BY FOCUSING AND INVOKING ONE'S INNER MAGIC...
A PERSON CAN CAST SPELLS ALIGNED WITH THEIR AFFINITY.
HOWEVER, ON VERY RARE OCCASIONS, A PERSON IS BORN WITH AN ATTRIBUTE OUTSIDE OF THESE SIX.
THIS PHENOMENON IS KNOWN AS THE MANIFESTATION OF A "RARE AFFINITY."
UGH...
Flum Apricot
Affinity: Reversal
STR: 0 MAG: 0
STM: 0 DEX: 0
INT: 0
SQUEEEEZE
AH...
Jean Inteige
Affinity: Nature
STR: 994 MAG: 8809
STM: 678 DEX: 1087
INT: 2886

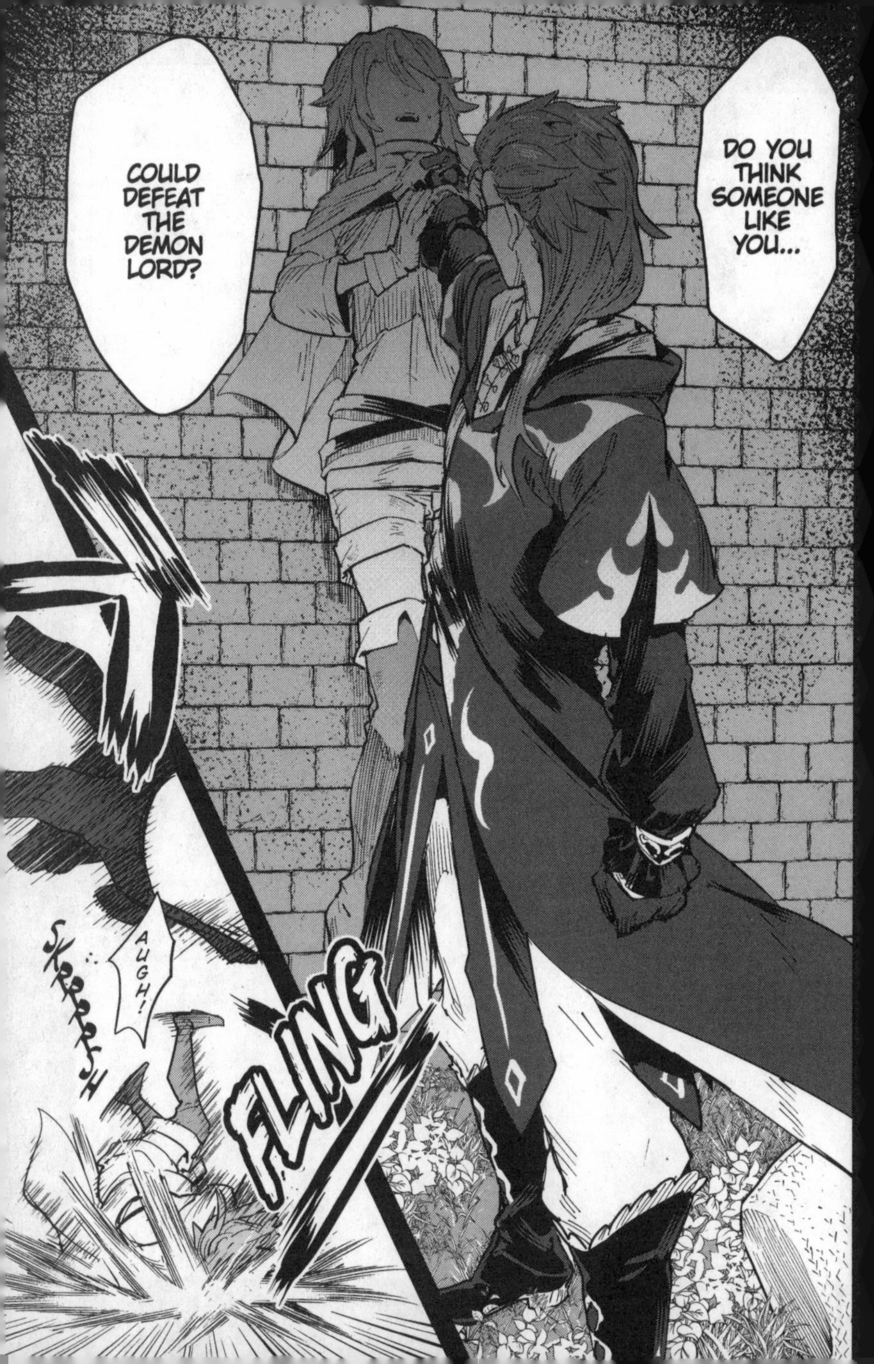
DO YOU THINK SOMEONE LIKE YOU...
COULD DEFEAT THE DEMON LORD?
FLING
AUGH!
SKRRRRSH

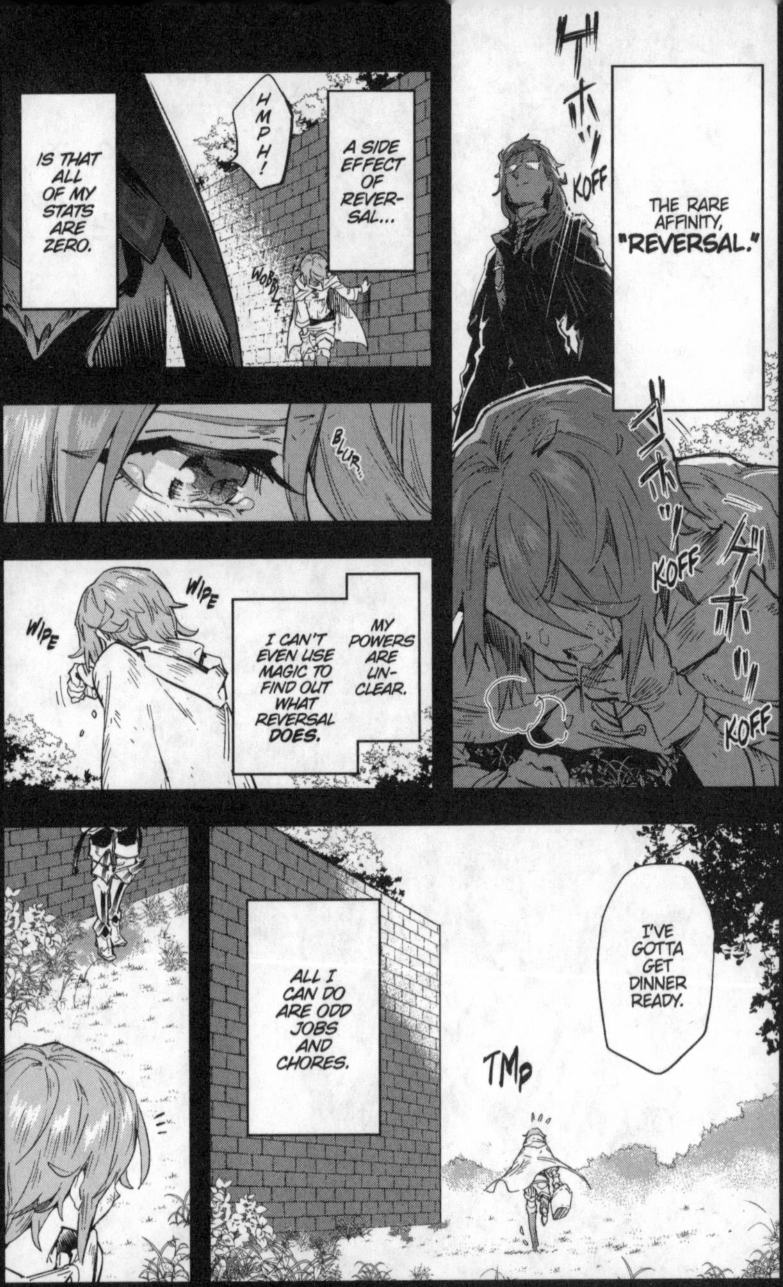
KOFF
THE RARE AFFINITY, "REVERSAL."
KOFF
KOFF
A SIDE EFFECT OF REVER-SAL...
HMPH!
WOBBLE
IS THAT ALL OF MY STATS ARE ZERO.
BLUR
MY POWERS ARE UN-CLEAR.
I CAN'T EVEN USE MAGIC TO FIND OUT WHAT REVERSAL DOES.
WIPE
WIPE
I'VE GOTTA GET DINNER READY.
TMP
ALL I CAN DO ARE ODD JOBS AND CHORES.

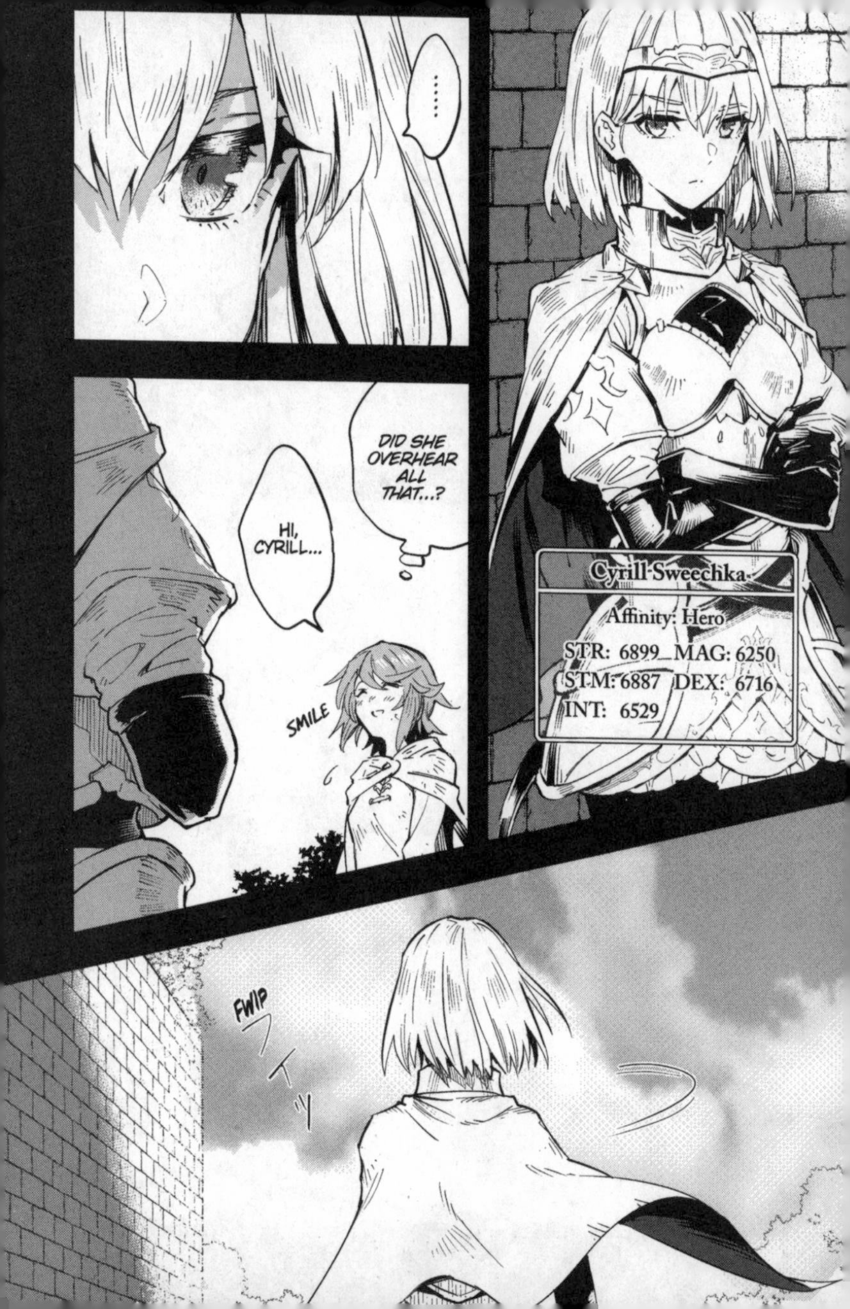
Cyrill Sweechka
Affinity: Hero
STR: 6899 MAG: 6250
STM: 6887 DEX: 6716
INT: 6529
......
DID SHE OVERHEAR ALL THAT...?
HI, CYRILL...
SMILE
FWIP

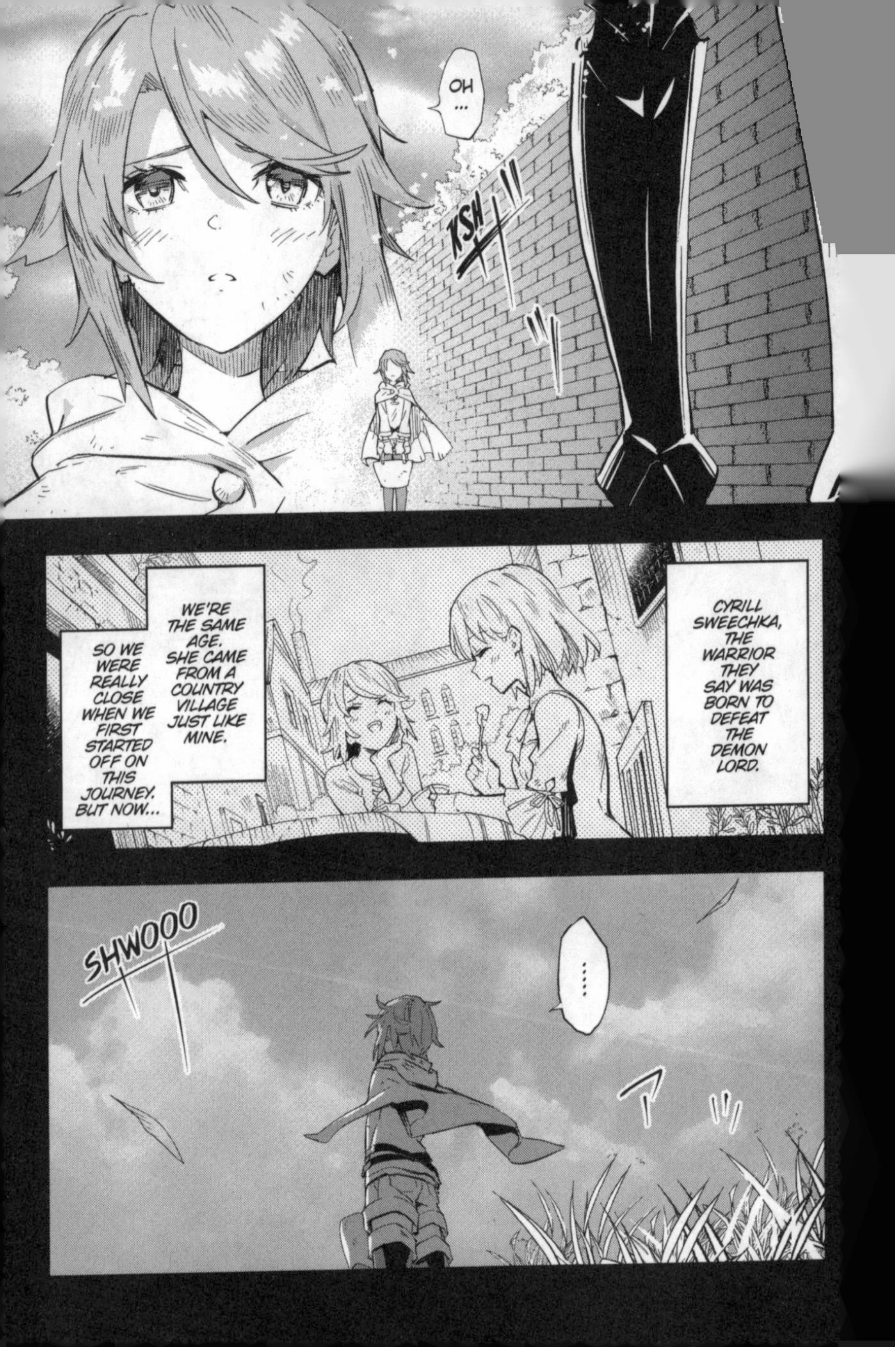
OH ...
KSH
CYRILL SWEECHKA, THE WARRIOR THEY SAY WAS BORN TO DEFEAT THE DEMON LORD.
WE'RE THE SAME AGE. SHE CAME FROM A COUNTRY VILLAGE JUST LIKE MINE.
SO WE WERE REALLY CLOSE WHEN WE FIRST STARTED OFF ON THIS JOURNEY. BUT NOW...
.....
SHWOOO

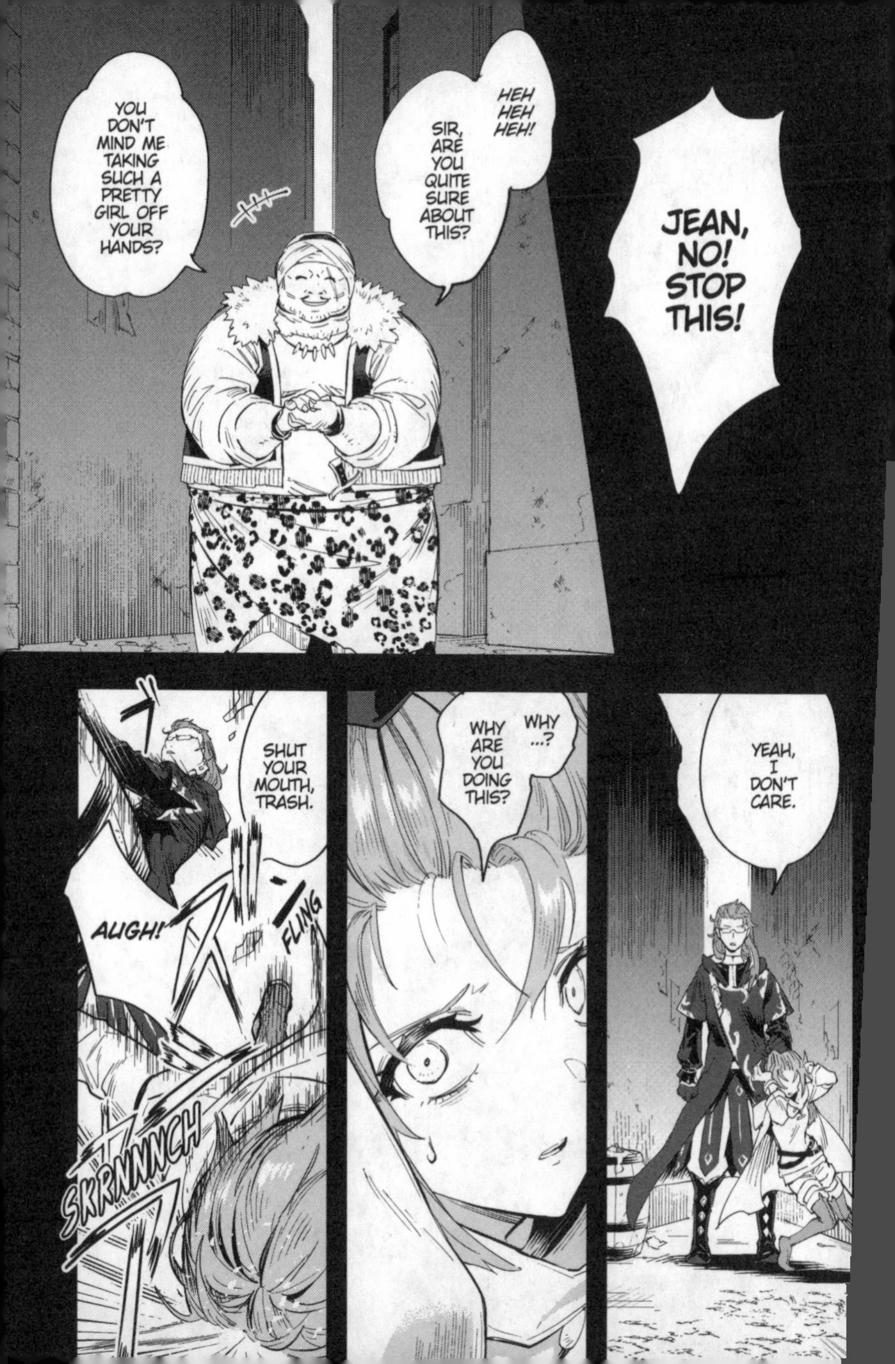
JEAN, NO! STOP THIS!
HEH HEH HEH!
SIR, ARE YOU QUITE SURE ABOUT THIS?
YOU DON'T MIND ME TAKING SUCH A PRETTY GIRL OFF YOUR HANDS?
YEAH, I DON'T CARE.
WHY ...?
WHY ARE YOU DOING THIS?
SHUT YOUR MOUTH, TRASH.
FLING
AUGH!
SKRNNNCH

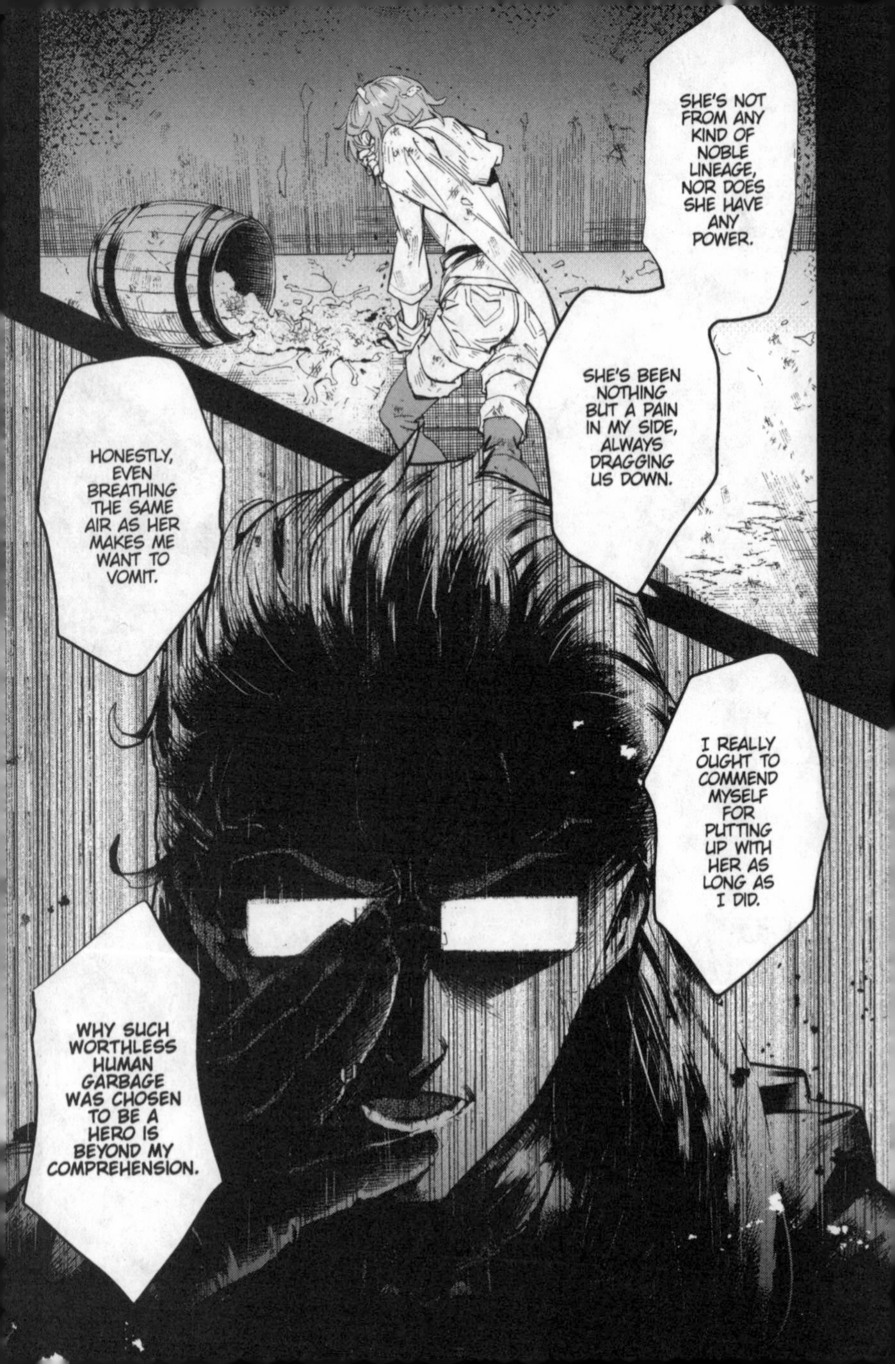
SHE'S NOT FROM ANY KIND OF NOBLE LINEAGE, NOR DOES SHE HAVE ANY POWER.
SHE'S BEEN NOTHING BUT A PAIN IN MY SIDE, ALWAYS DRAGGING US DOWN.
HONESTLY, EVEN BREATHING THE SAME AIR AS HER MAKES ME WANT TO VOMIT.
I REALLY OUGHT TO COMMEND MYSELF FOR PUTTING UP WITH HER AS LONG AS I DID.
WHY SUCH WORTHLESS HUMAN GARBAGE WAS CHOSEN TO BE A HERO IS BEYOND MY COMPREHENSION.

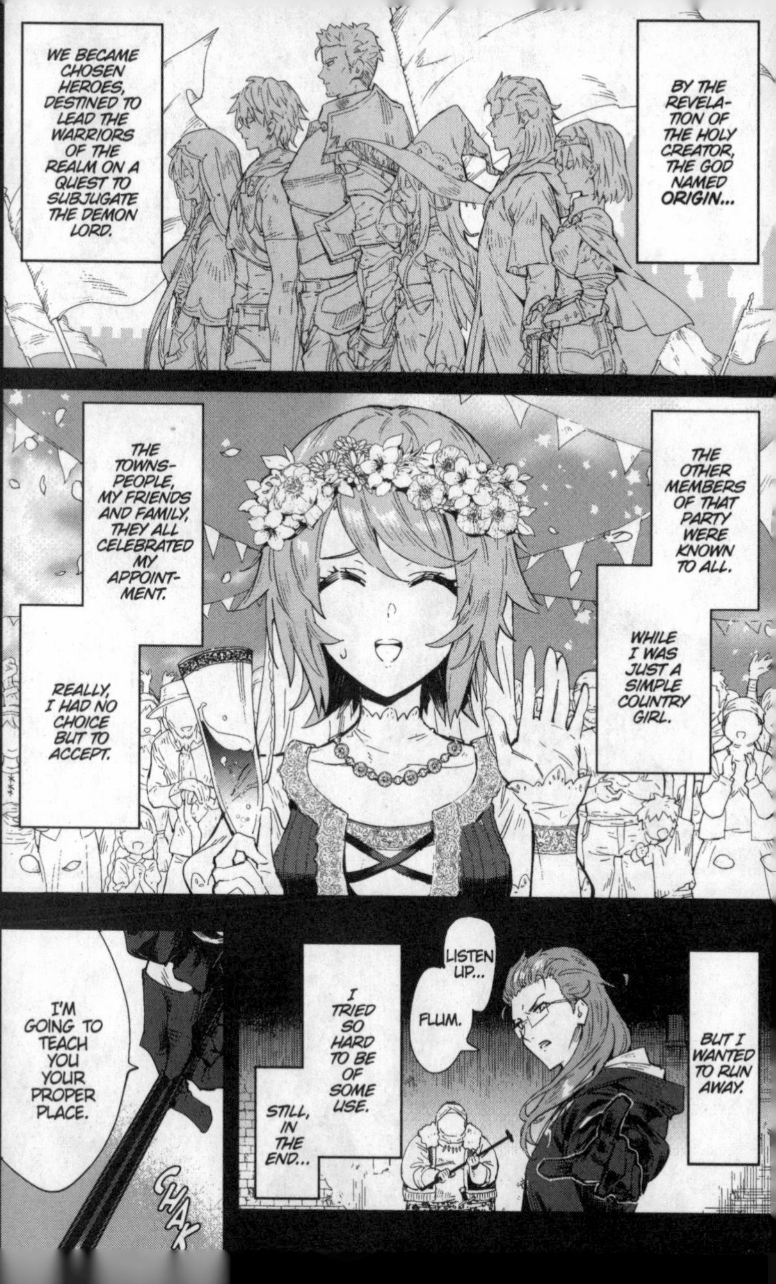
BY THE REVELATION OF THE HOLY CREATOR, THE GOD NAMED ORIGIN...
WE BECAME CHOSEN HEROES, DESTINED TO LEAD THE WARRIORS OF THE REALM ON A QUEST TO SUBJUGATE THE DEMON LORD.
THE OTHER MEMBERS OF THAT PARTY WERE KNOWN TO ALL.
WHILE I WAS JUST A SIMPLE COUNTRY GIRL.
THE TOWNSPEOPLE, MY FRIENDS AND FAMILY, THEY ALL CELEBRATED MY APPOINTMENT.
REALLY, I HAD NO CHOICE BUT TO ACCEPT.
BUT I WANTED TO RUN AWAY.
LISTEN UP...
FLUM.
I TRIED SO HARD TO BE OF SOME USE.
STILL, IN THE END...
I'M GOING TO TEACH YOU YOUR PROPER PLACE.
CHAK

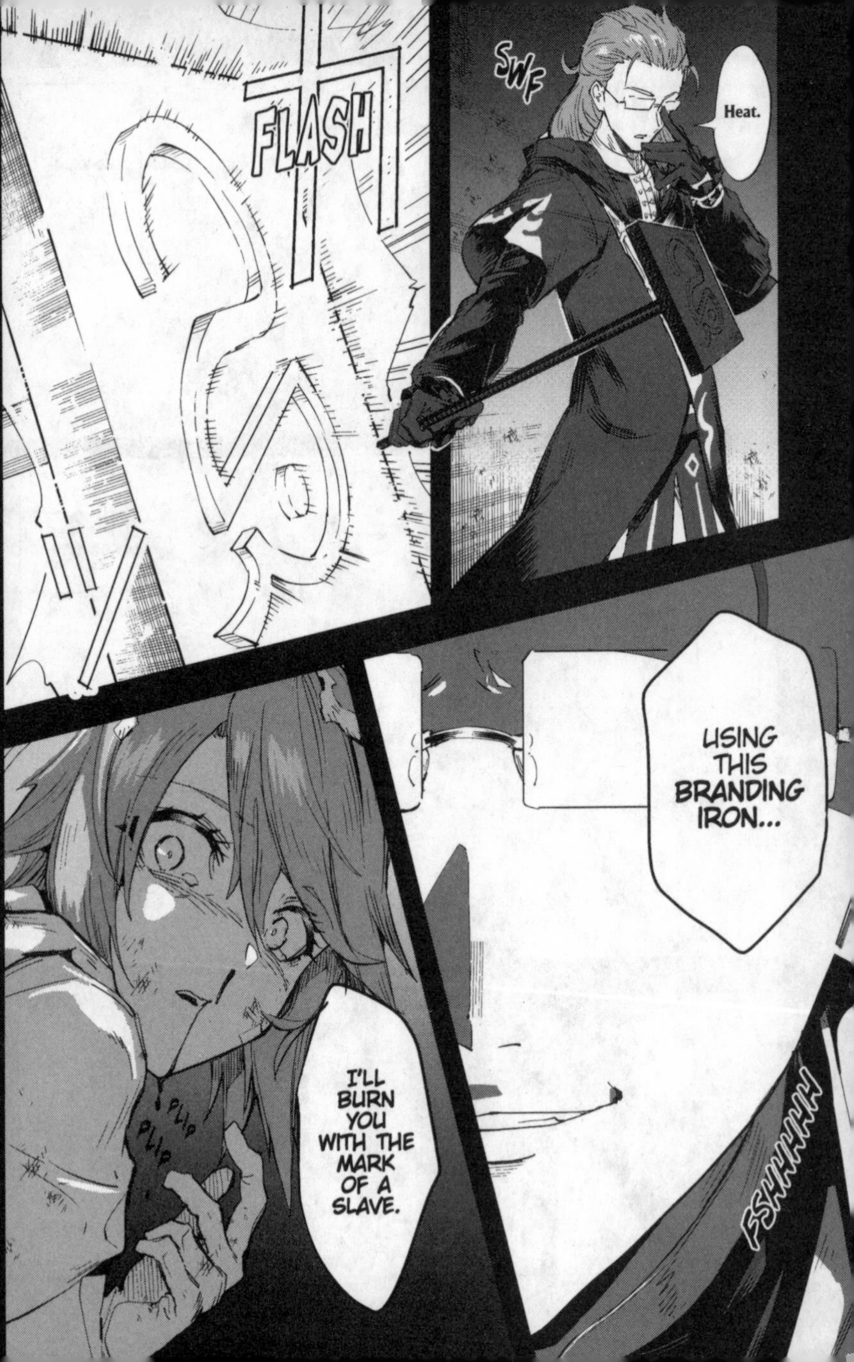
SWF
Heat.
FLASH
USING THIS BRANDING IRON...
FSHHHHH
I'LL BURN YOU WITH THE MARK OF A SLAVE.
PLIP
PLIP

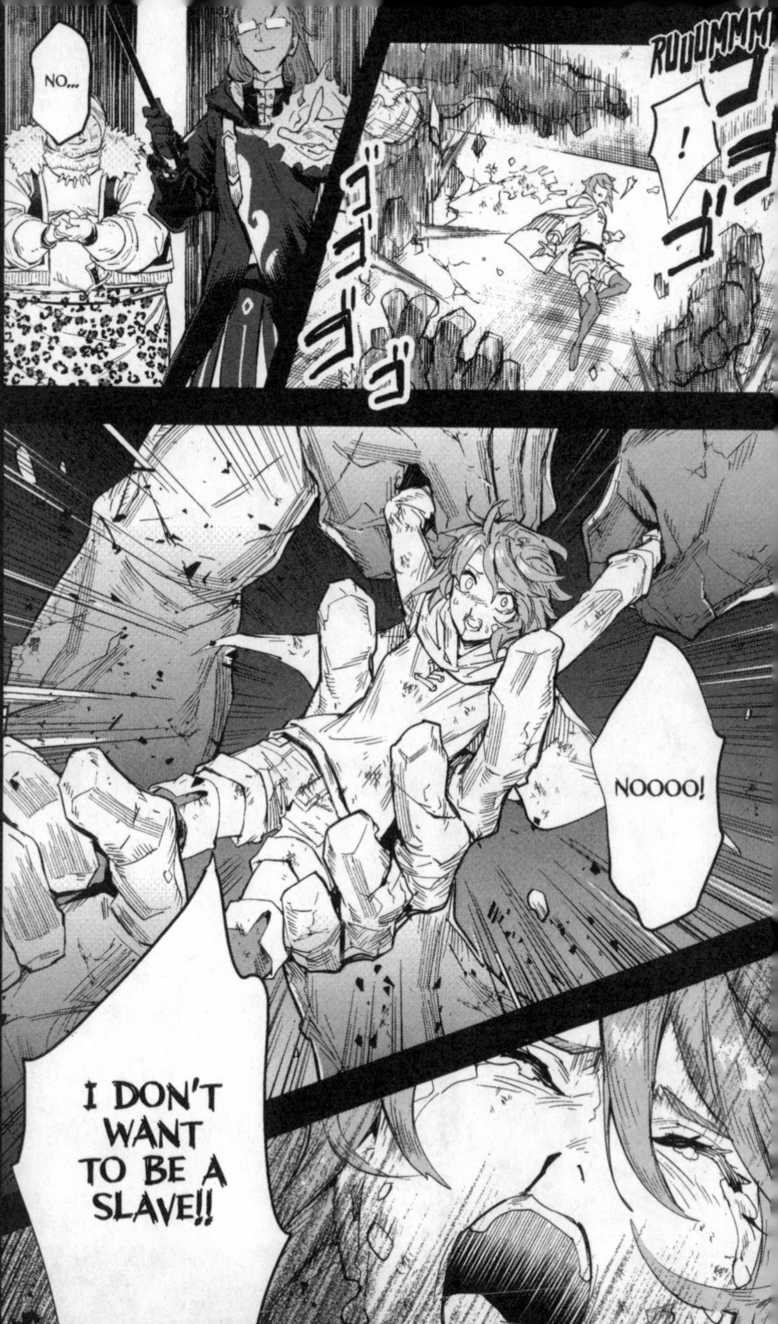

RUUUMMM
!
ゴゴゴゴ
NO...
NOOOO!
I DON'T WANT TO BE A SLAVE!!

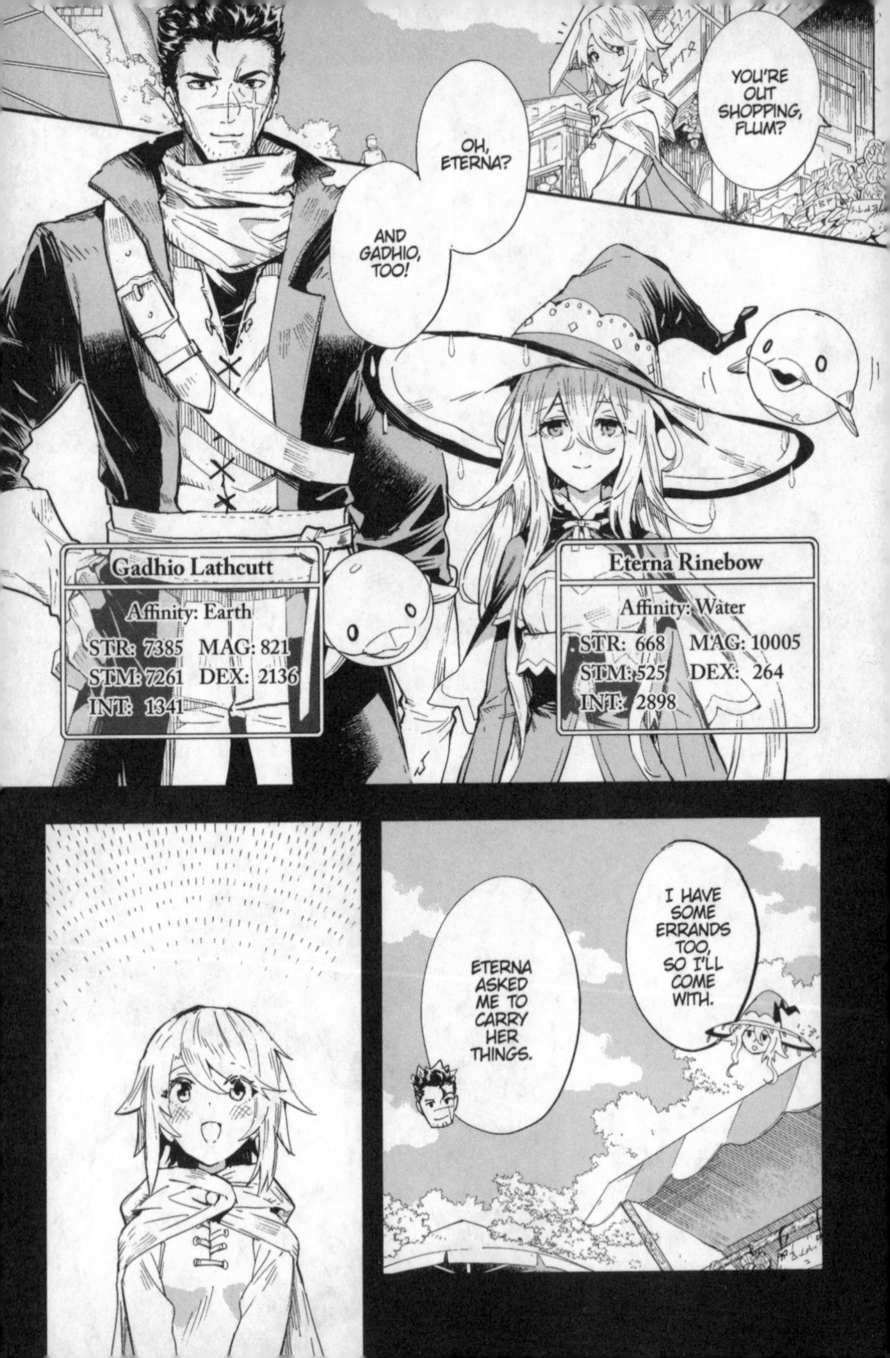
YOU'RE OUT SHOPPING, FLUM?
OH, ETERNA?
AND GADHIO, TOO!
Eterna Rinebow
Affinity: Water
STR: 668 MAG: 10005
STM: 525 DEX: 264
INT: 2898
Gadhio Lathcutt
Affinity: Earth
STR: 7385 MAG: 821
STM: 7261 DEX: 2136
INT: 1341
I HAVE SOME ERRANDS TOO, SO I'LL COME WITH.
ETERNA ASKED ME TO CARRY HER THINGS.

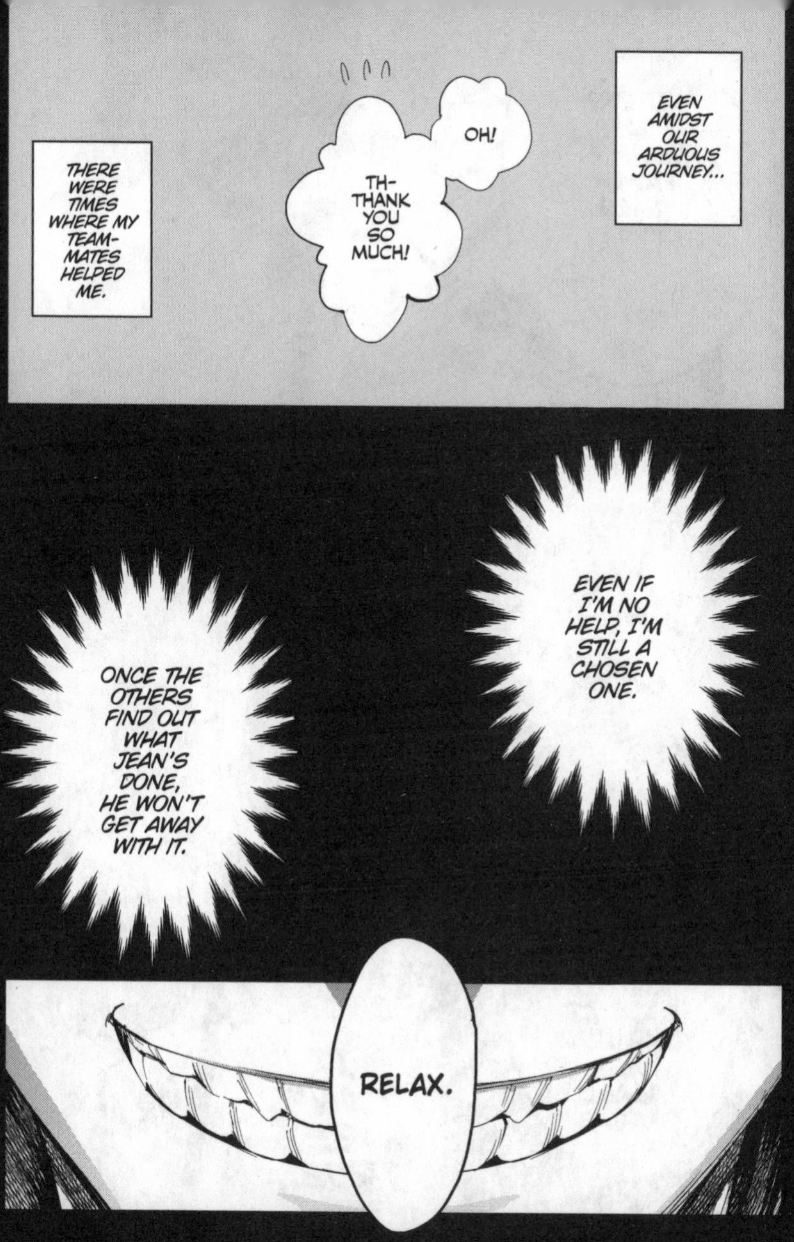
EVEN AMIDST OUR ARDUOUS JOURNEY...
OH!
TH-THANK YOU SO MUCH!
THERE WERE TIMES WHERE MY TEAM-MATES HELPED ME.
EVEN IF I'M NO HELP, I'M STILL A CHOSEN ONE.
ONCE THE OTHERS FIND OUT WHAT JEAN'S DONE, HE WON'T GET AWAY WITH IT.
RELAX.

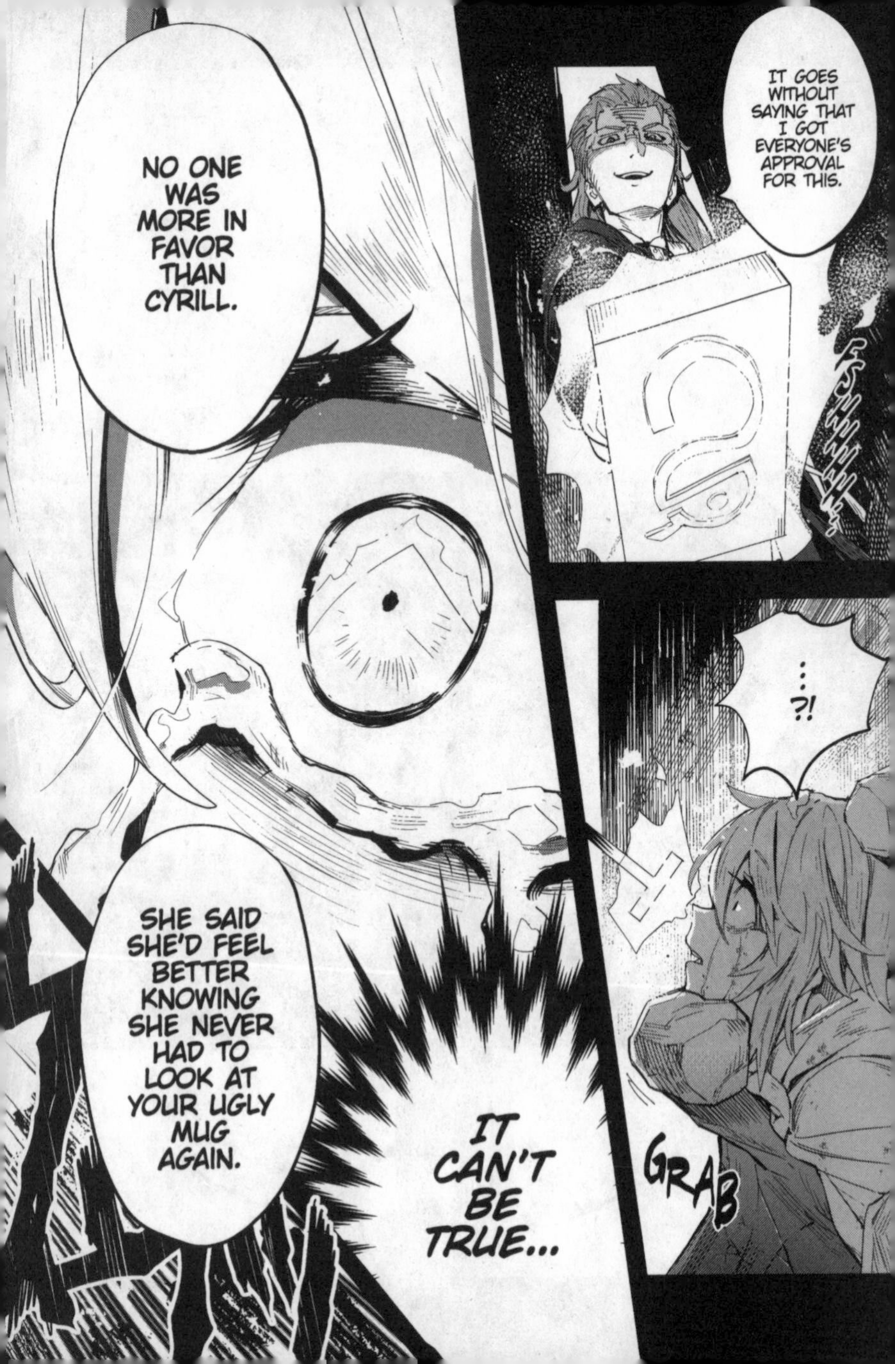
IT GOES WITHOUT SAYING THAT I GOT EVERYONE'S APPROVAL FOR THIS.
...?!
GRAB
NO ONE WAS MORE IN FAVOR THAN CYRILL.
SHE SAID SHE'D FEEL BETTER KNOWING SHE NEVER HAD TO LOOK AT YOUR UGLY MUG AGAIN.
IT CAN'T BE TRUE...

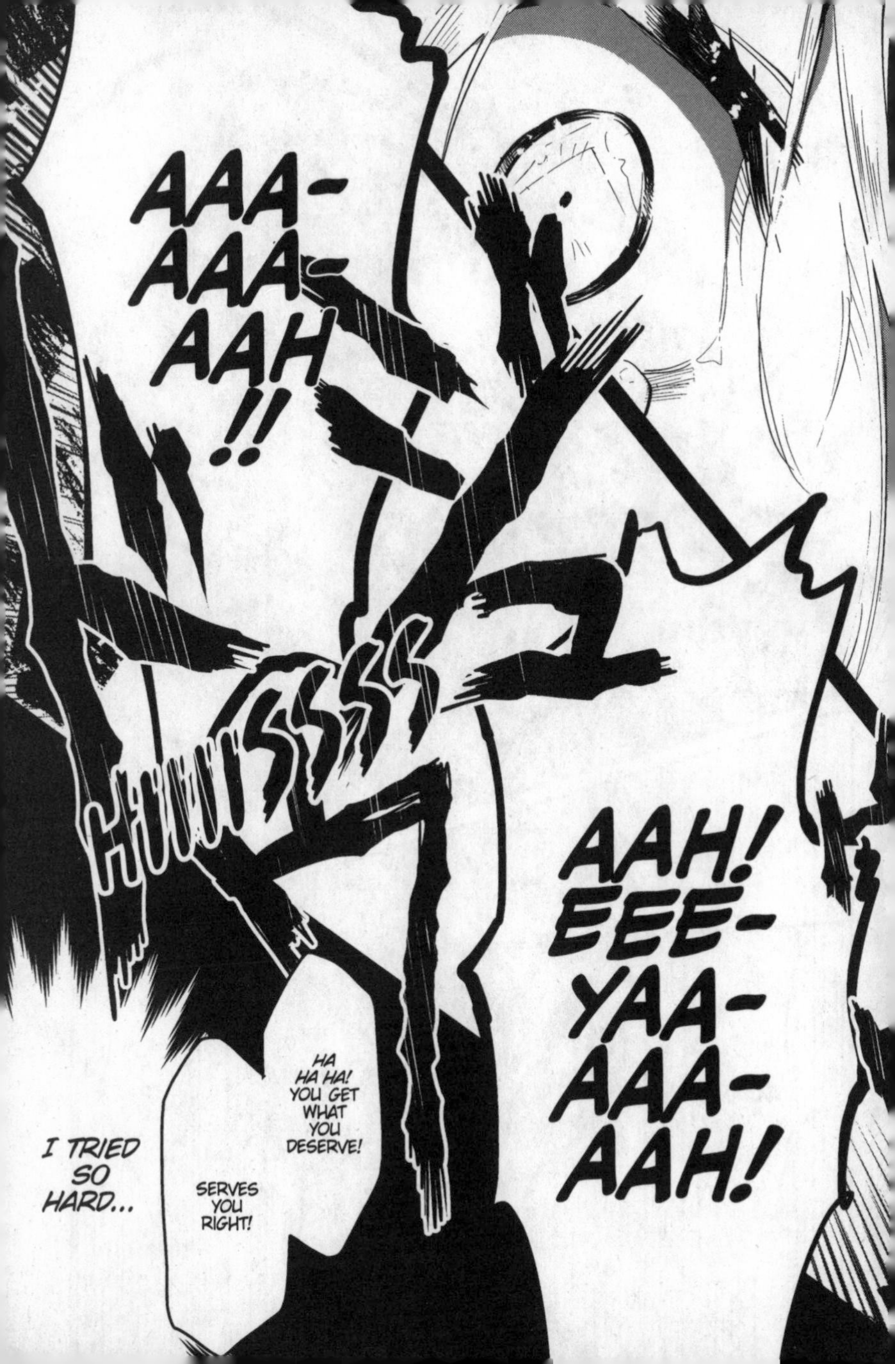
AAA-AAA-AAH!!
HIIISSSSS
AAH! EEE-YAA-AAA-AAH!
HA HA HA! YOU GET WHAT YOU DESERVE!
SERVES YOU RIGHT!
I TRIED SO HARD...

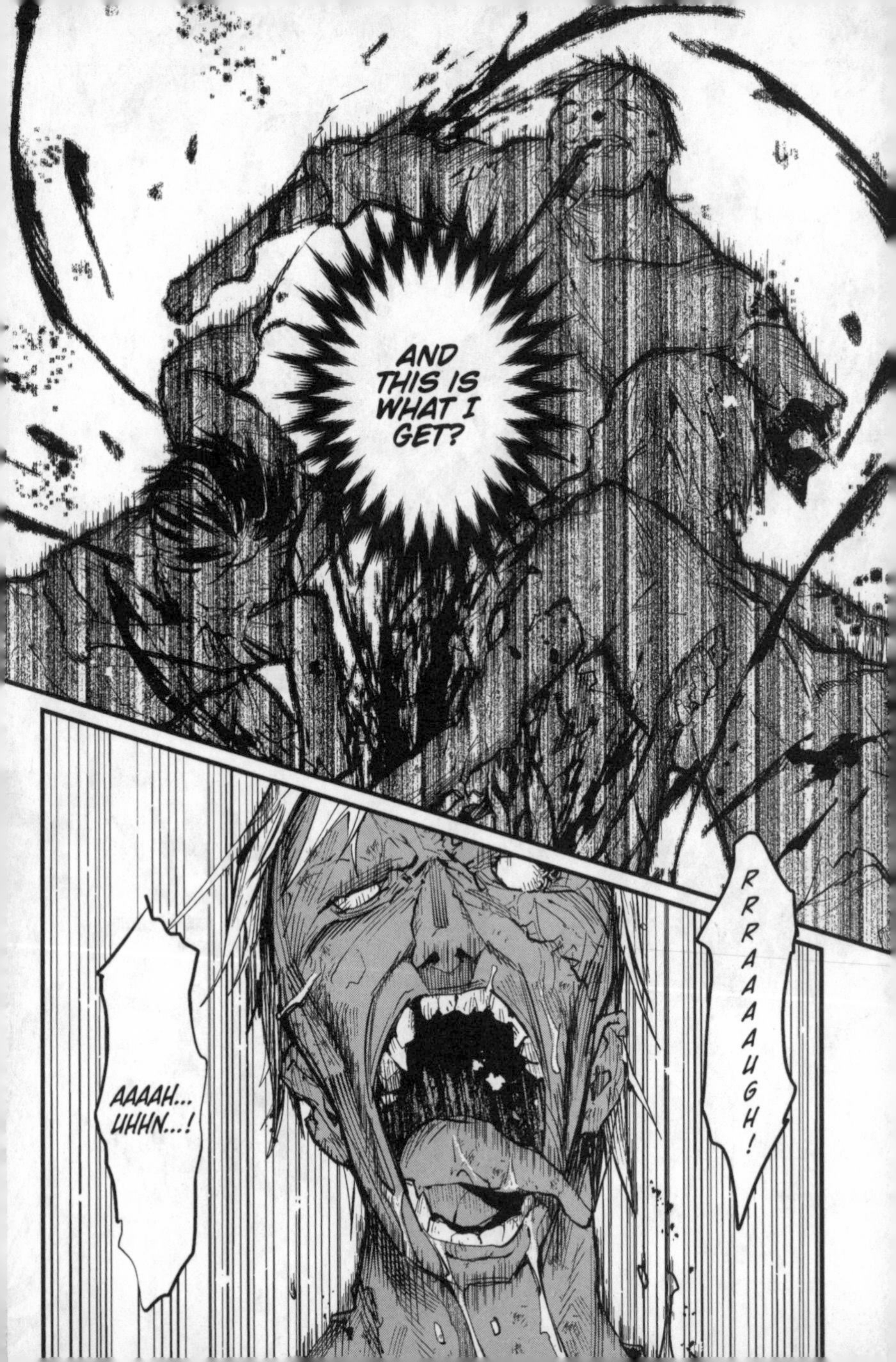
AND THIS IS WHAT I GET?
RRRAAAAUGH!
AAAAH... UHHN...!

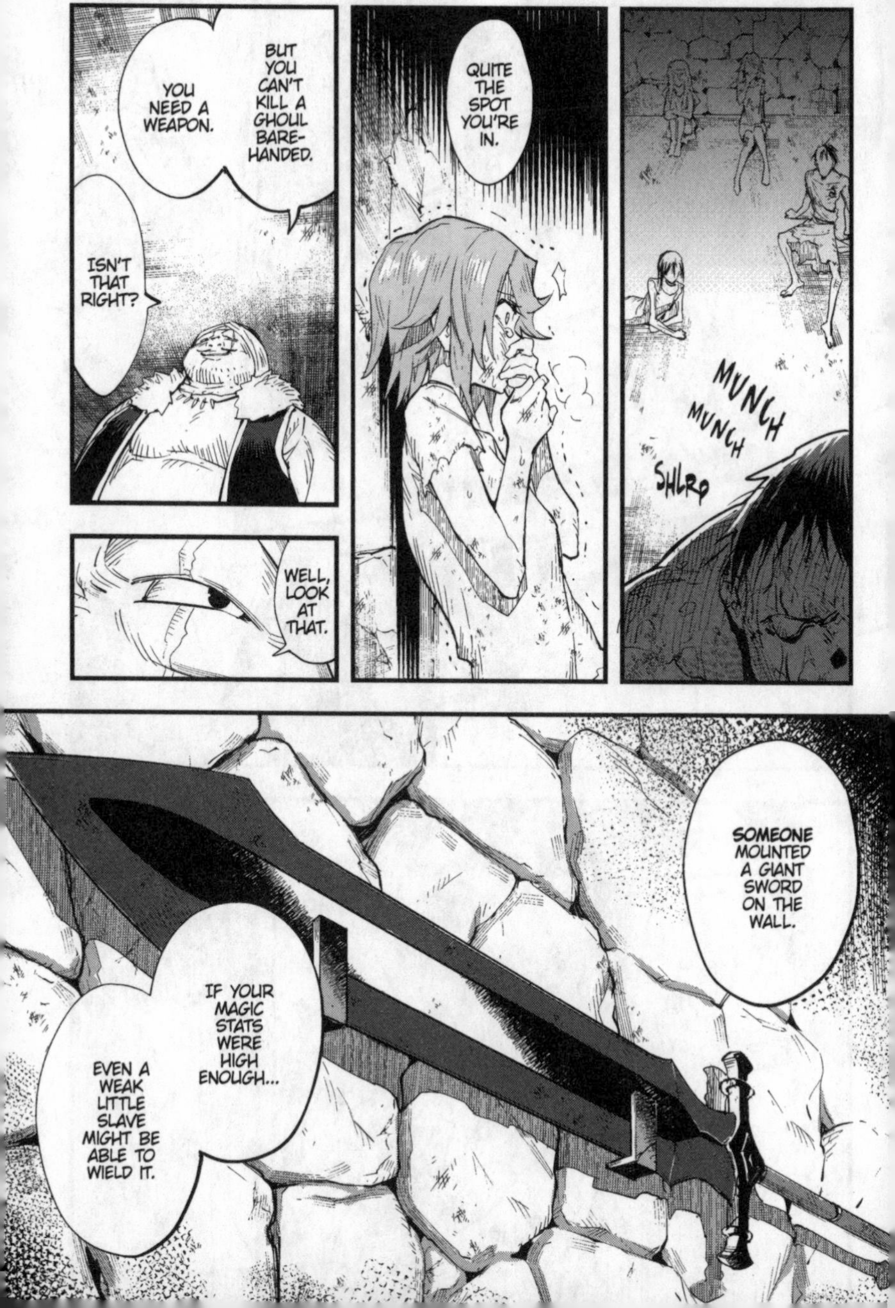
MUNCH
MUNCH
SHLRP
QUITE THE SPOT YOU'RE IN.
BUT YOU CAN'T KILL A GHOUL BARE-HANDED.
YOU NEED A WEAPON.
ISN'T THAT RIGHT?
WELL, LOOK AT THAT.
SOMEONE MOUNTED A GIANT SWORD ON THE WALL.
IF YOUR MAGIC STATS WERE HIGH ENOUGH...
EVEN A WEAK LITTLE SLAVE MIGHT BE ABLE TO WIELD IT.

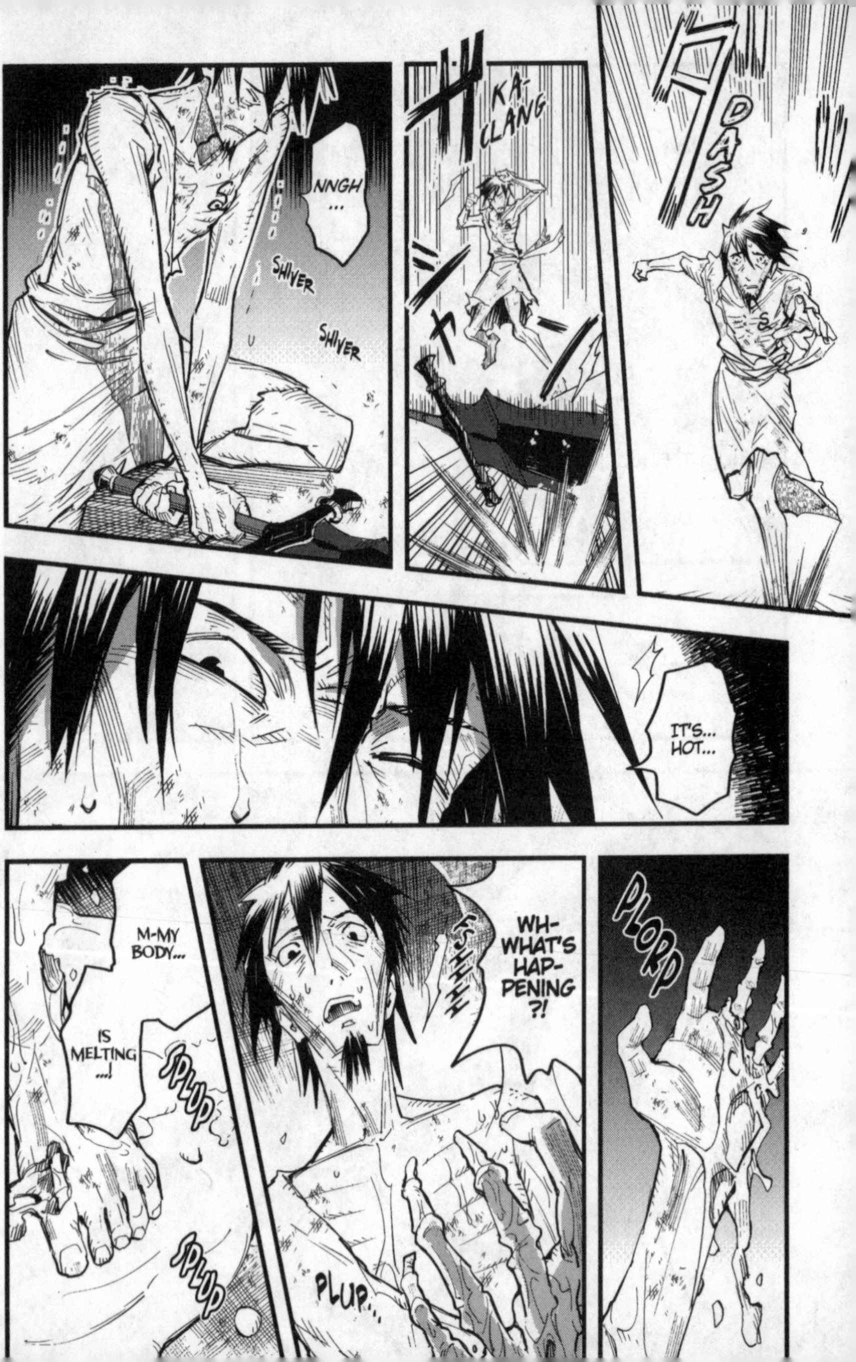
DASH
KA-CLANG
NNGH...
SHIVER
SHIVER
IT'S... HOT...
PLORP
WH-WHAT'S HAP-PENING?!
M-MY BODY...
IS MELTING...!
SPLUP
SPLUP
PLUP...

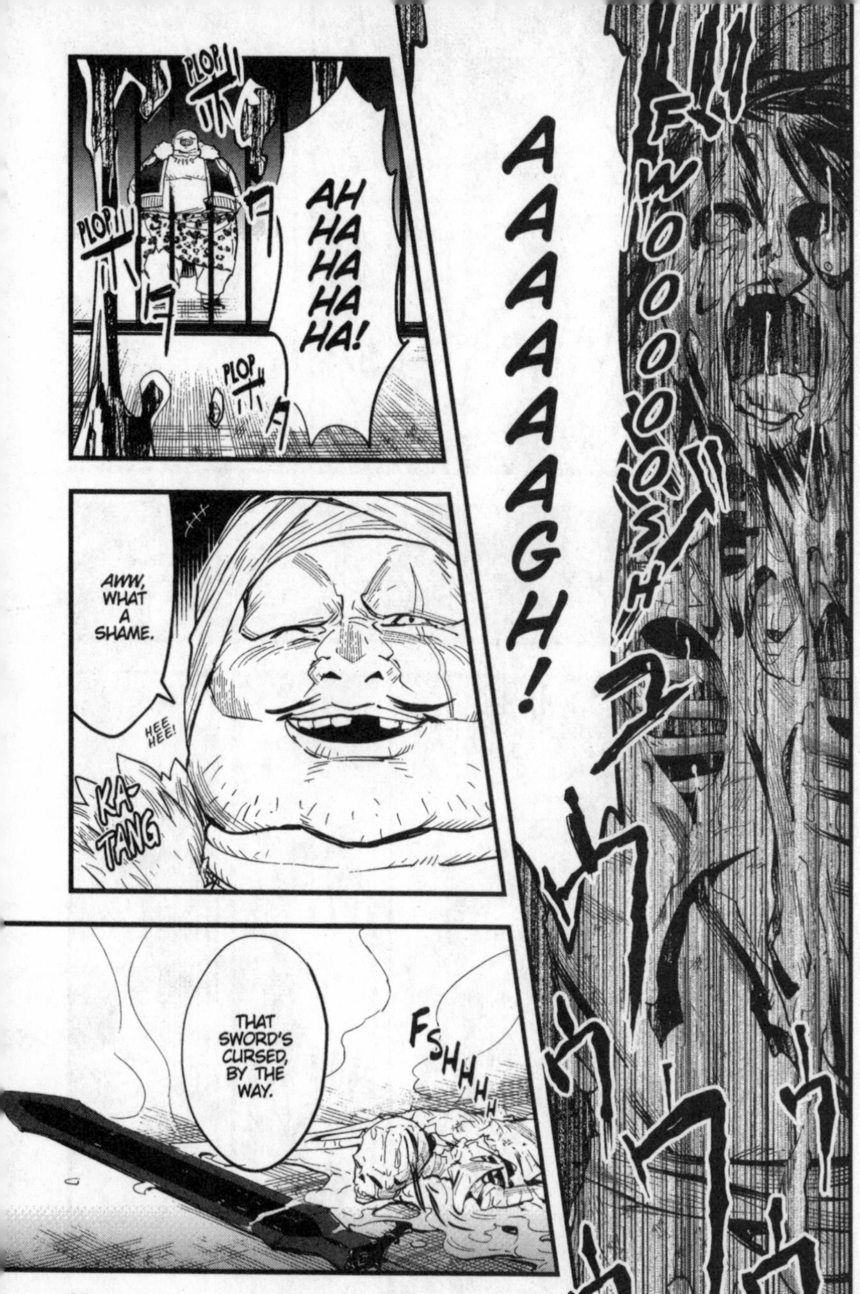
FWOOOOOOSH
AAAAAAAGH!
PLOP
AH HA HA HA HA!
PLOP
PLOP
AWW, WHAT A SHAME.
HEE HEE!
KA-TANG
THAT SWORD'S CURSED, BY THE WAY.
FSHHHHH

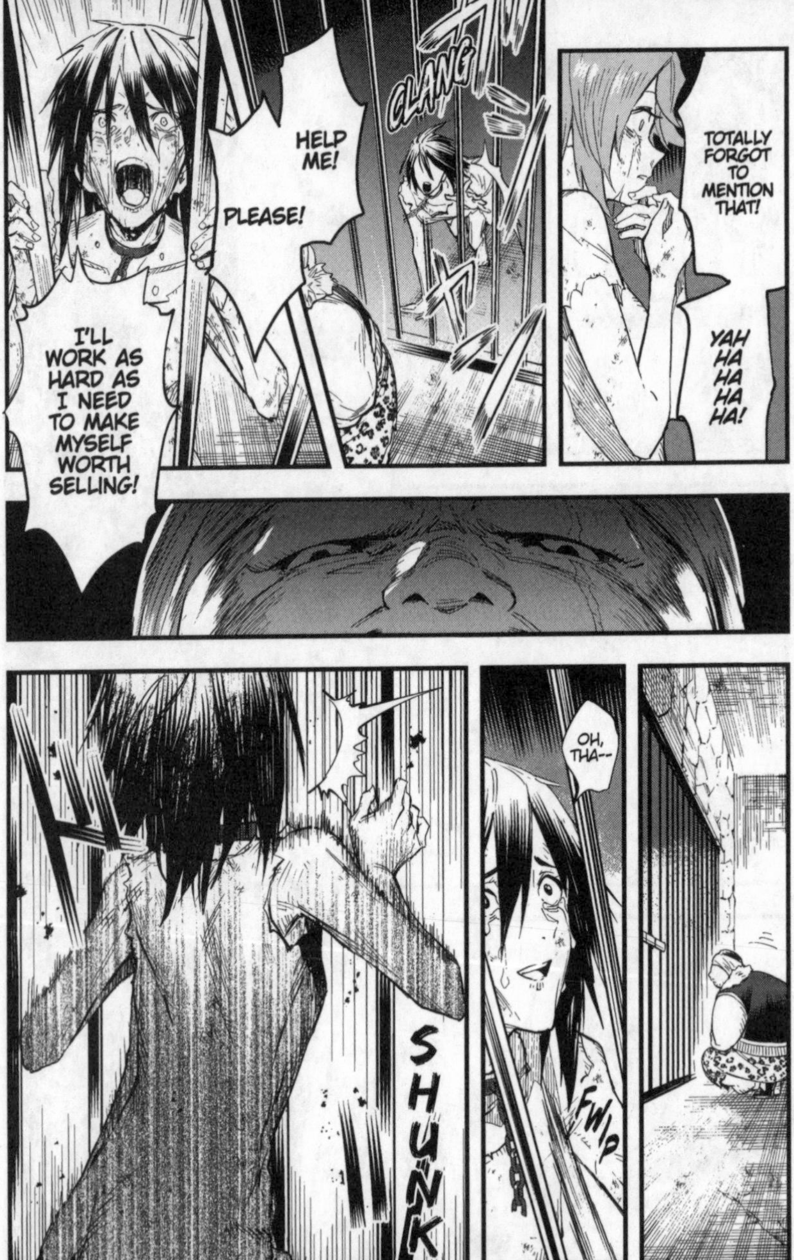
TOTALLY FORGOT TO MENTION THAT!
YAH HA HA HA HA!
CLANG
HELP ME!
PLEASE!
I'LL WORK AS HARD AS I NEED TO MAKE MYSELF WORTH SELLING!
OH, THA--
FWIP
SHUNK

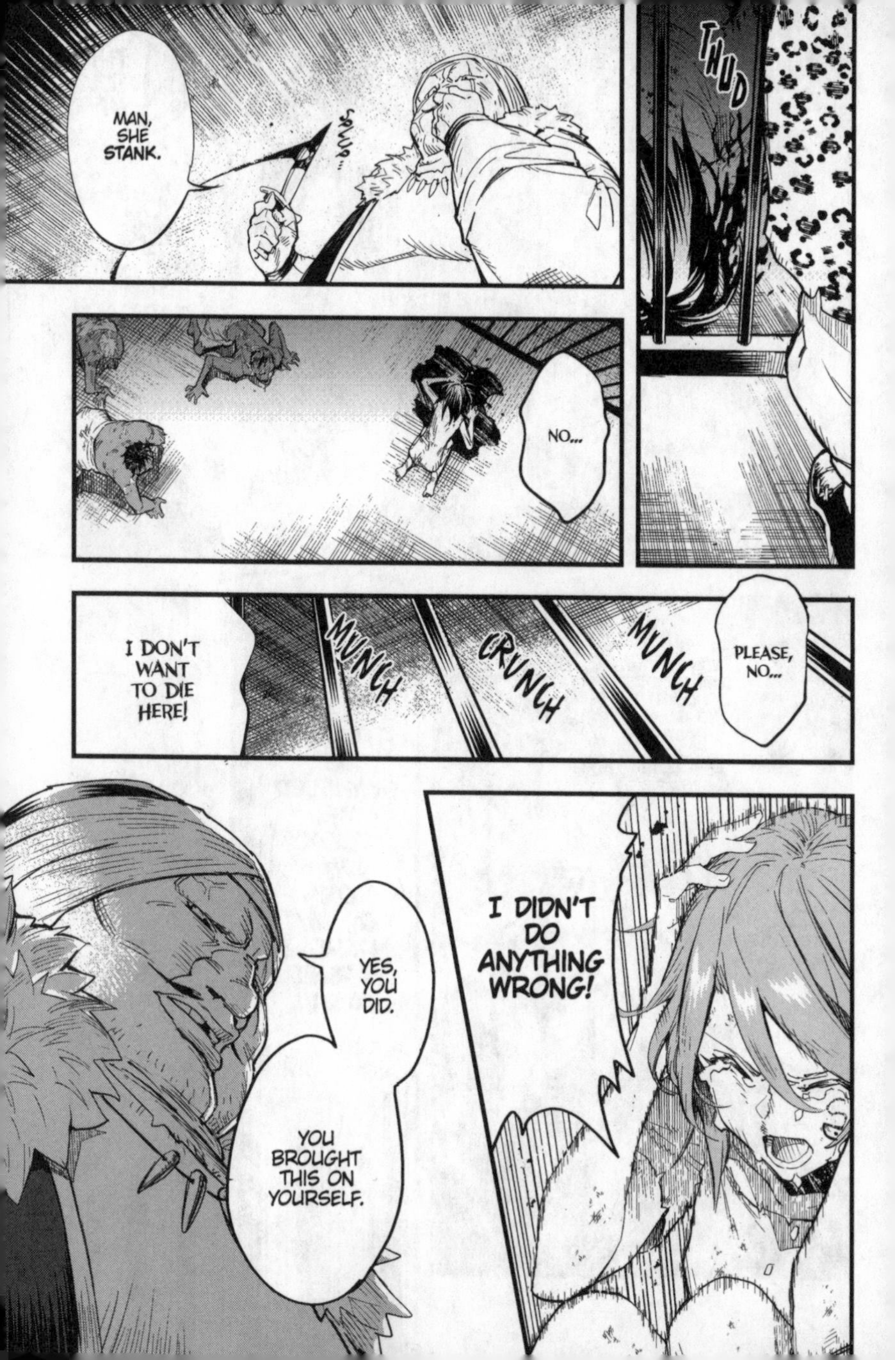
THUD
MAN, SHE STANK.
NO...
PLEASE, NO...
MUNCH
CRUNCH
MUNCH
I DON'T WANT TO DIE HERE!
I DIDN'T DO ANYTHING WRONG!
YES, YOU DID.
YOU BROUGHT THIS ON YOURSELF.

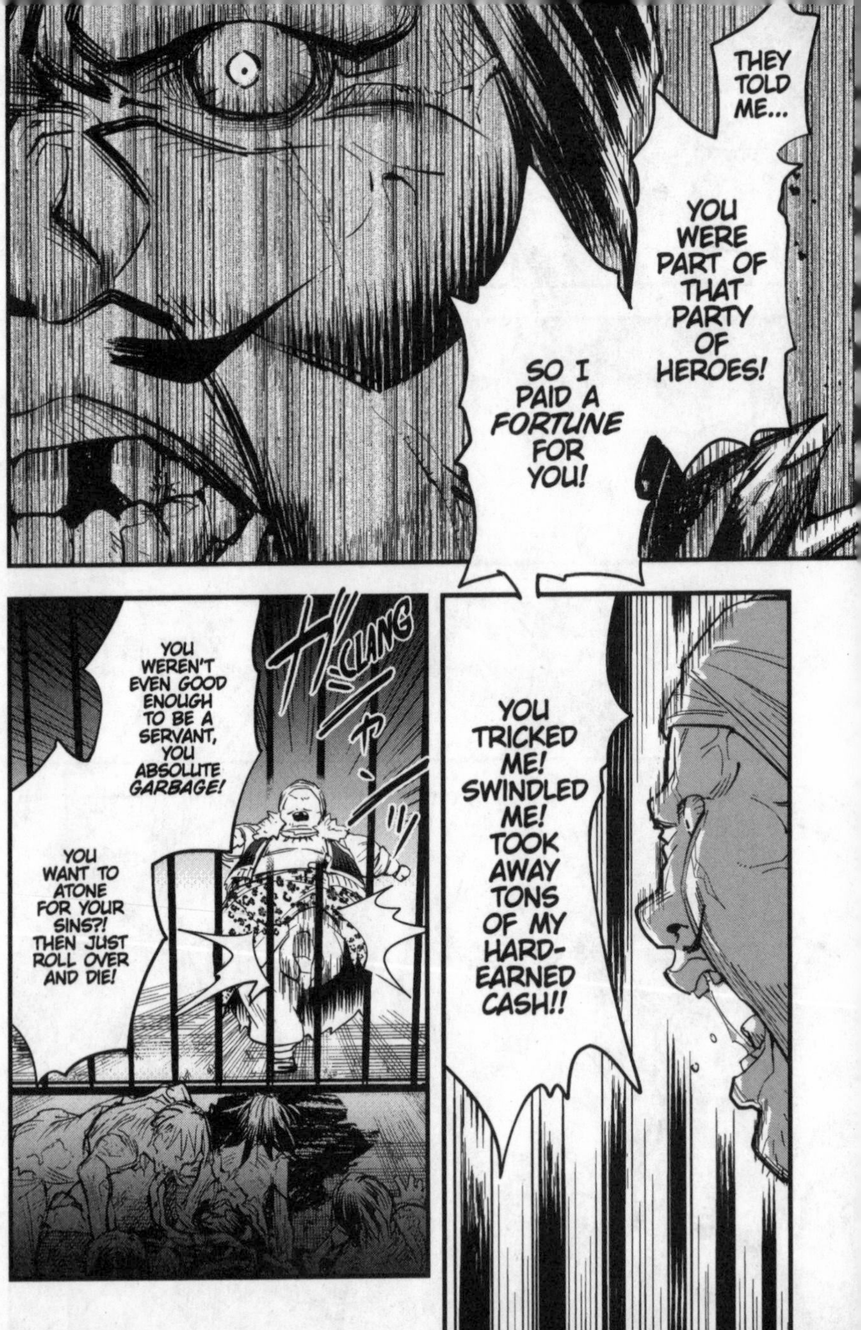
THEY TOLD ME...
YOU WERE PART OF THAT PARTY OF HEROES!
SO I PAID A *FORTUNE* FOR YOU!
YOU TRICKED ME! SWINDLED ME! TOOK AWAY TONS OF MY HARD-EARNED CASH!!
CLANG
YOU WEREN'T EVEN GOOD ENOUGH TO BE A SERVANT, YOU ABSOLUTE *GARBAGE!*
YOU WANT TO ATONE FOR YOUR SINS?! THEN JUST ROLL OVER AND DIE!

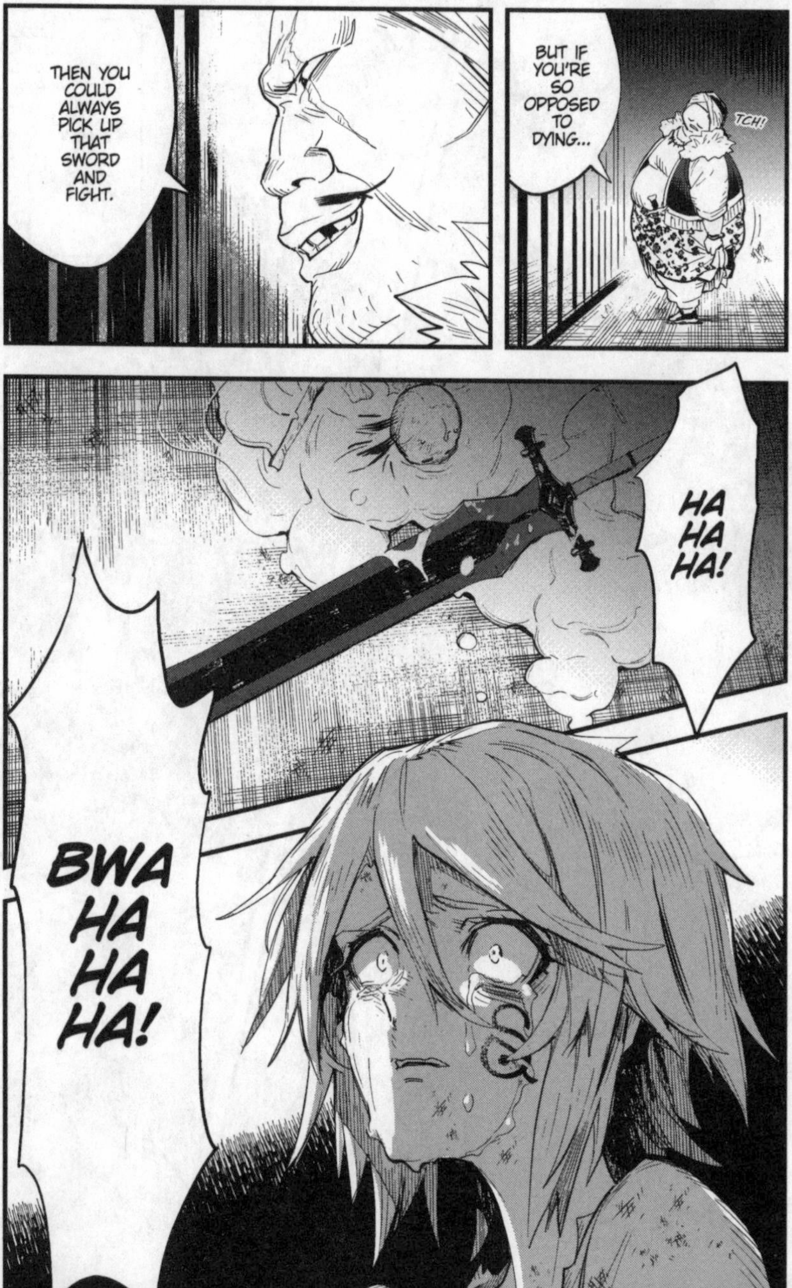
BUT IF YOU'RE SO OPPOSED TO DYING...
TCH!
THEN YOU COULD ALWAYS PICK UP THAT SWORD AND FIGHT.
HA HA HA!
BWA HA HA HA HA!

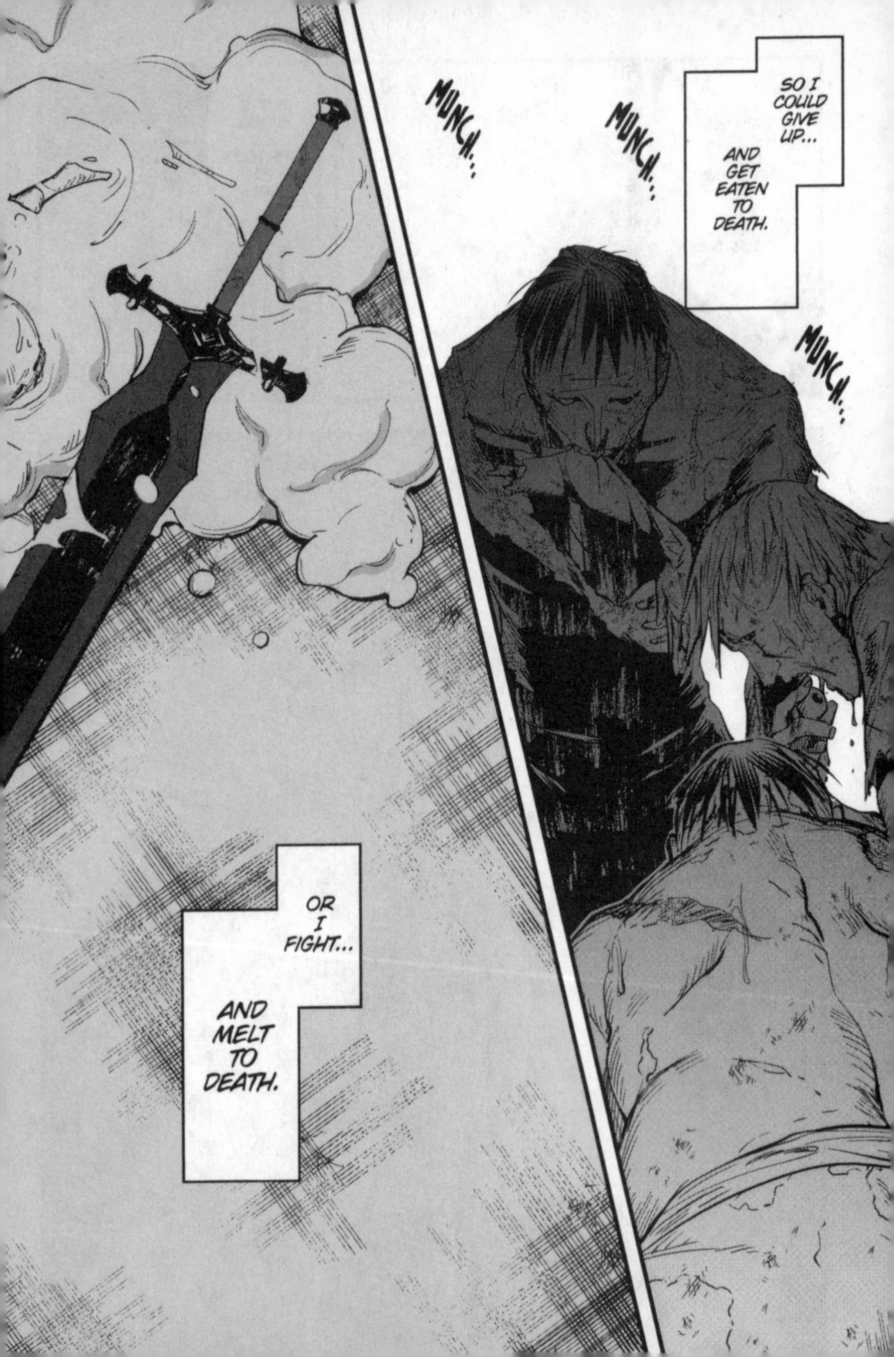
SO I COULD GIVE UP... AND GET EATEN TO DEATH.
MUNCH...
MUNCH...
MUNCH...
OR I FIGHT...
AND MELT TO DEATH.

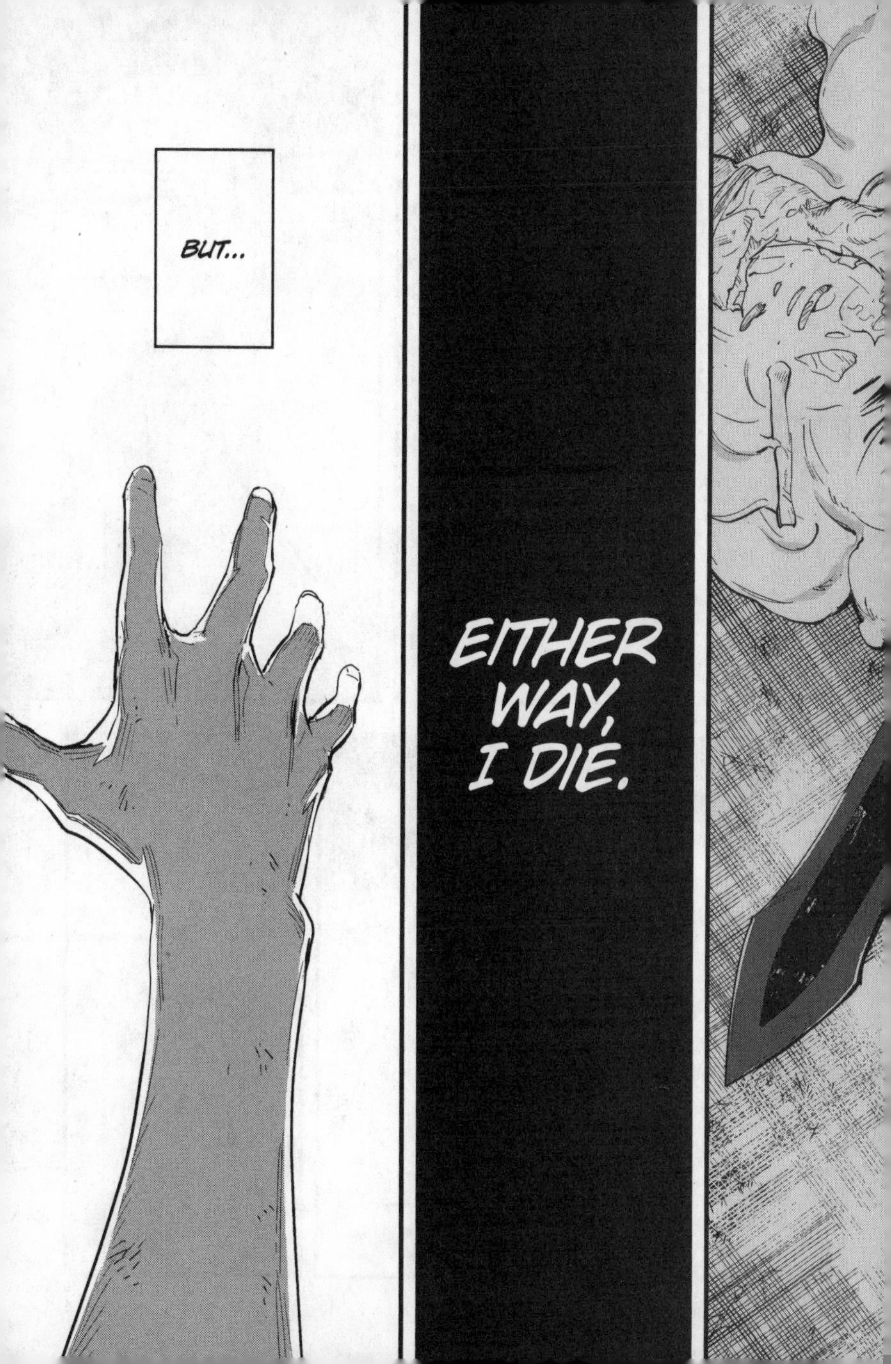
EITHER WAY, I DIE.
BUT...

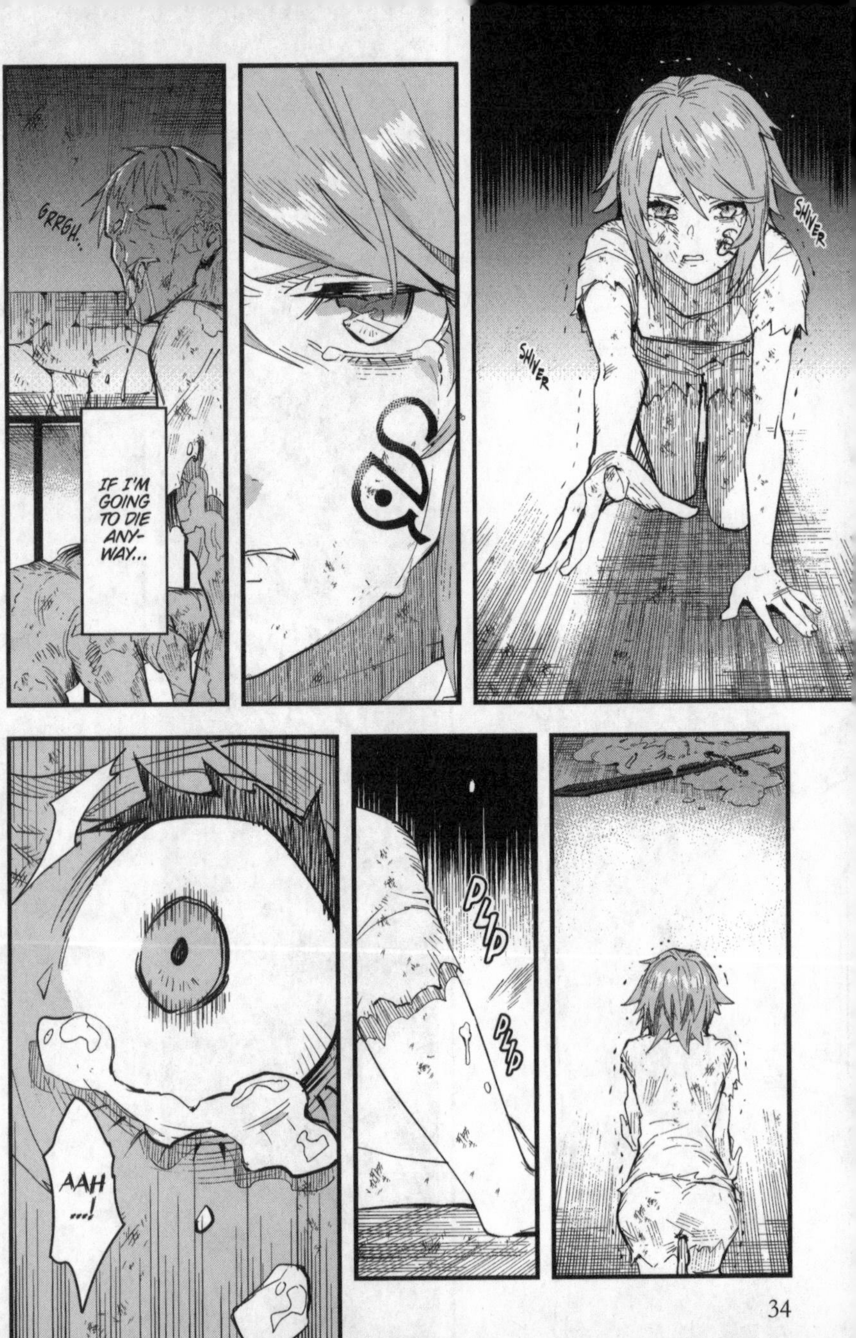
SHIVER
SHIVER
GRRGH...
IF I'M GOING TO DIE ANY-WAY...
PLIP
PLIP
AAH ...!

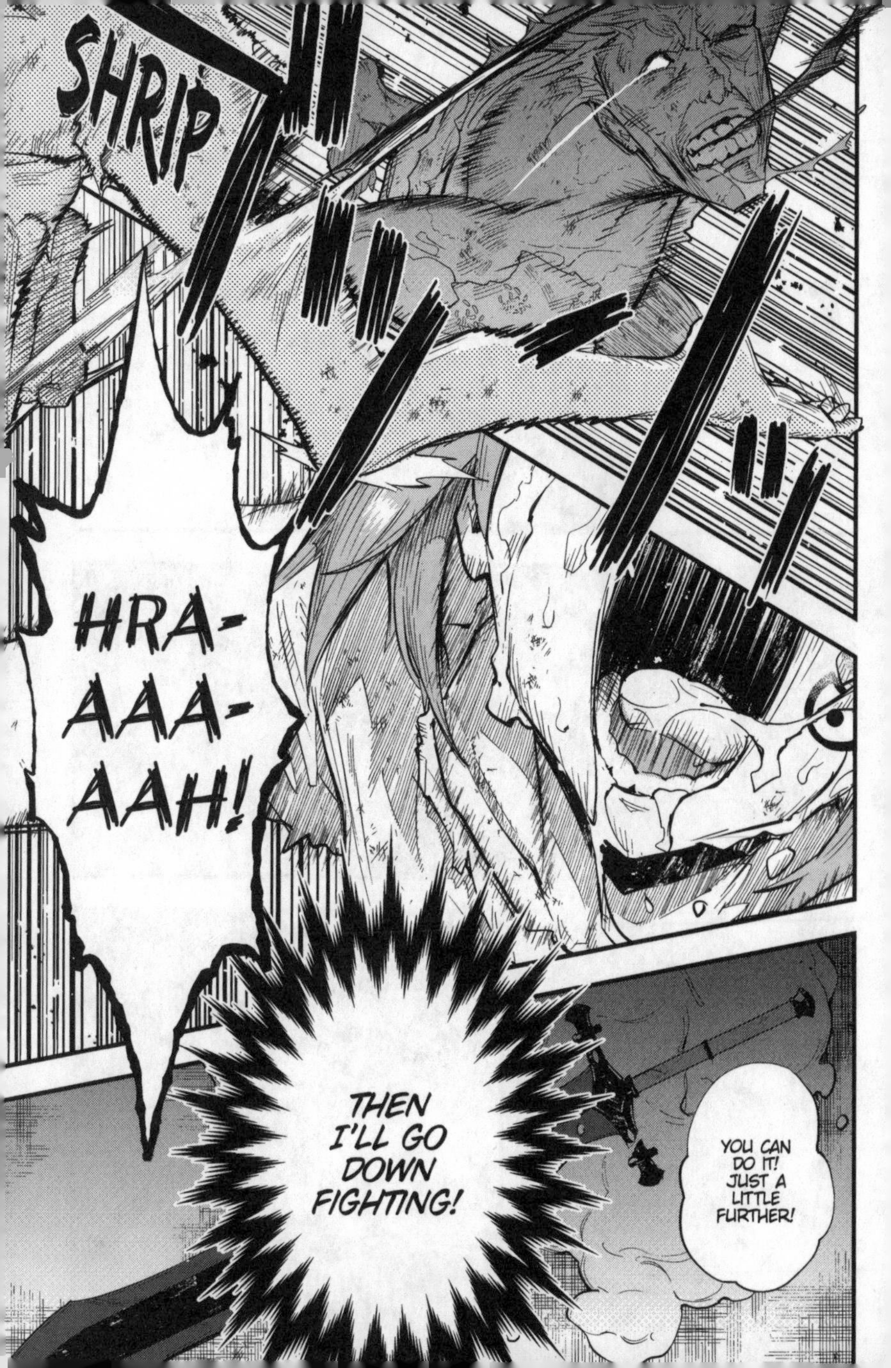
SHRIP
HRA-AAA-AAH!
YOU CAN DO IT! JUST A LITTLE FURTHER!
THEN I'LL GO DOWN FIGHTING!

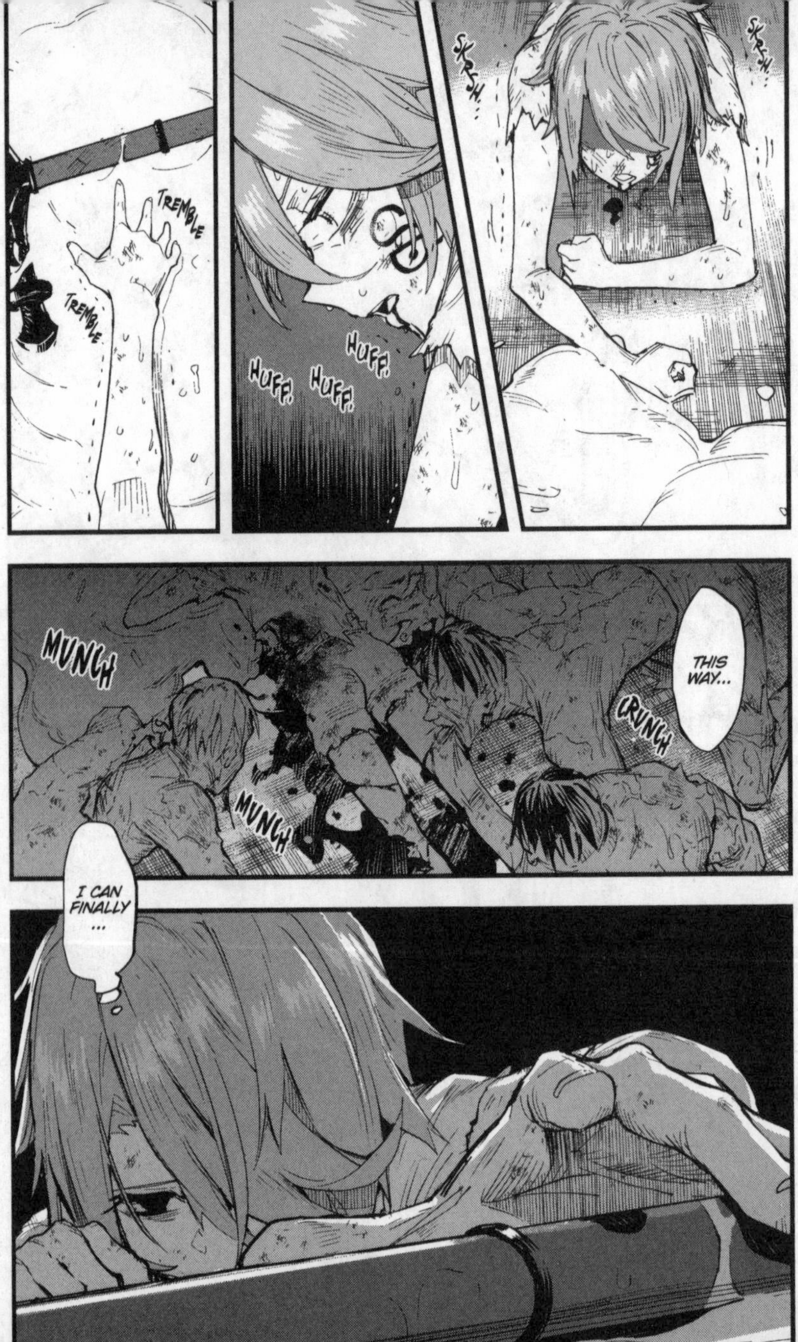
SKRSH...
SKRSH...
HUFF!
HUFF!
HUFF!
TREMBLE
TREMBLE
THIS WAY...
CRUNCH
MUNCH
MUNCH
I CAN FINALLY...

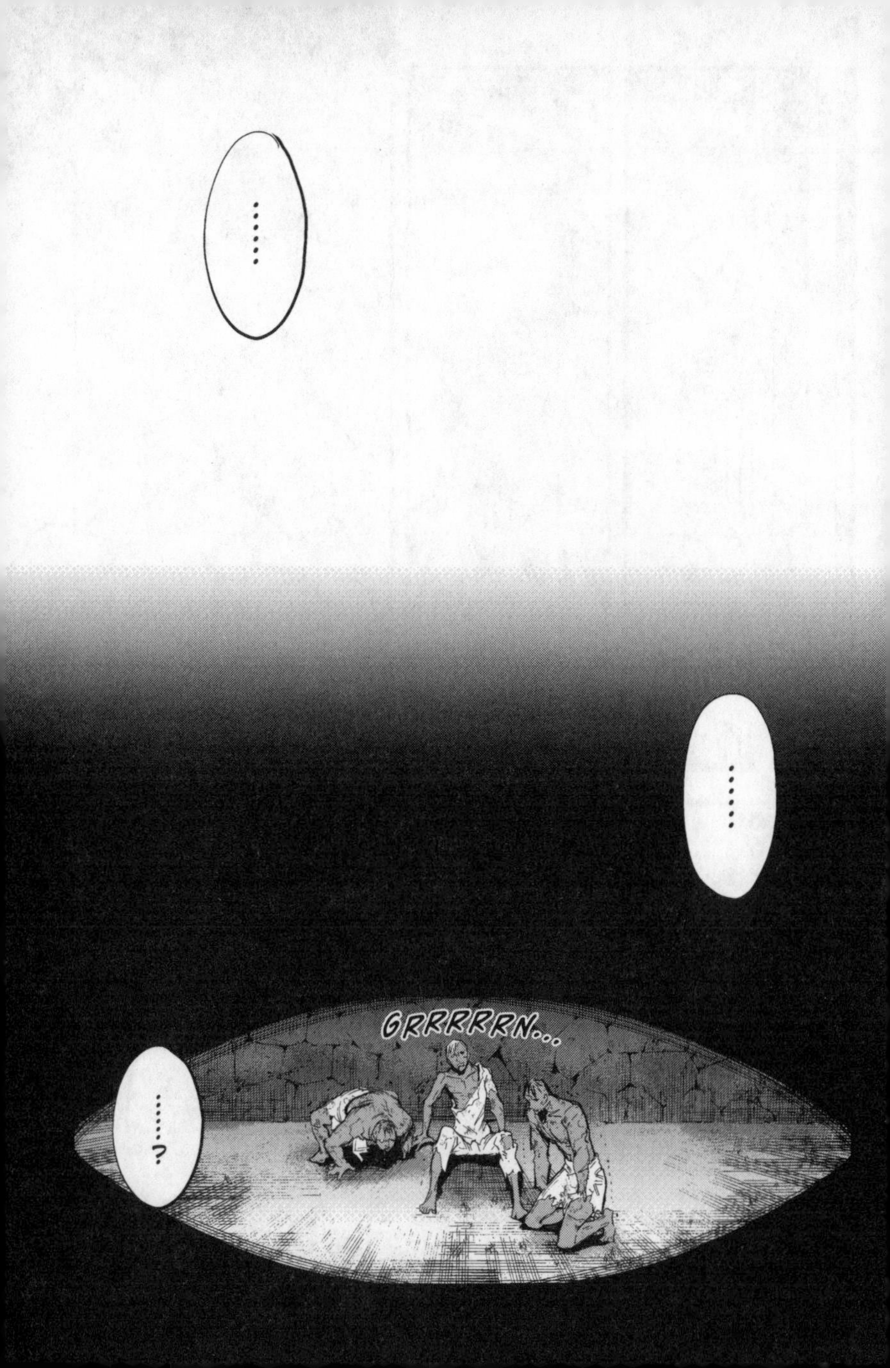
......
......
GRRRRRN...
......?

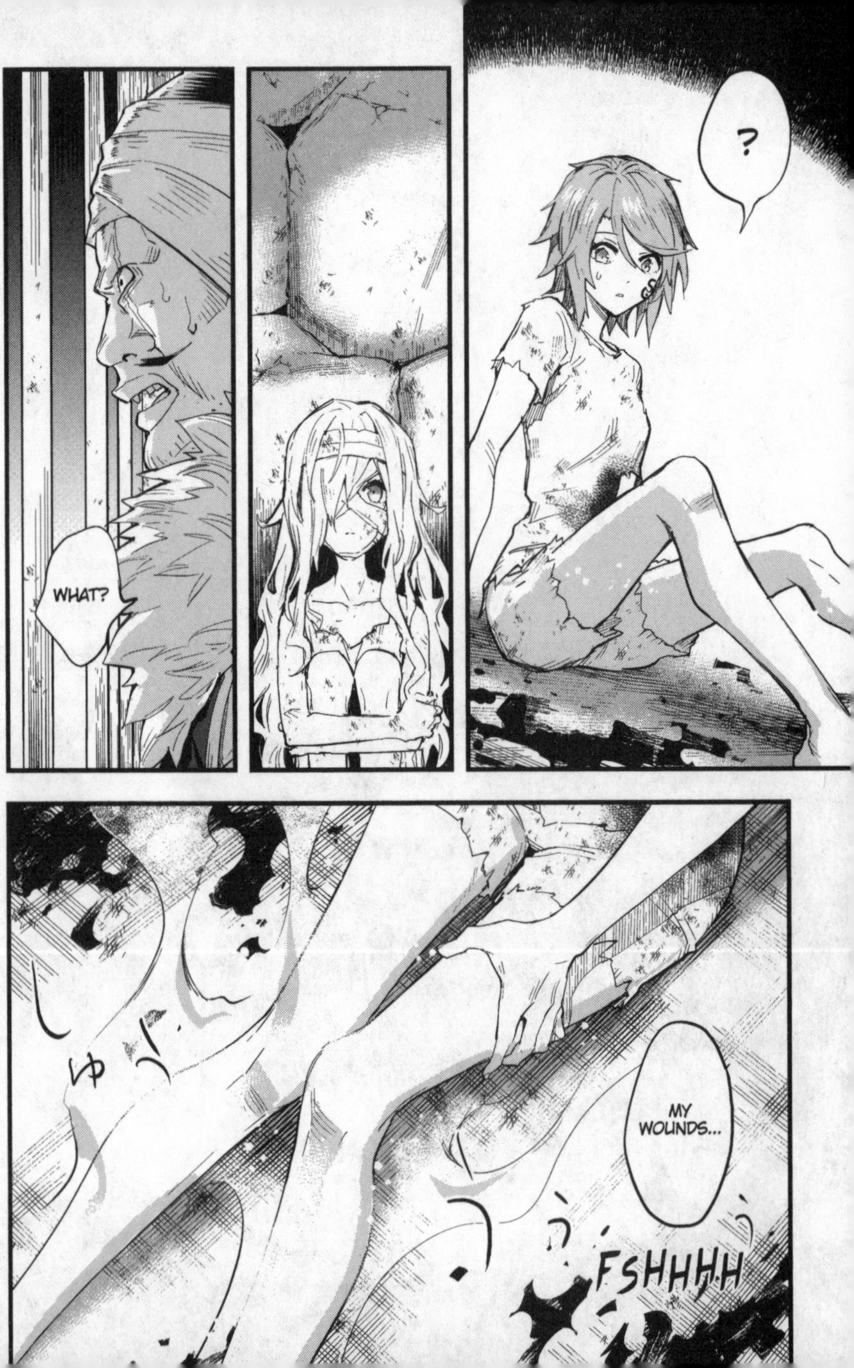
?
WHAT?
MY WOUNDS...
FSHHHH

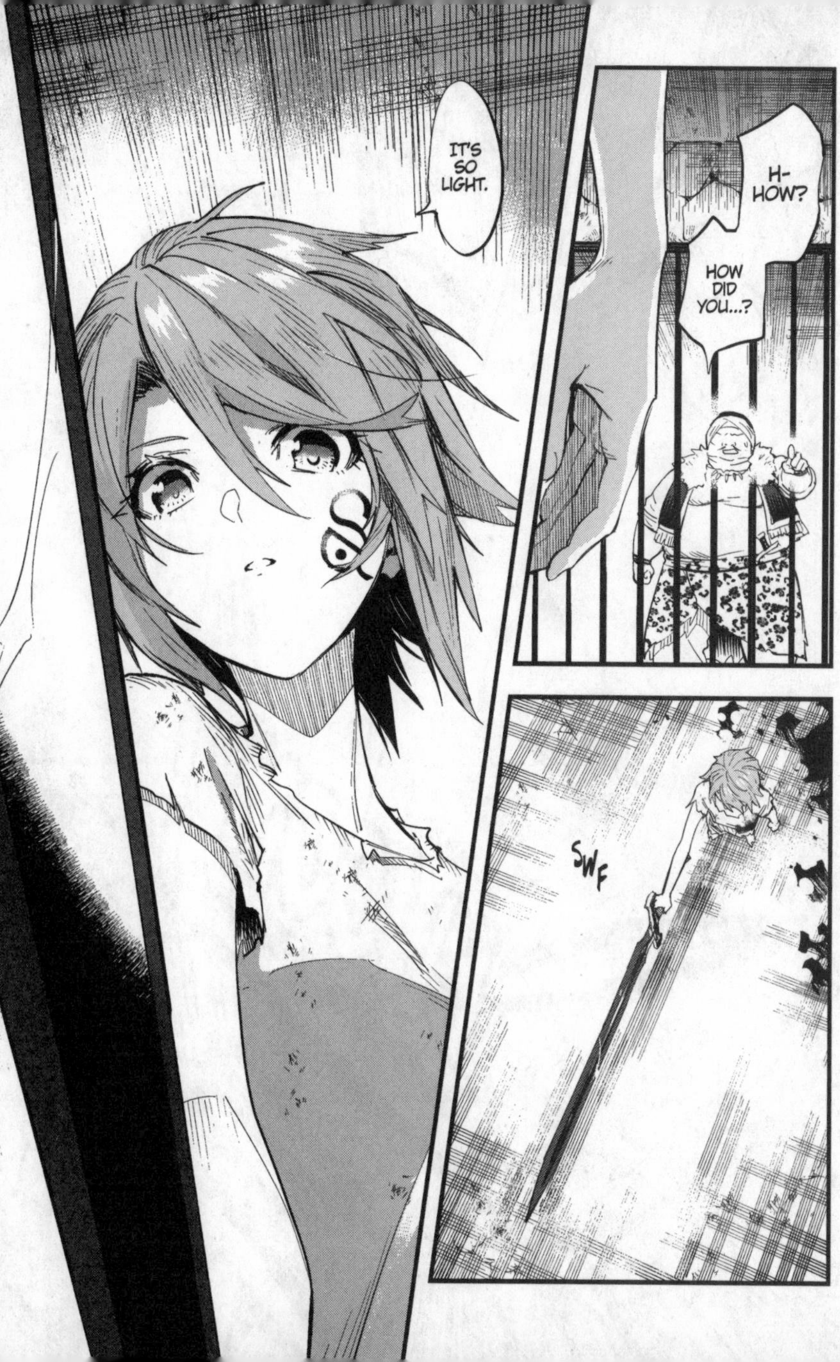
H-HOW?
HOW DID YOU...?
SWF
IT'S SO LIGHT.

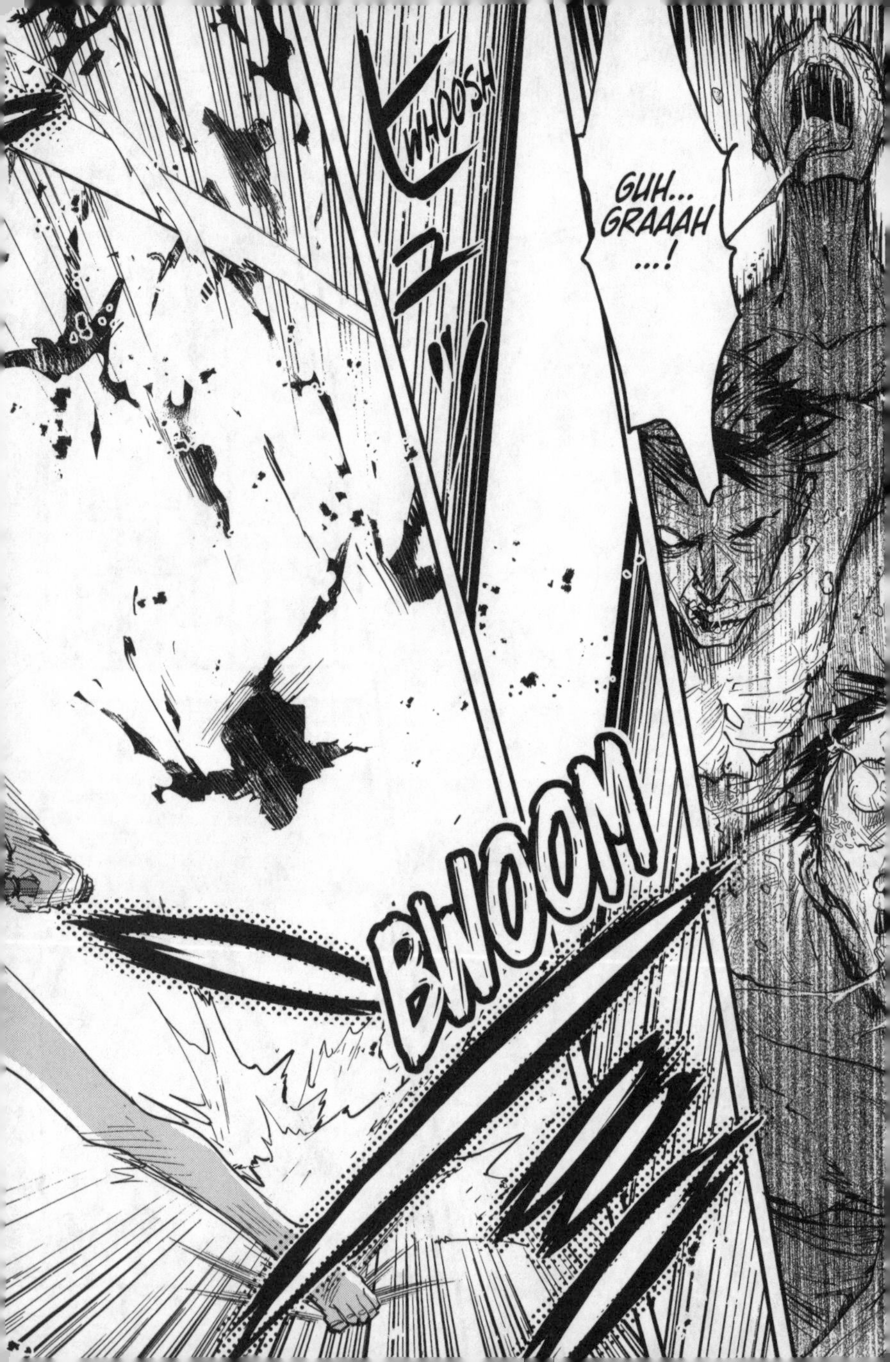
GUH... GRAAAH ...!
WHOOSH
BWOOM

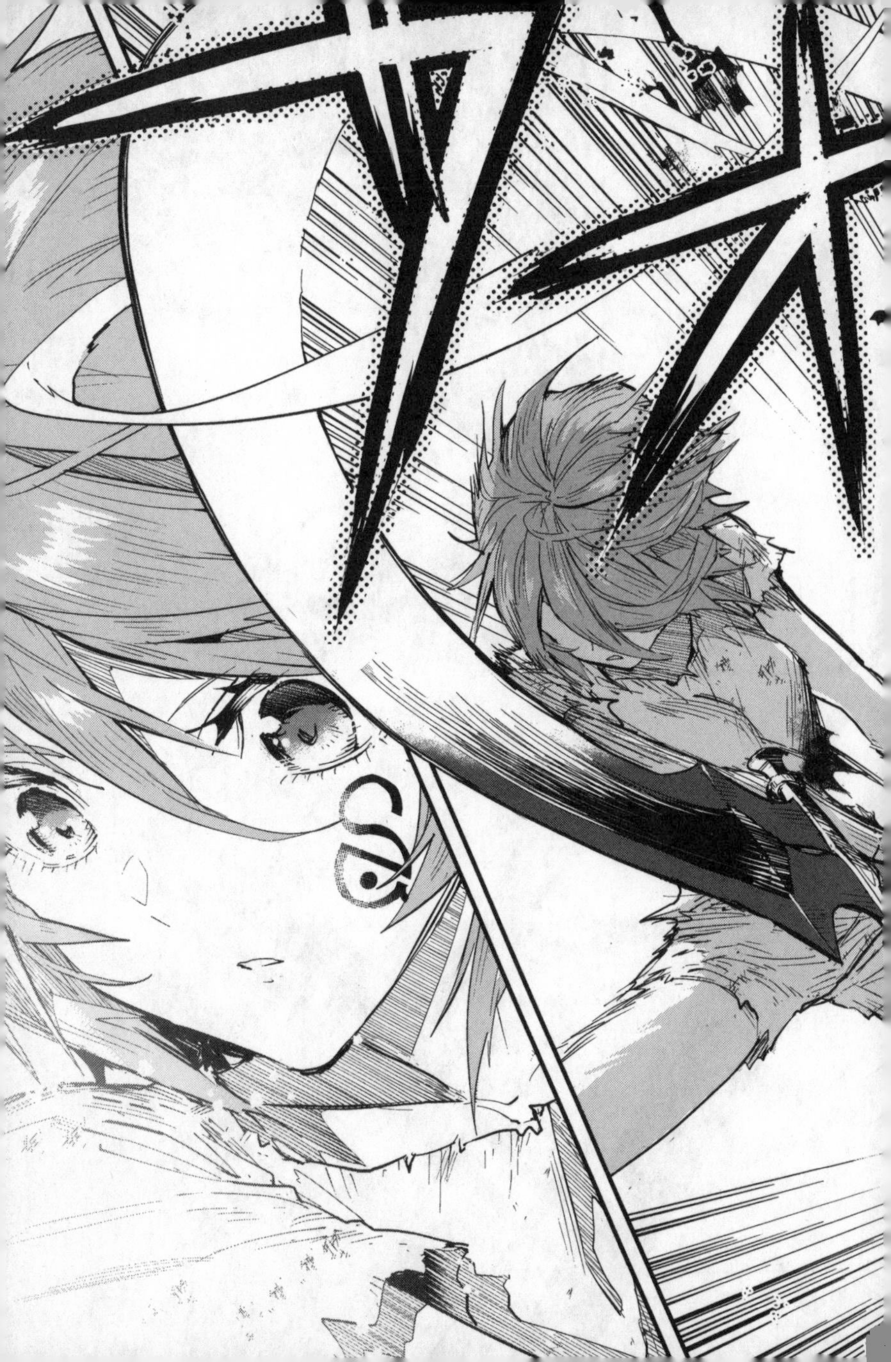

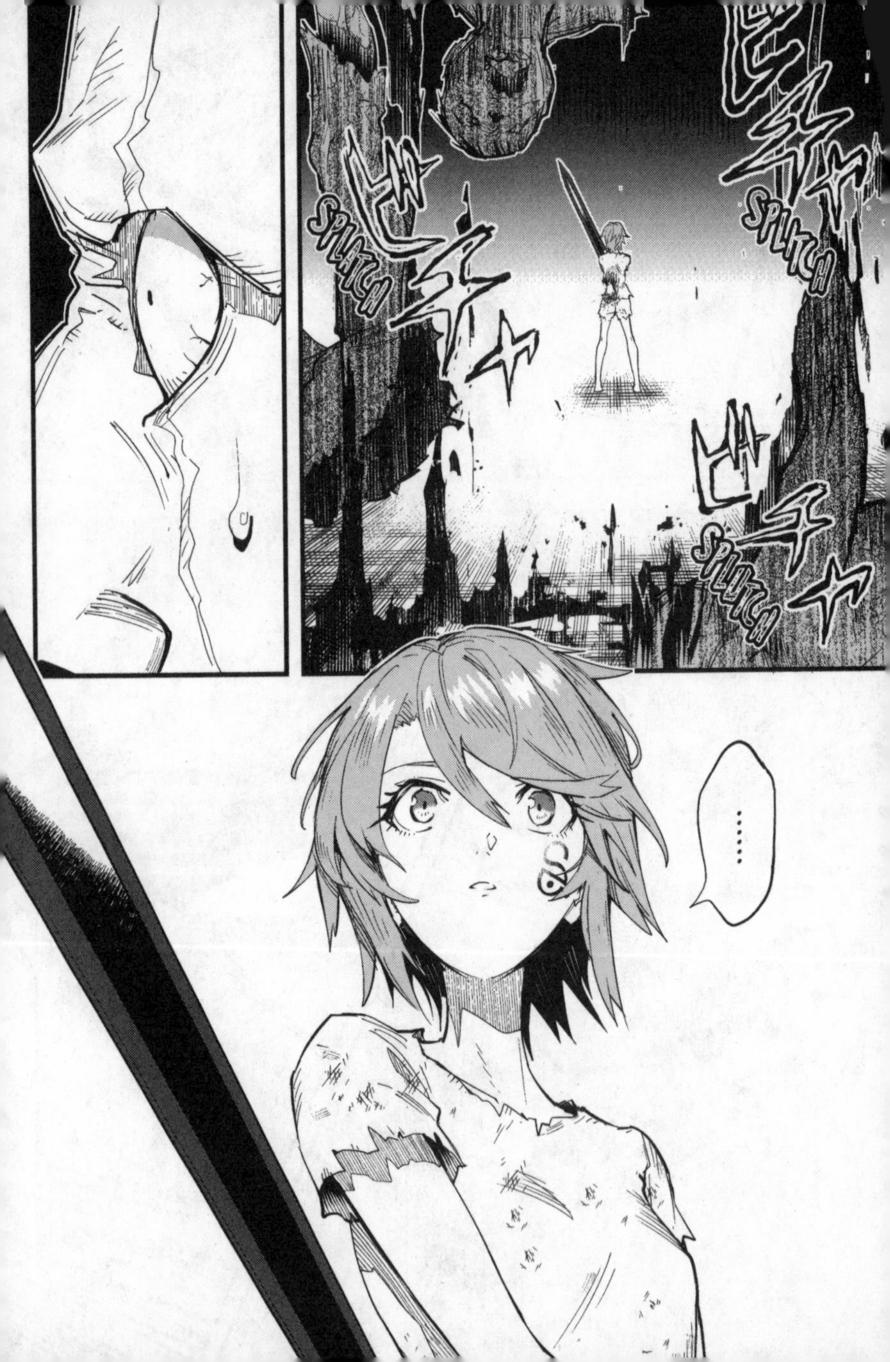
SPLATCH
SPLATCH
SPLATCH
......

EEP!

CREEEAK

KA-TIING

W...

Y-YOU'RE FREE TO LEAVE!

WAIT! PLEASE!

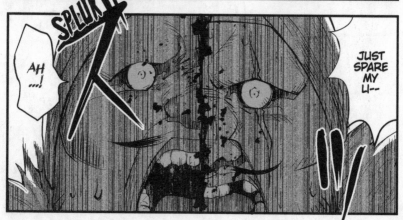

SPLUK!!

AH...!

JUST SPARE MY LI--

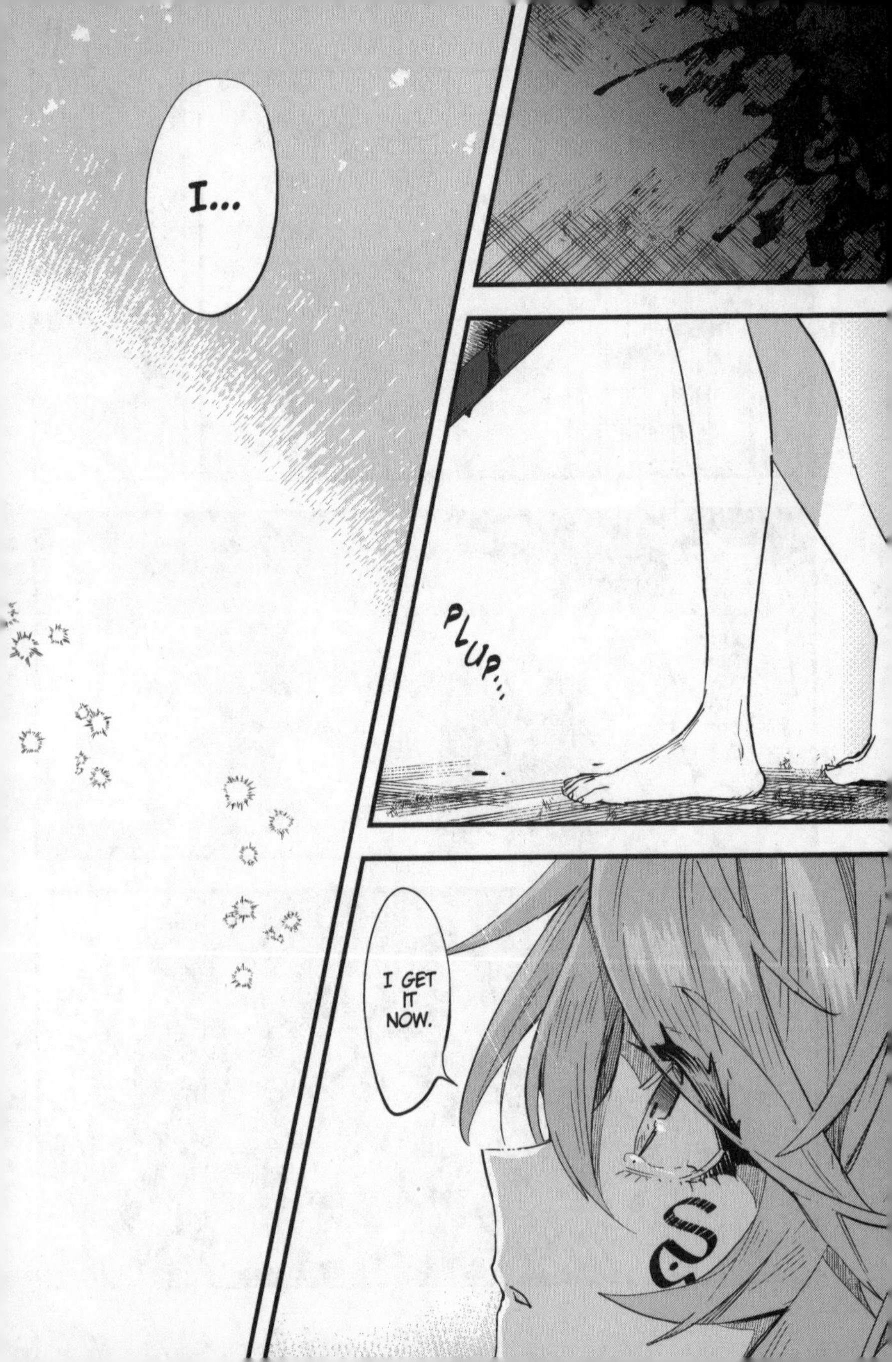
PLUP...
I GET IT NOW.
I...

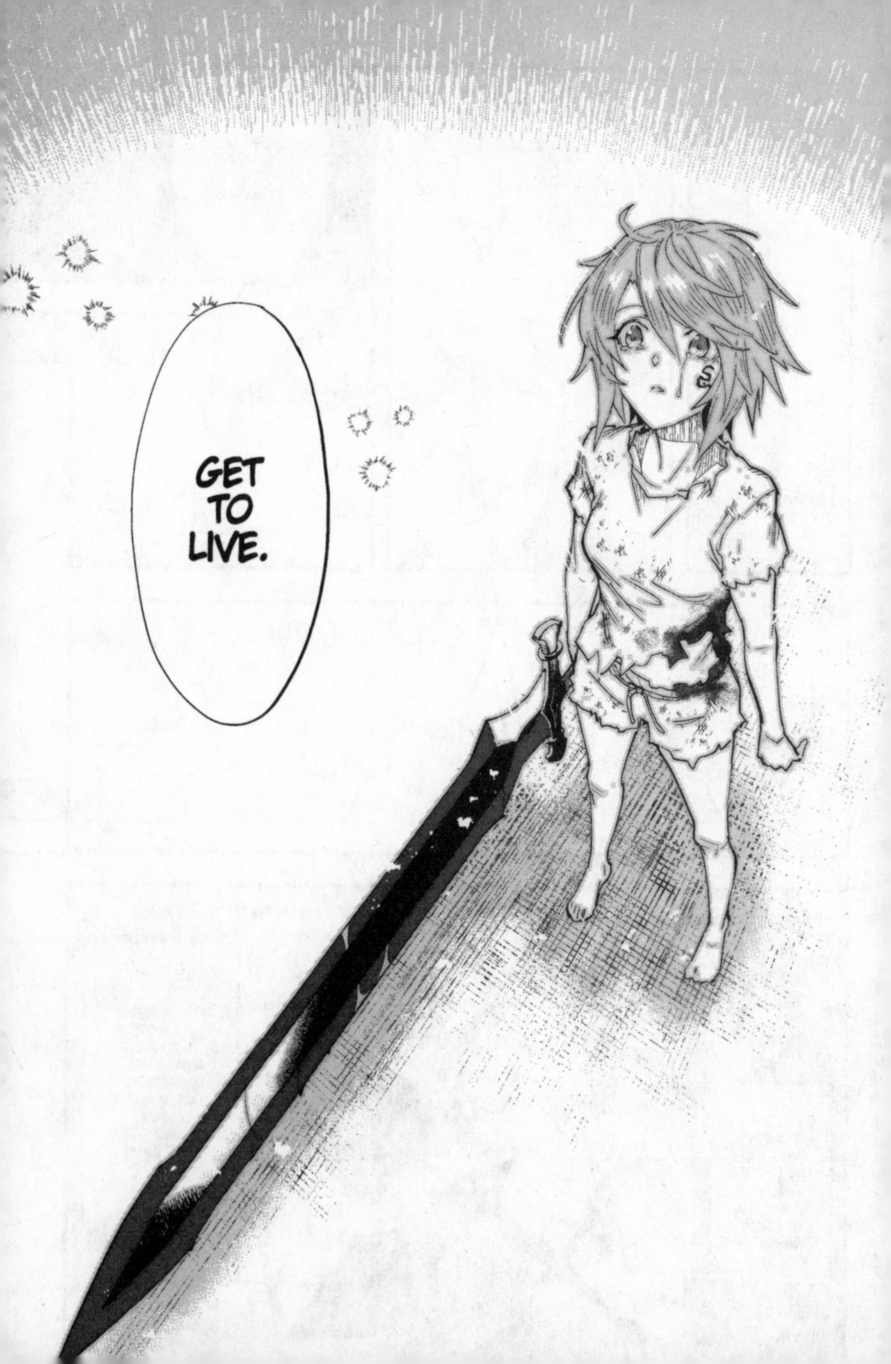
GET TO LIVE.

CREAK...
NOW THEN.
HOW DO I USE THIS THING?
!
GLO OOW
IT'S EPIC GRADE...
BUT I THOUGHT HE SAID IT WAS CURSED. SO WHY...?
Epic
Legend
Rare
Uncommon
Common
EQUIPMENT IS DIVIDED INTO FIVE RANKINGS: COMMON, UNCOMMON, RARE, LEGENDARY, AND EPIC.
THE HIGHER THE WEAPON'S RANK, THE STRONGER IT IS.
WITH A MERE THOUGHT, THE OWNER OF AN EPIC ARMAMENT...
CAN STORE OR RETRIEVE THEIR ITEM FROM A PERSONAL POCKET DIMENSION.

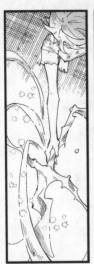

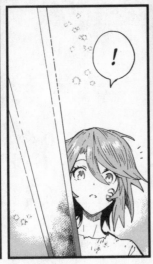

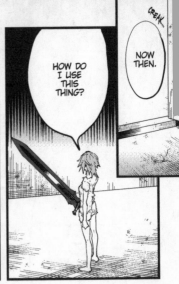

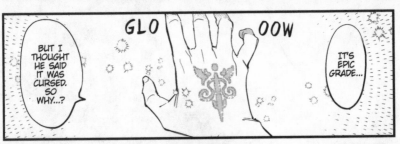

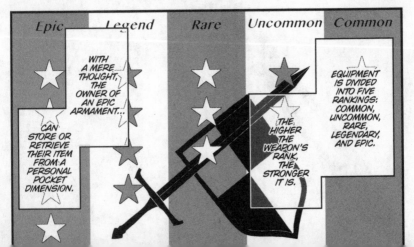

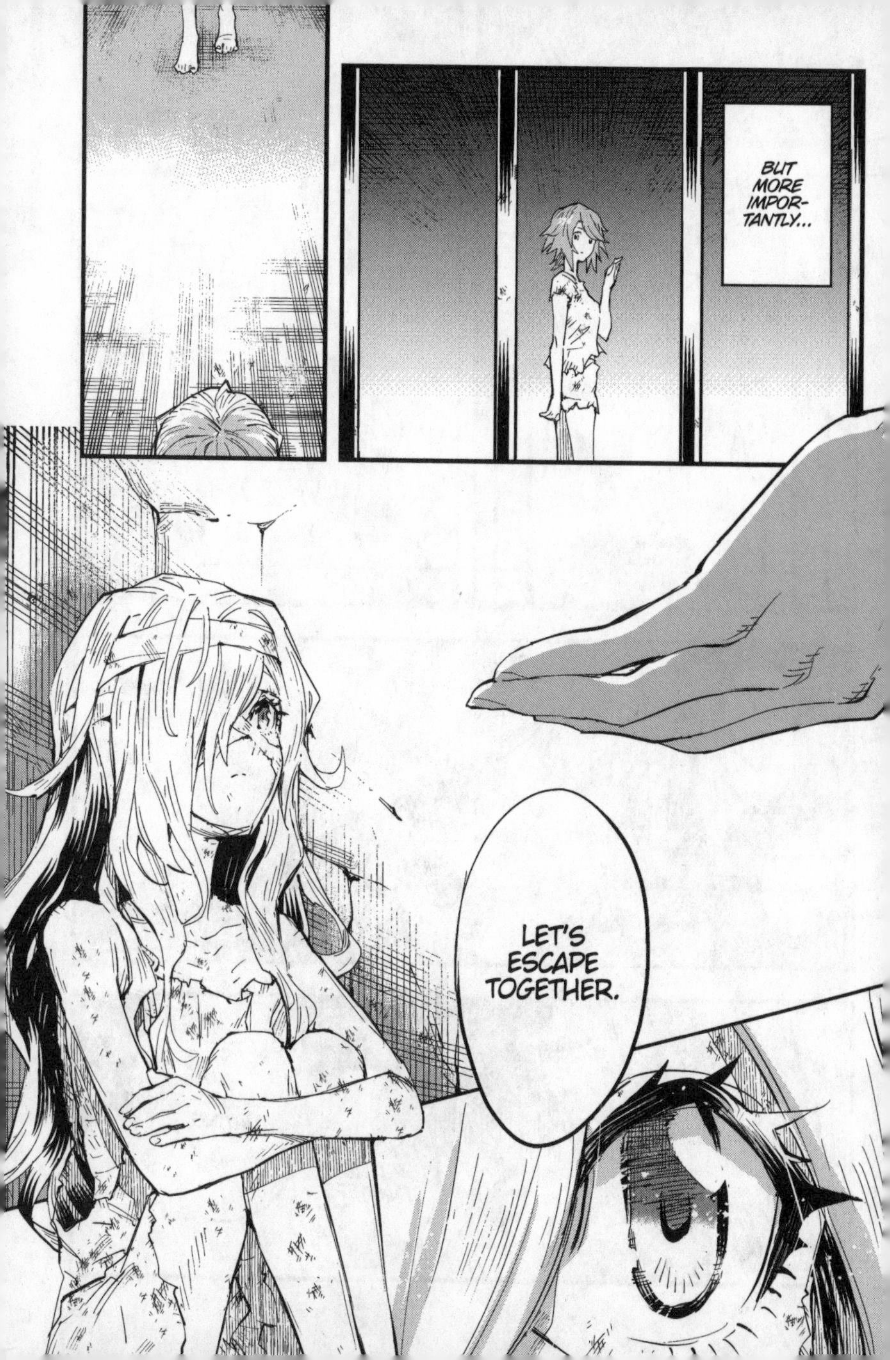
BUT MORE IMPOR-TANTLY...
LET'S ESCAPE TOGETHER.

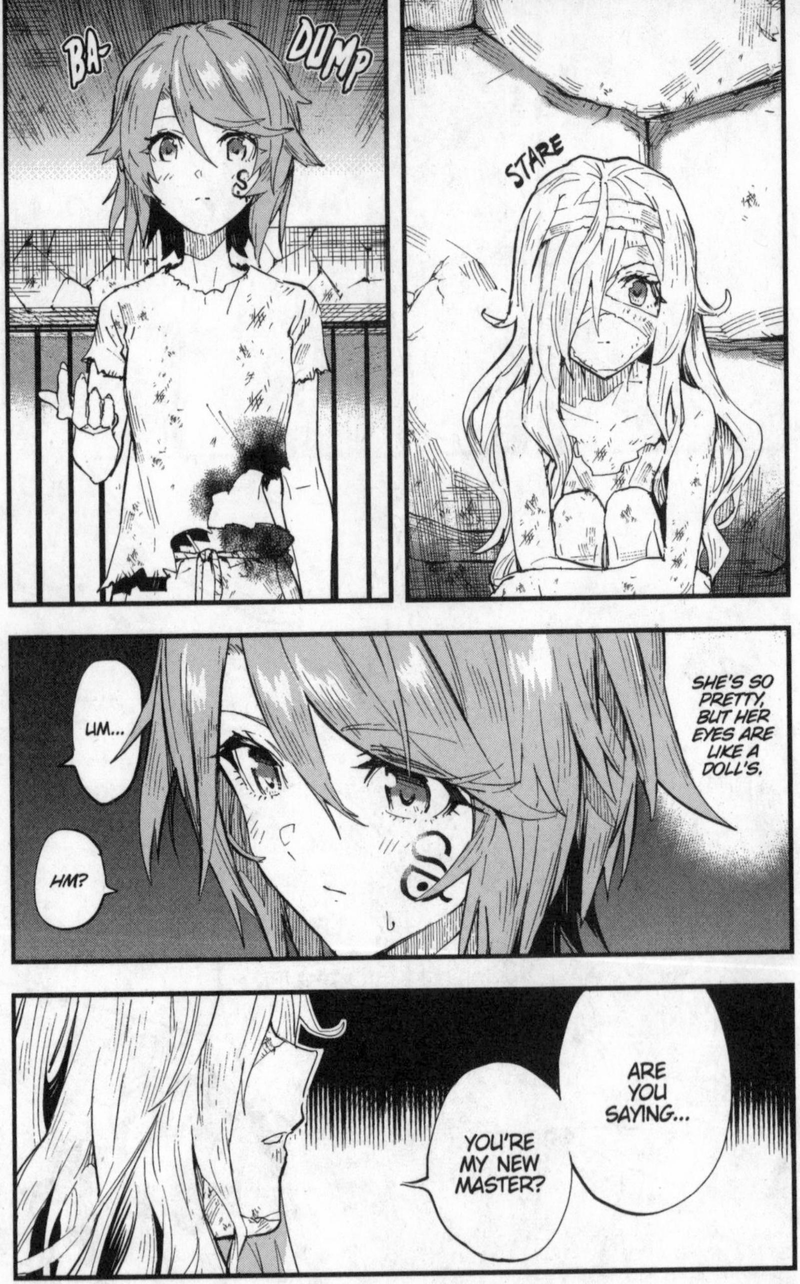
STARE
BA-
DUMP
SHE'S SO PRETTY, BUT HER EYES ARE LIKE A DOLL'S.
UM...
HM?
ARE YOU SAYING...
YOU'RE MY NEW MASTER?

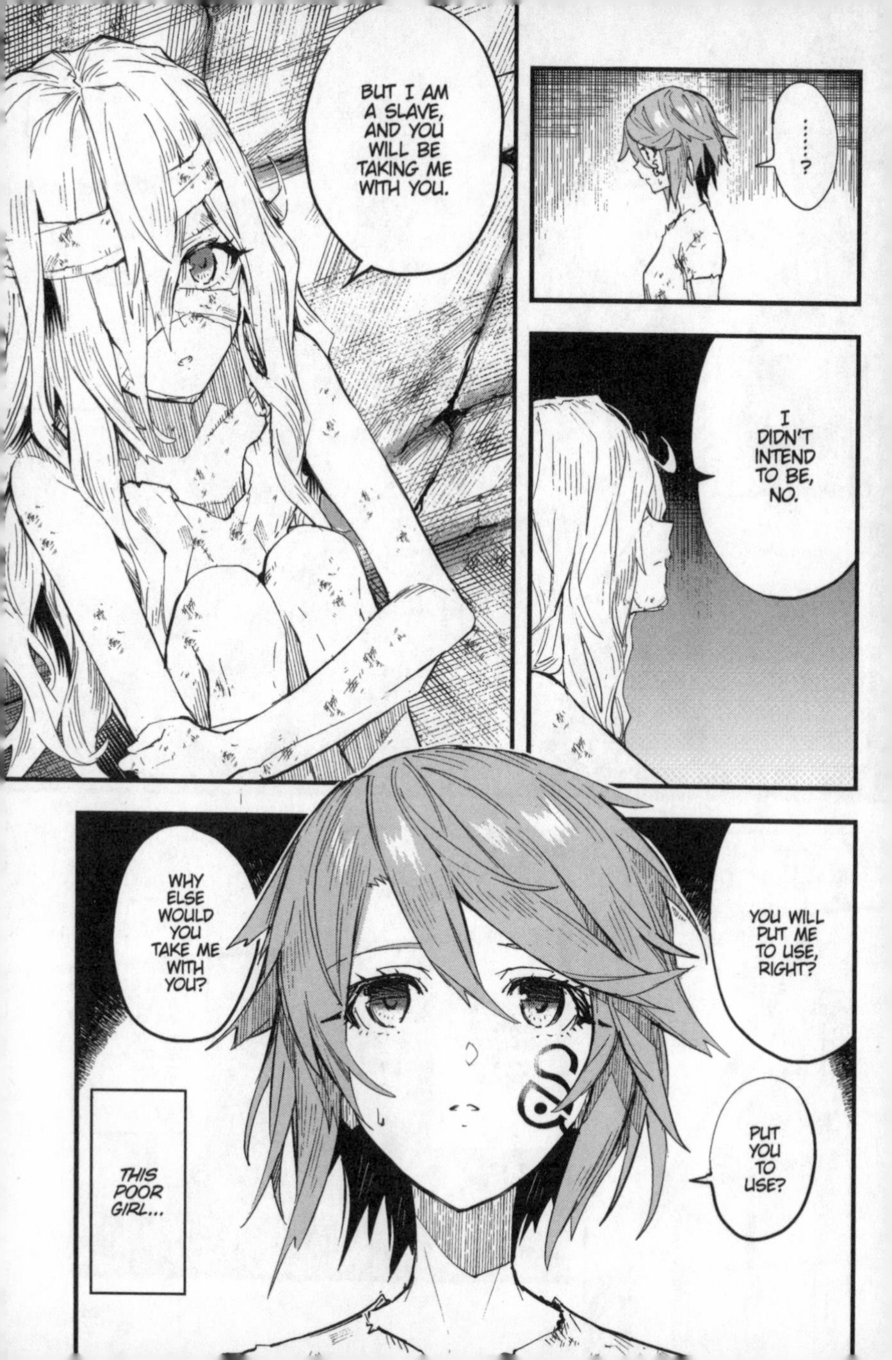
......?
I DIDN'T INTEND TO BE, NO.
BUT I AM A SLAVE, AND YOU WILL BE TAKING ME WITH YOU.
YOU WILL PUT ME TO USE, RIGHT?
WHY ELSE WOULD YOU TAKE ME WITH YOU?
PUT YOU TO USE?
THIS POOR GIRL...

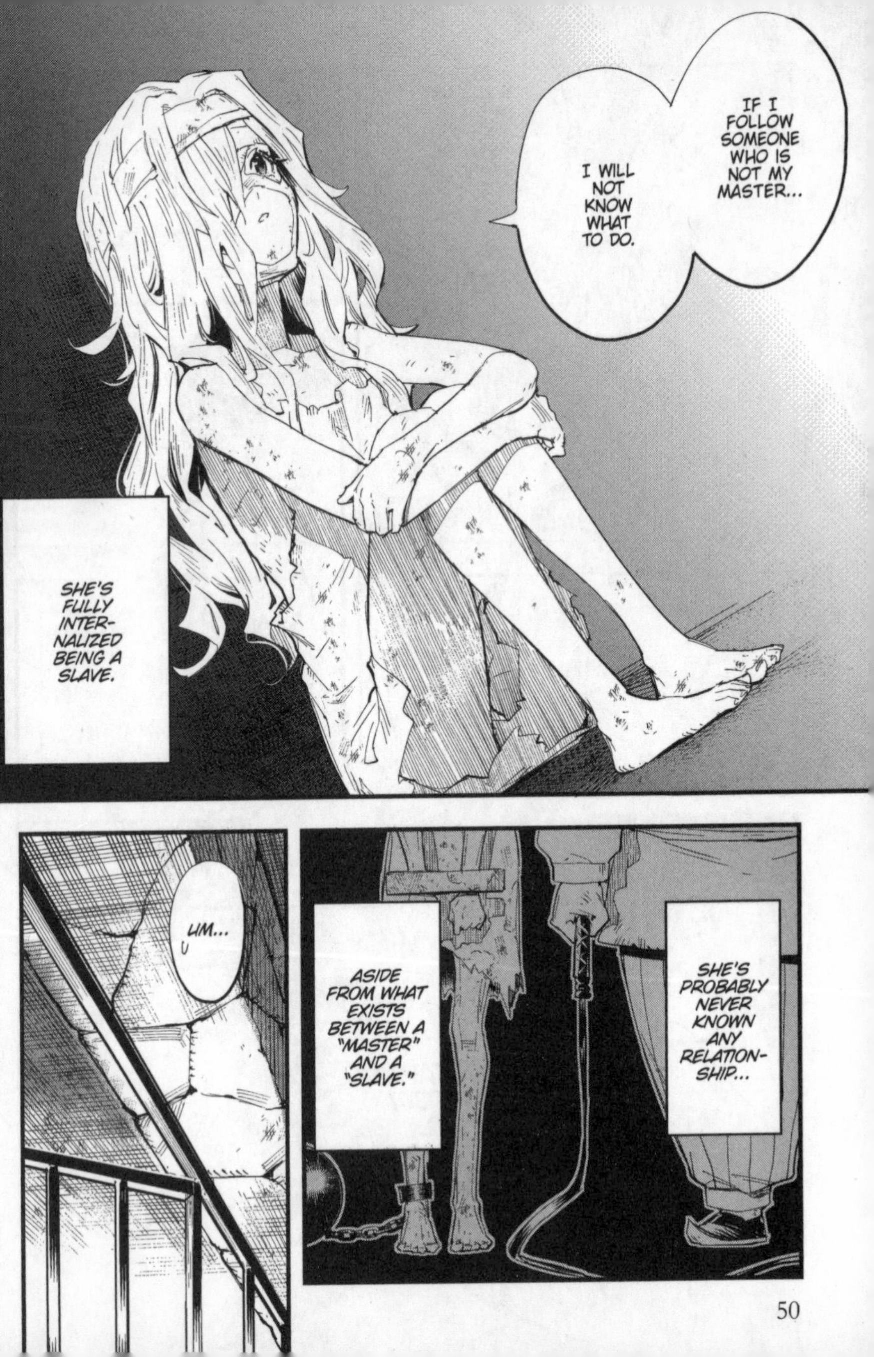
IF I FOLLOW SOMEONE WHO IS NOT MY MASTER...
I WILL NOT KNOW WHAT TO DO.
SHE'S FULLY INTERNALIZED BEING A SLAVE.
SHE'S PROBABLY NEVER KNOWN ANY RELATIONSHIP...
ASIDE FROM WHAT EXISTS BETWEEN A "MASTER" AND A "SLAVE."
UM...

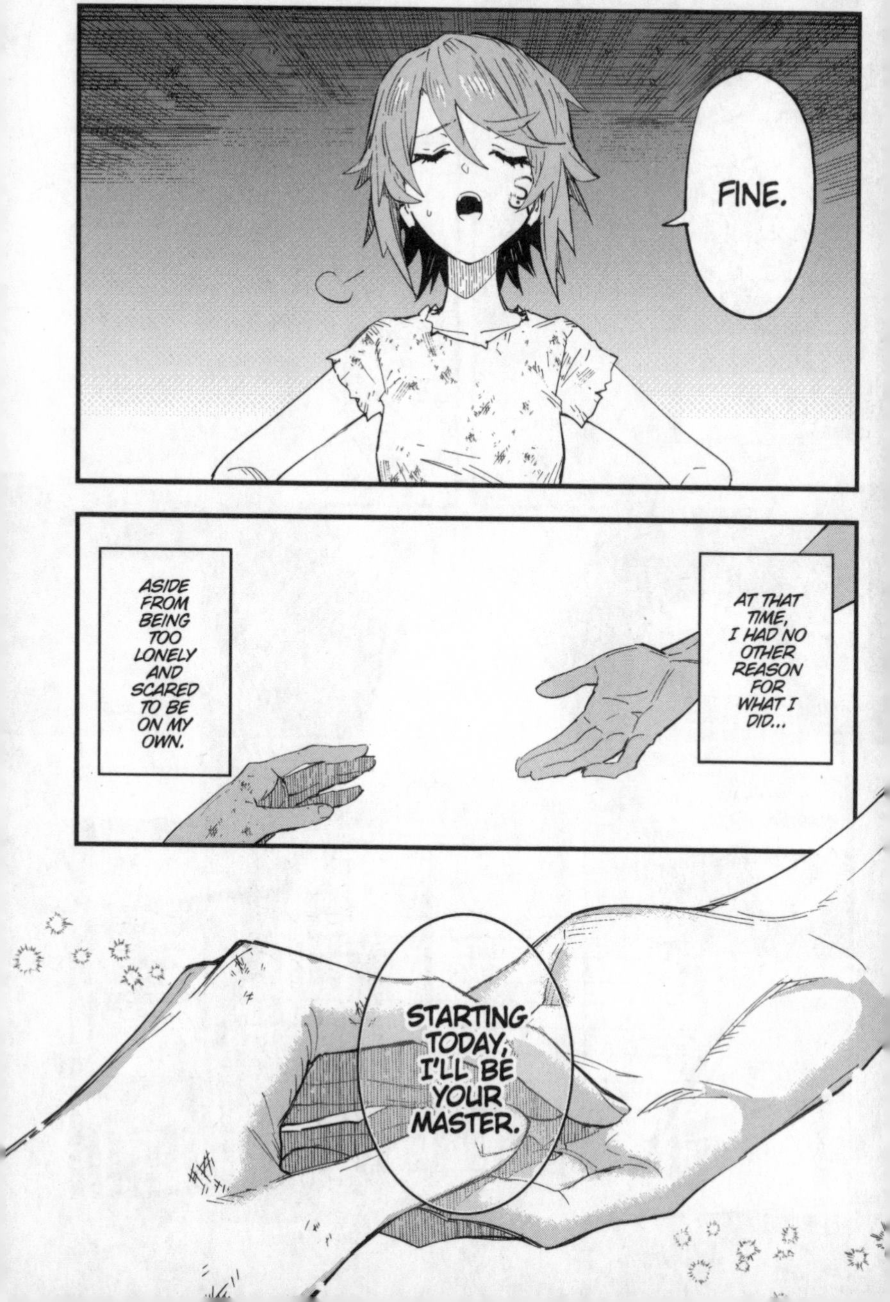
FINE.
AT THAT TIME, I HAD NO OTHER REASON FOR WHAT I DID...
ASIDE FROM BEING TOO LONELY AND SCARED TO BE ON MY OWN.
STARTING TODAY, I'LL BE YOUR MASTER.

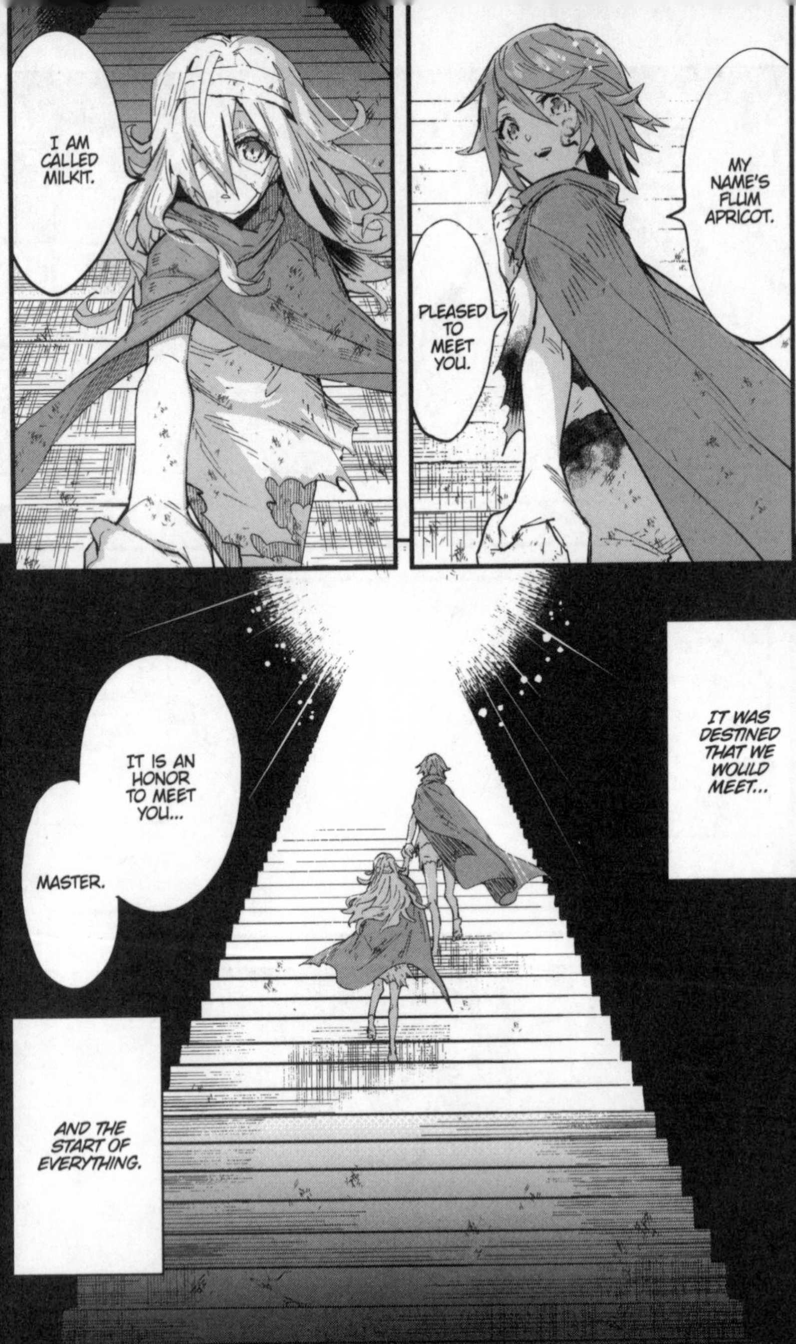
MY NAME'S FLUM APRICOT.
PLEASED TO MEET YOU.
I AM CALLED MILKIT.
IT WAS DESTINED THAT WE WOULD MEET...
IT IS AN HONOR TO MEET YOU...
MASTER.
AND THE START OF EVERYTHING.

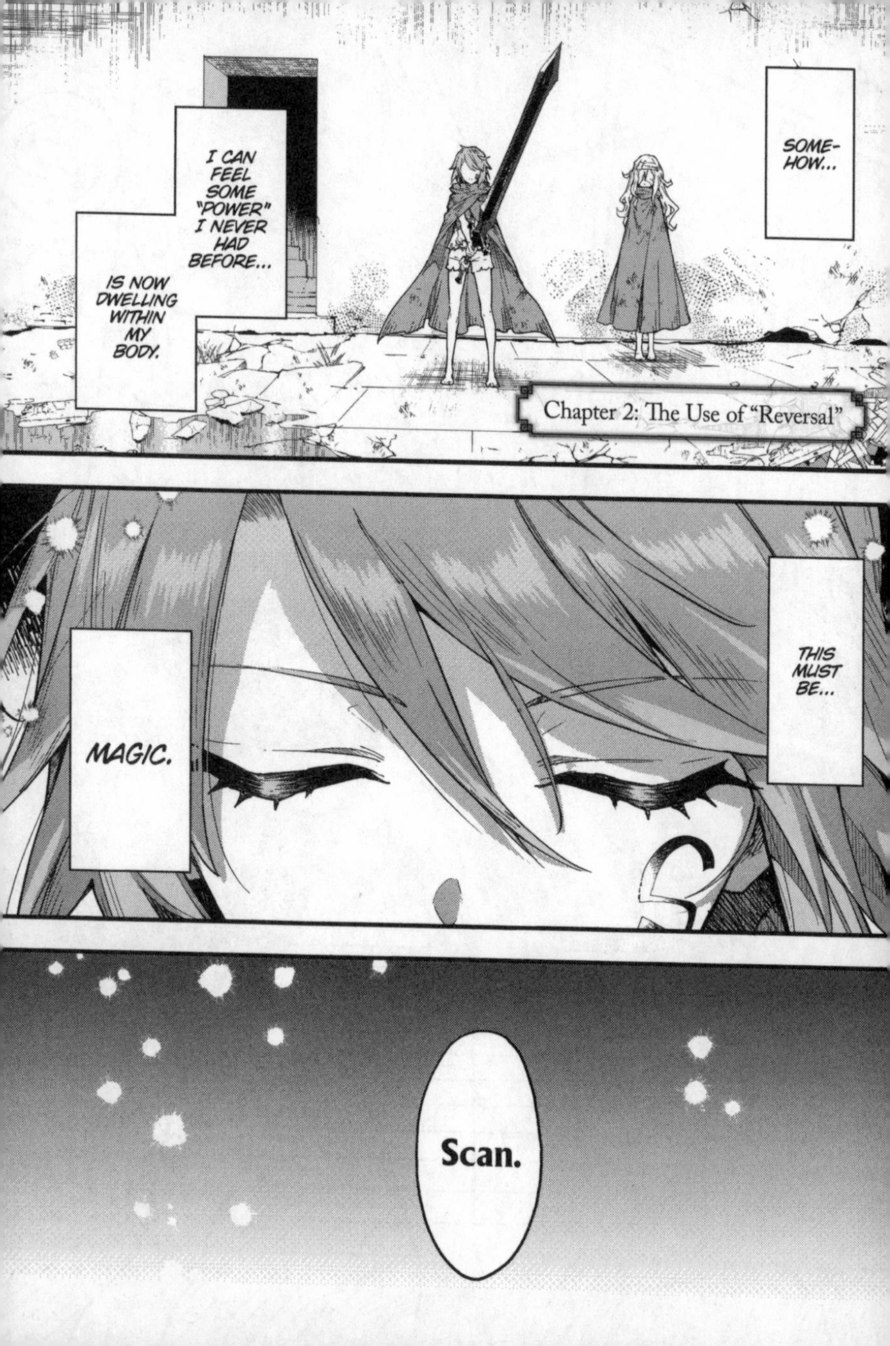
SOME-HOW...
I CAN FEEL SOME "POWER" I NEVER HAD BEFORE...
IS NOW DWELLING WITHIN MY BODY.
Chapter 2: The Use of "Reversal"
THIS MUST BE...
MAGIC.
Scan.

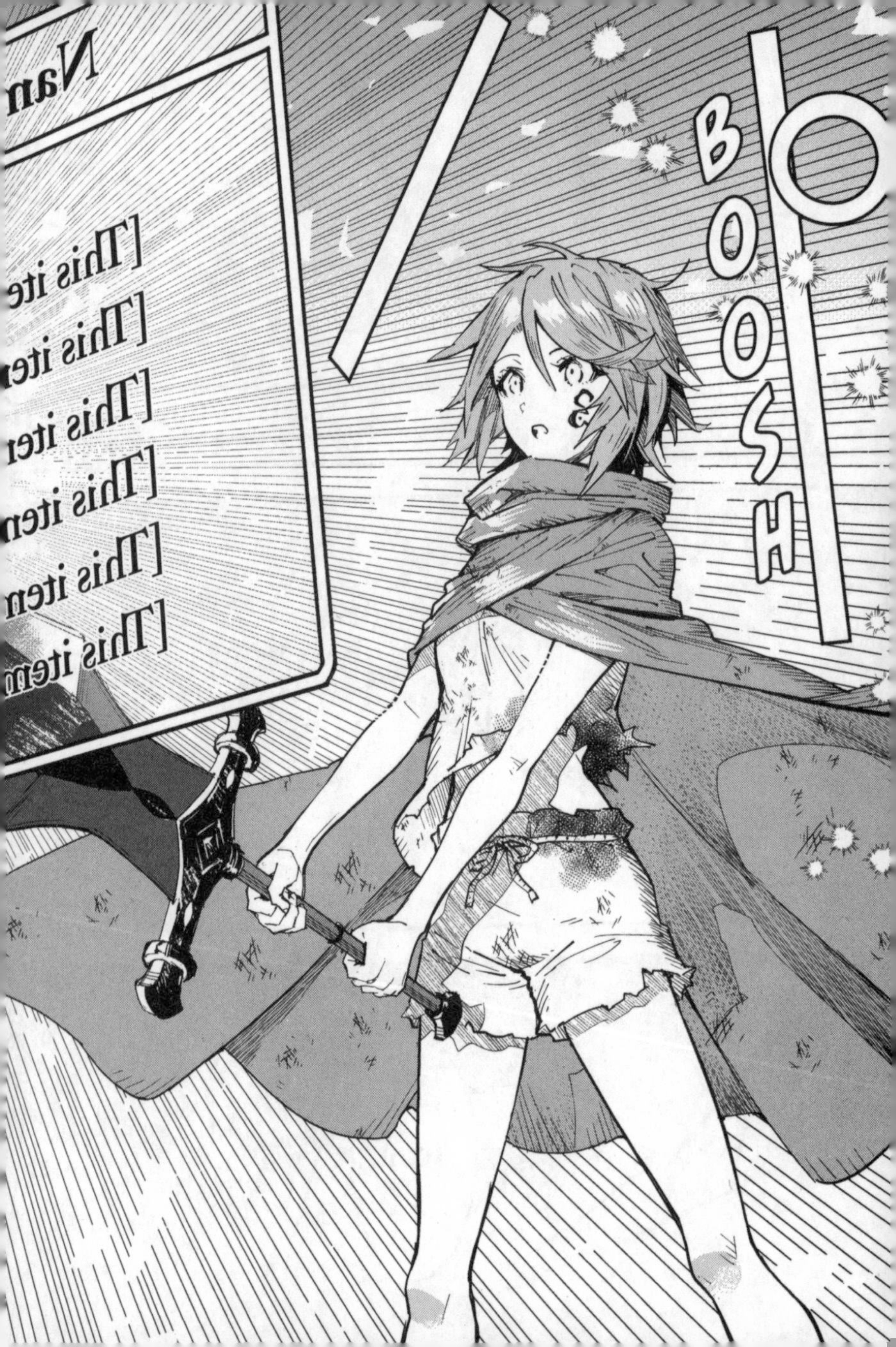
BOOSH

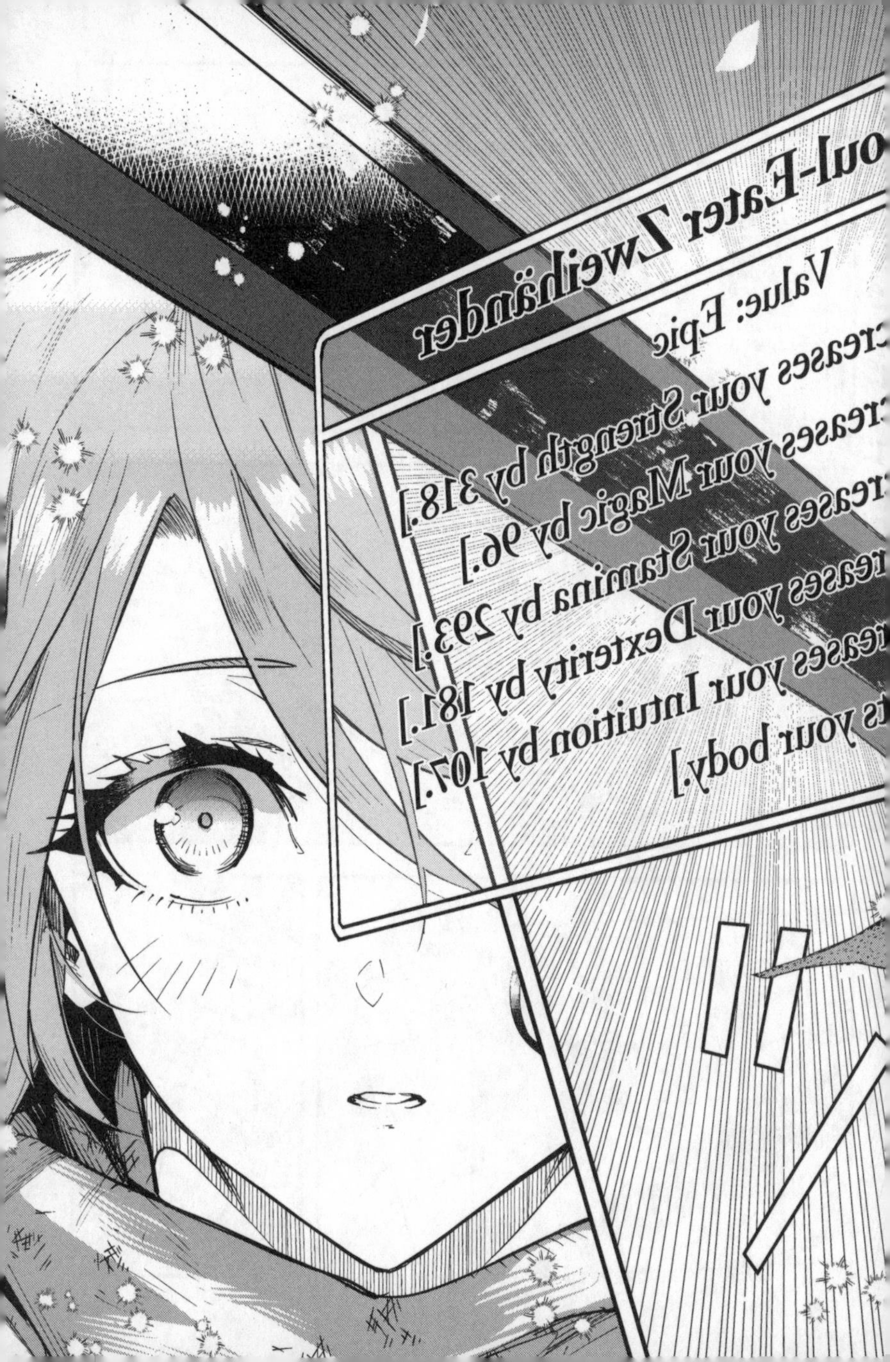

oul-Eater Zweihänder
Value: Epic
creases your Strength by 318.]
creases your Magic by 96.]
creases your Stamina by 293.]
creases your Dexterity by 181.]
creases your Intuition by 107.]
ts your body.]

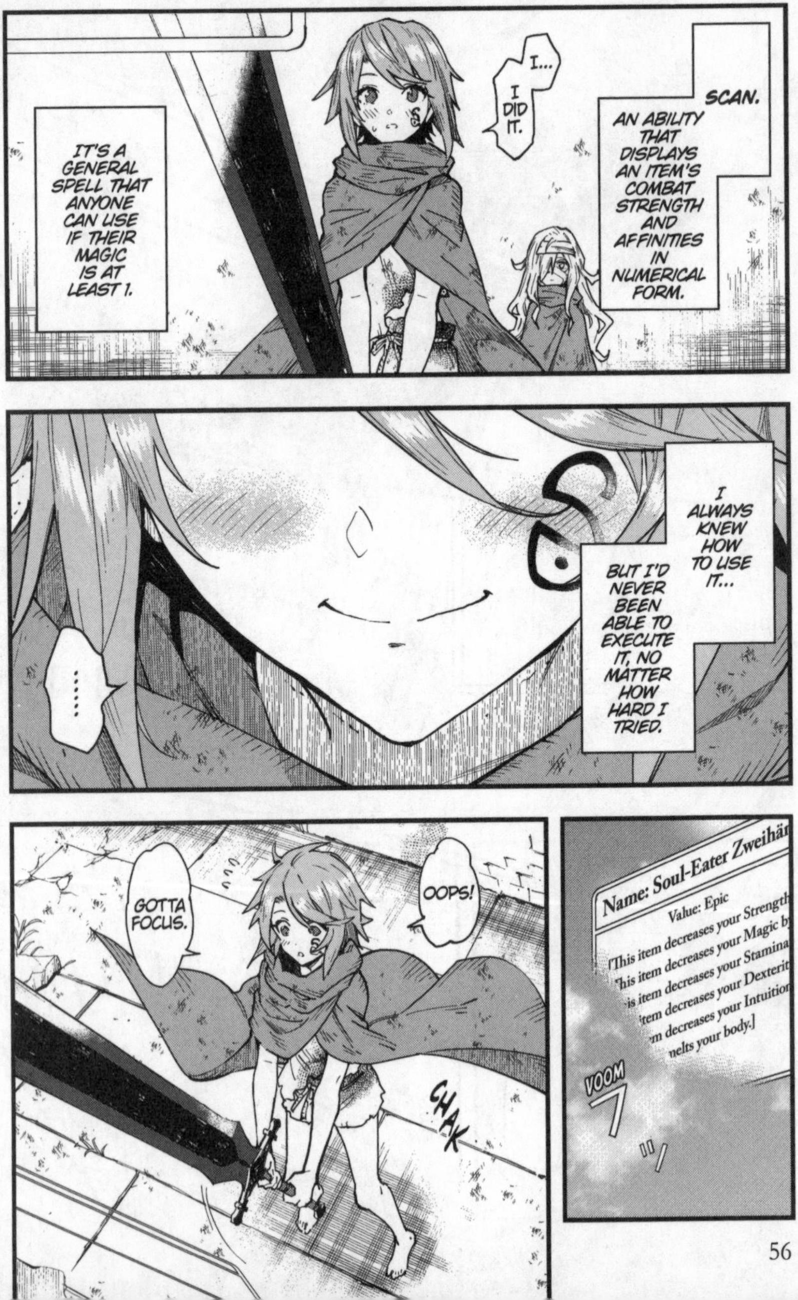
SCAN.
AN ABILITY THAT DISPLAYS AN ITEM'S COMBAT STRENGTH AND AFFINITIES IN NUMERICAL FORM.
I... I DID IT.
IT'S A GENERAL SPELL THAT ANYONE CAN USE IF THEIR MAGIC IS AT LEAST 1.
I ALWAYS KNEW HOW TO USE IT...
BUT I'D NEVER BEEN ABLE TO EXECUTE IT, NO MATTER HOW HARD I TRIED.
......
Name: Soul-Eater Zweihän
Value: Epic
[This item decreases your Strength
This item decreases your Magic by
is item decreases your Stamina
item decreases your Dexterit
item decreases your Intuition
m decreases your body.]
nelts your body.]
VOOM
OOPS!
GOTTA FOCUS.
CHAK

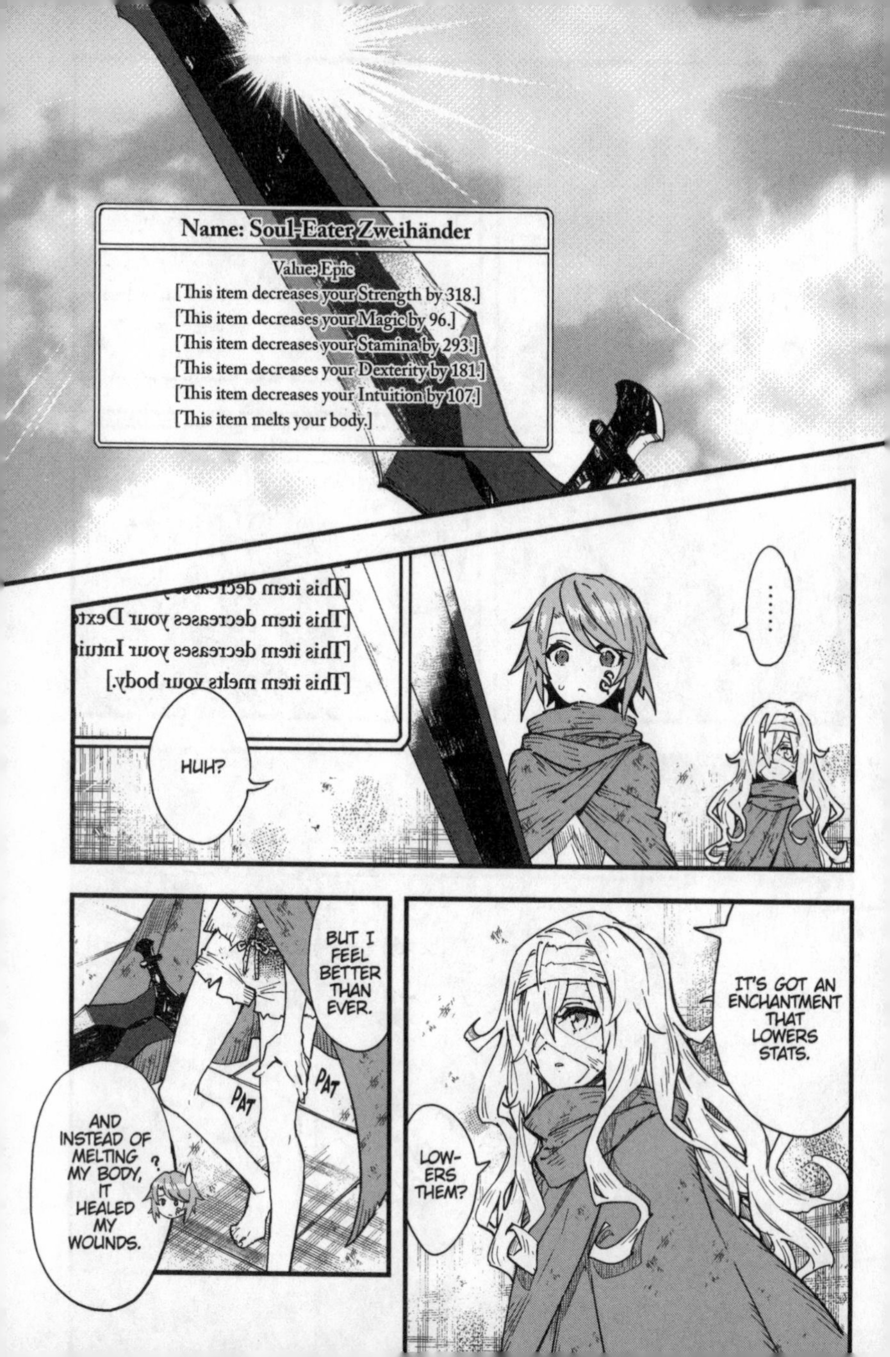

Name: Soul-Eater Zweihänder
Value: Epic
[This item decreases your Strength by 318.]
[This item decreases your Magic by 96.]
[This item decreases your Stamina by 293.]
[This item decreases your Dexterity by 181.]
[This item decreases your Intuition by 107.]
[This item melts your body.]
......
HUH?
IT'S GOT AN ENCHANTMENT THAT LOWERS STATS.
LOW-ERS THEM?
BUT I FEEL BETTER THAN EVER.
PAT
PAT
AND INSTEAD OF MELTING MY BODY, IT HEALED MY WOUNDS.

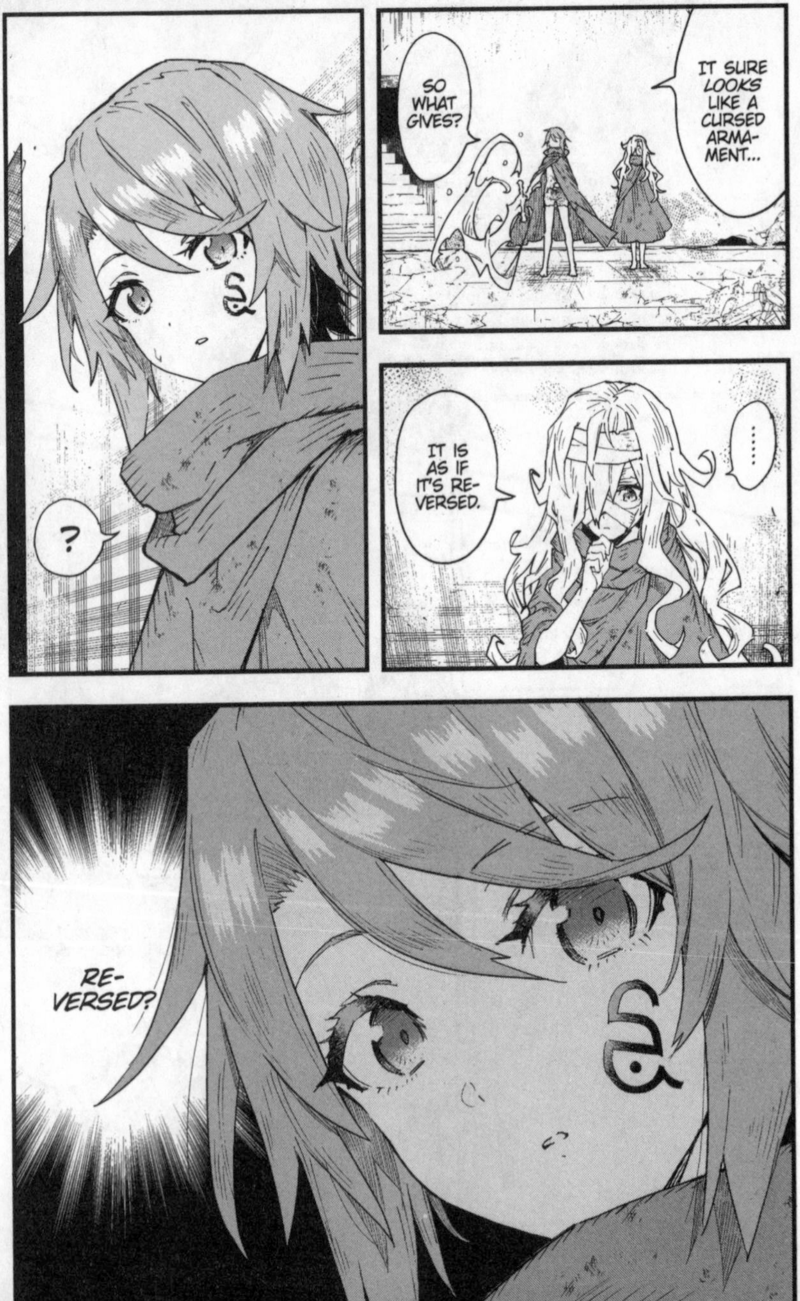
IT SURE LOOKS LIKE A CURSED ARMAMENT...
SO WHAT GIVES?
......
IT IS AS IF IT'S REVERSED.
?
REVERSED?

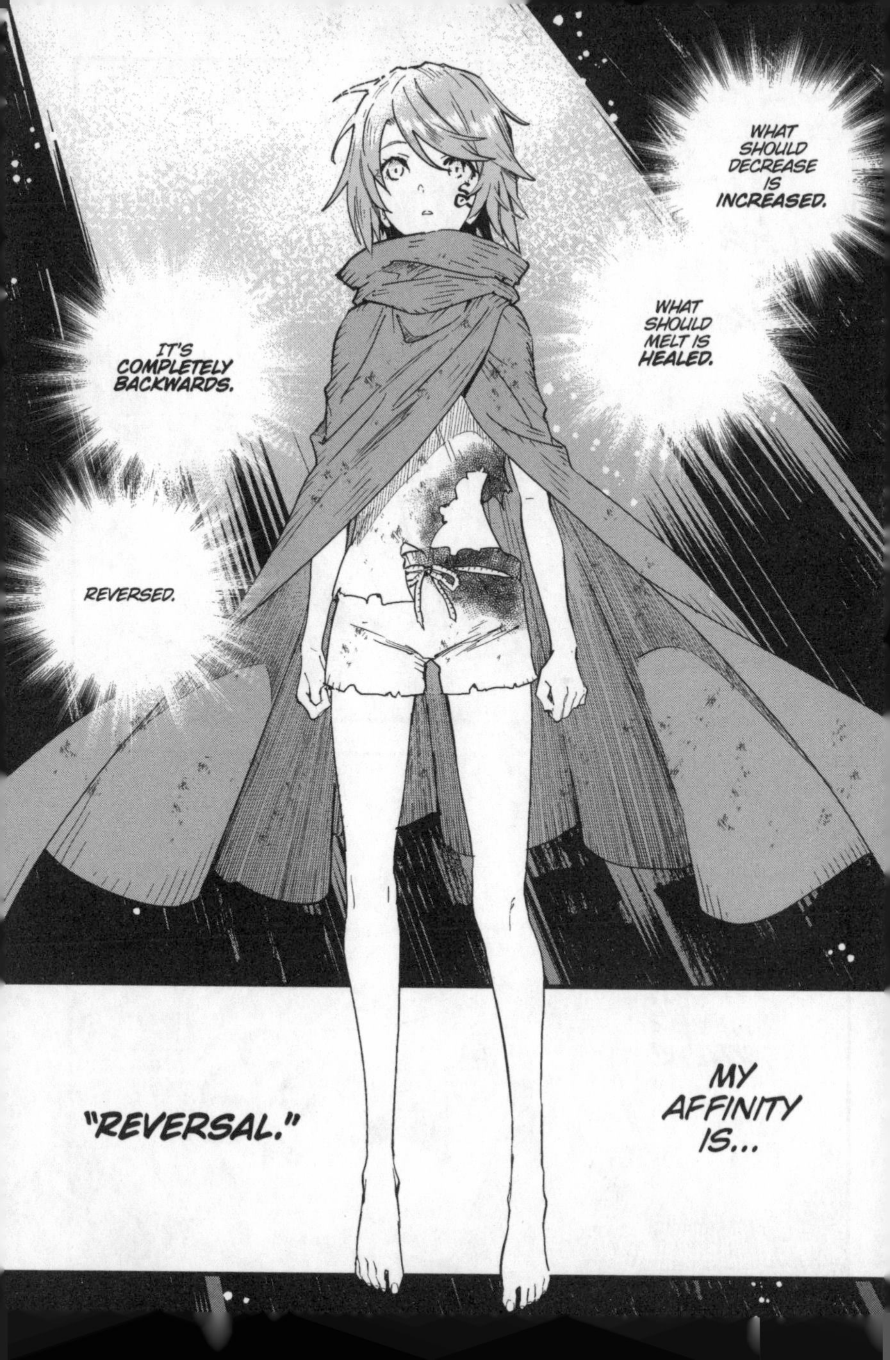
WHAT SHOULD DECREASE IS INCREASED.
WHAT SHOULD MELT IS HEALED.
IT'S COMPLETELY BACKWARDS.
REVERSED.
MY AFFINITY IS...
"REVERSAL."

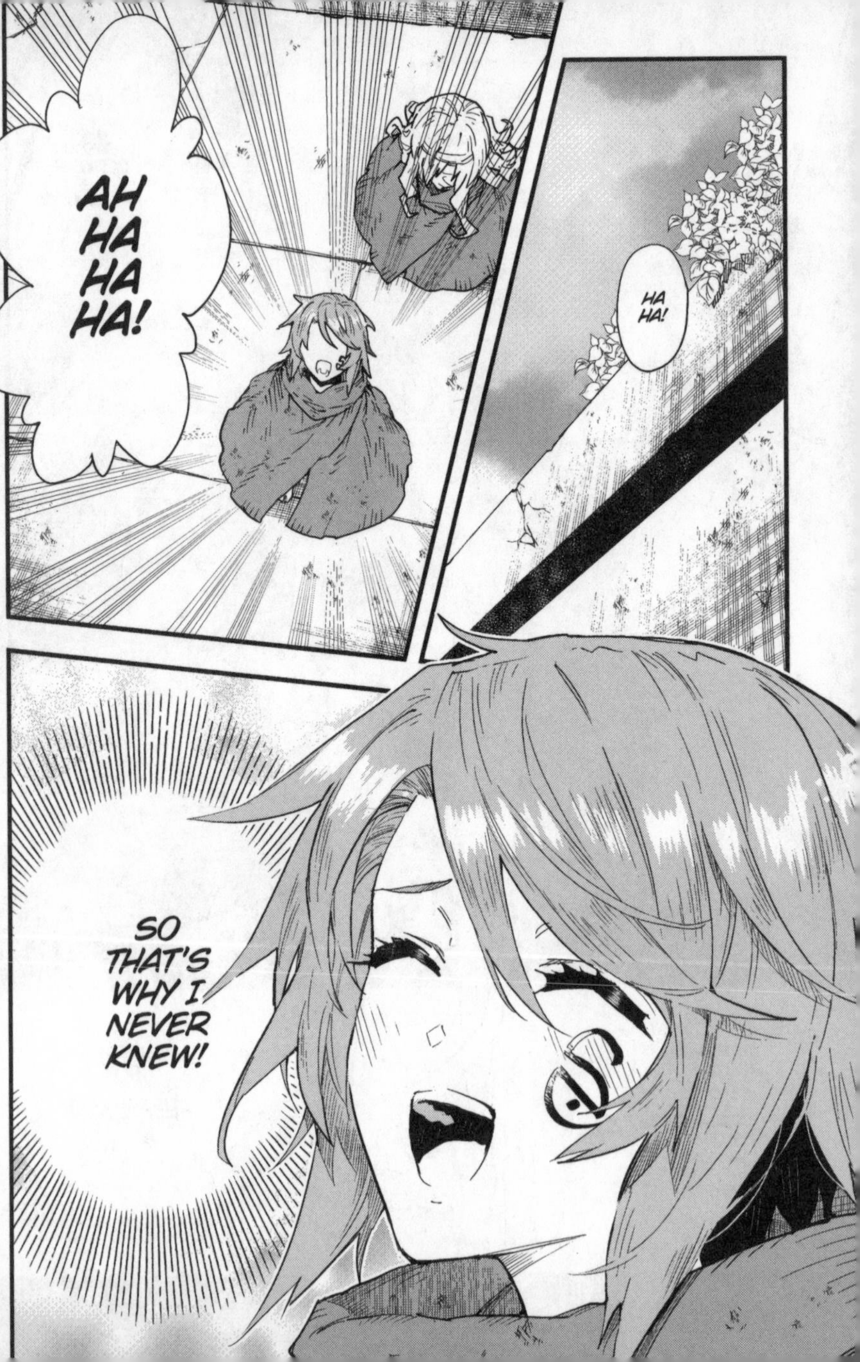
HA HA!
AH HA HA HA!
SO THAT'S WHY I NEVER KNEW!

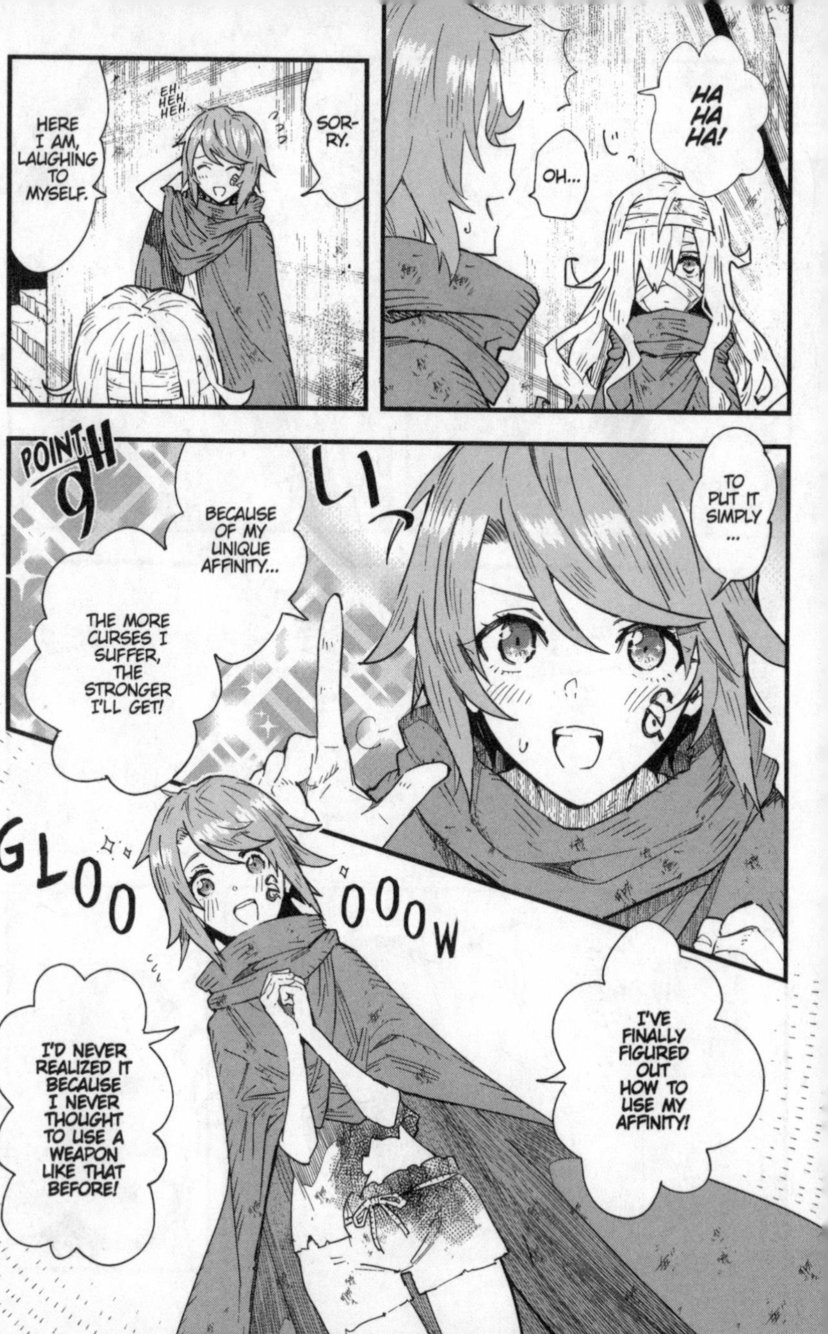
HA HA HA!
OH...
EH HEH HEH.
SOR-RY.
HERE I AM, LAUGHING TO MYSELF.
TO PUT IT SIMPLY...
POINT
BECAUSE OF MY UNIQUE AFFINITY...
THE MORE CURSES I SUFFER, THE STRONGER I'LL GET!
GLOOOOOW
I'VE FINALLY FIGURED OUT HOW TO USE MY AFFINITY!
I'D NEVER REALIZED IT BECAUSE I NEVER THOUGHT TO USE A WEAPON LIKE THAT BEFORE!

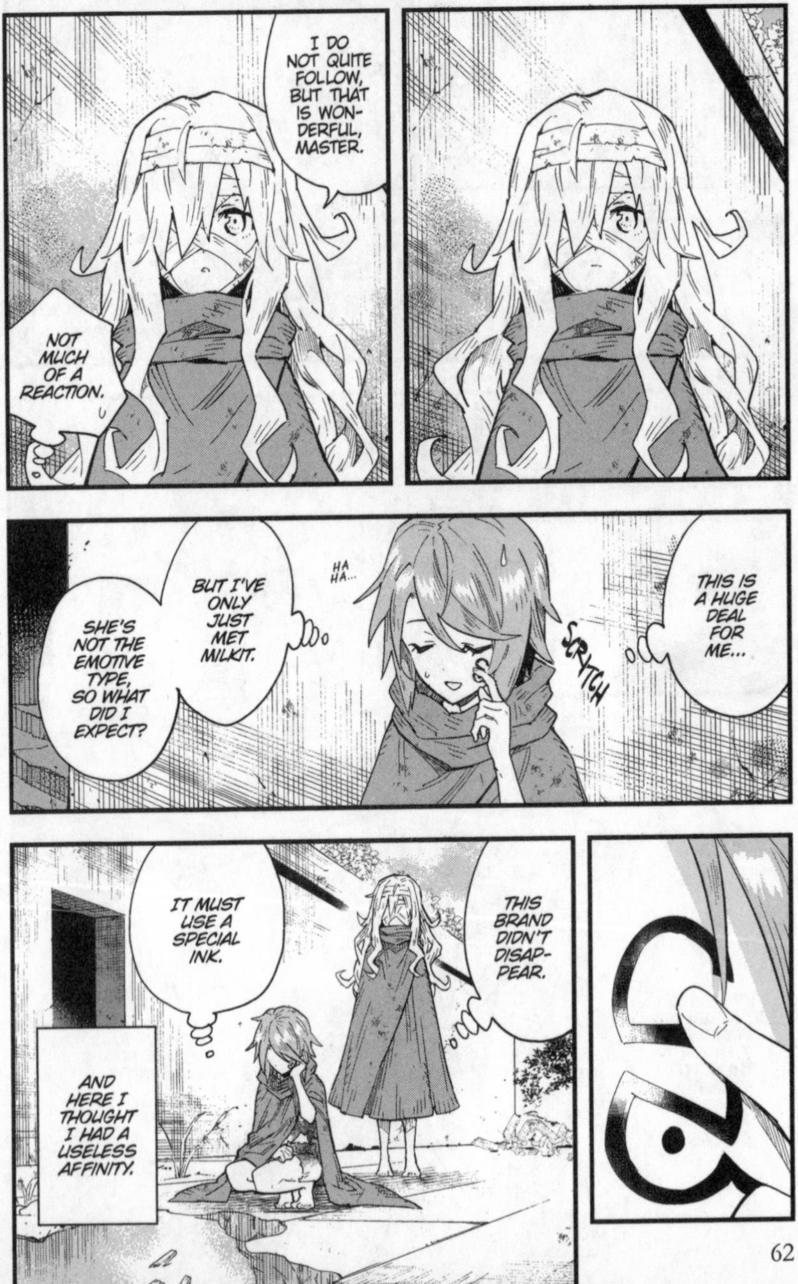
I DO NOT QUITE FOLLOW, BUT THAT IS WON-DERFUL, MASTER.
NOT MUCH OF A REACTION.
THIS IS A HUGE DEAL FOR ME...
SCRYTCH
HA HA...
BUT I'VE ONLY JUST MET MILKIT.
SHE'S NOT THE EMOTIVE TYPE, SO WHAT DID I EXPECT?
THIS BRAND DIDN'T DISAP-PEAR.
IT MUST USE A SPECIAL INK.
AND HERE I THOUGHT I HAD A USELESS AFFINITY.

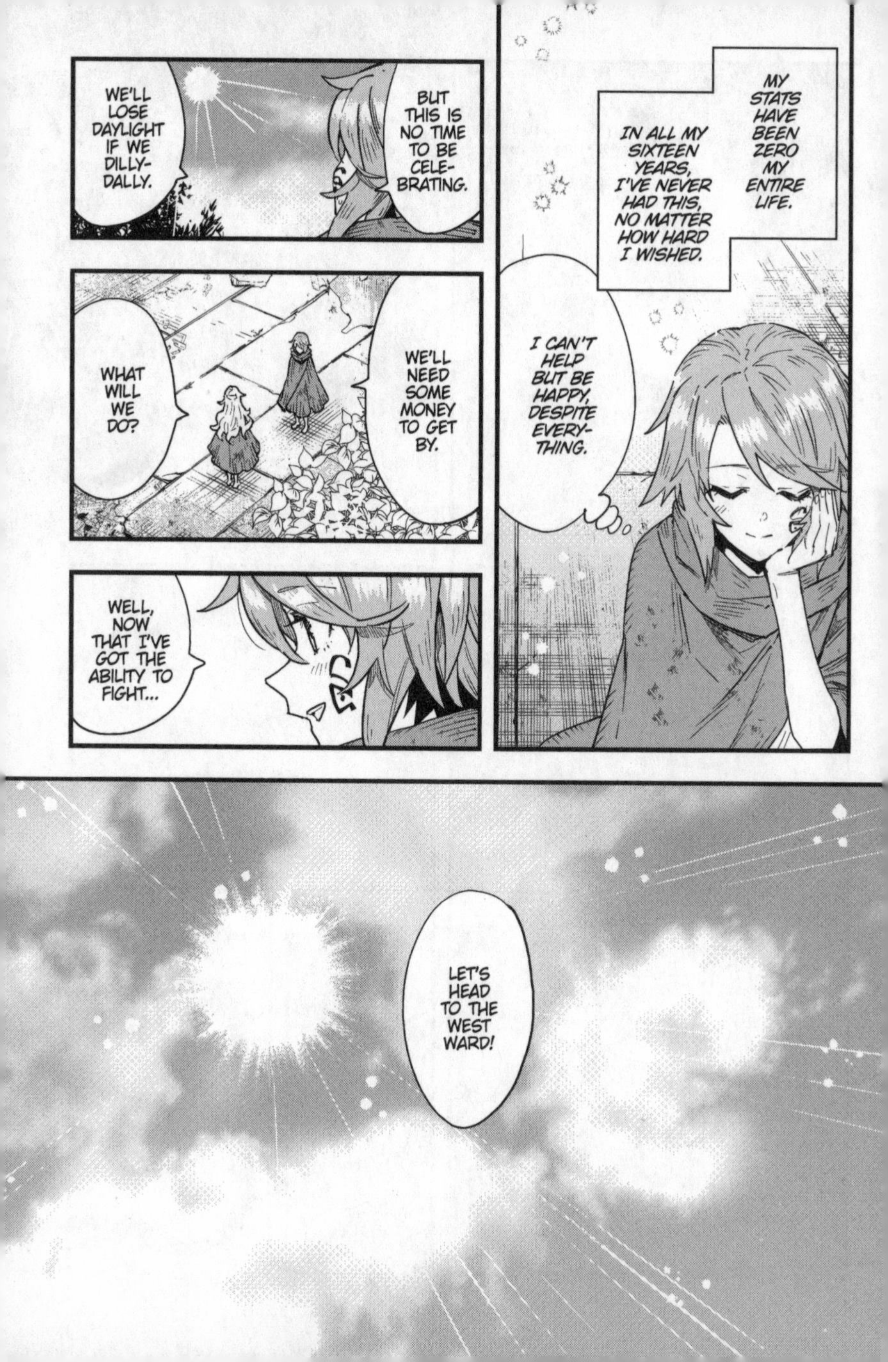
MY STATS HAVE BEEN ZERO MY ENTIRE LIFE.
IN ALL MY SIXTEEN YEARS, I'VE NEVER HAD THIS, NO MATTER HOW HARD I WISHED.
I CAN'T HELP BUT BE HAPPY, DESPITE EVERYTHING.
BUT THIS IS NO TIME TO BE CELEBRATING.
WE'LL LOSE DAYLIGHT IF WE DILLY-DALLY.
WE'LL NEED SOME MONEY TO GET BY.
WHAT WILL WE DO?
WELL, NOW THAT I'VE GOT THE ABILITY TO FIGHT...
LET'S HEAD TO THE WEST WARD!

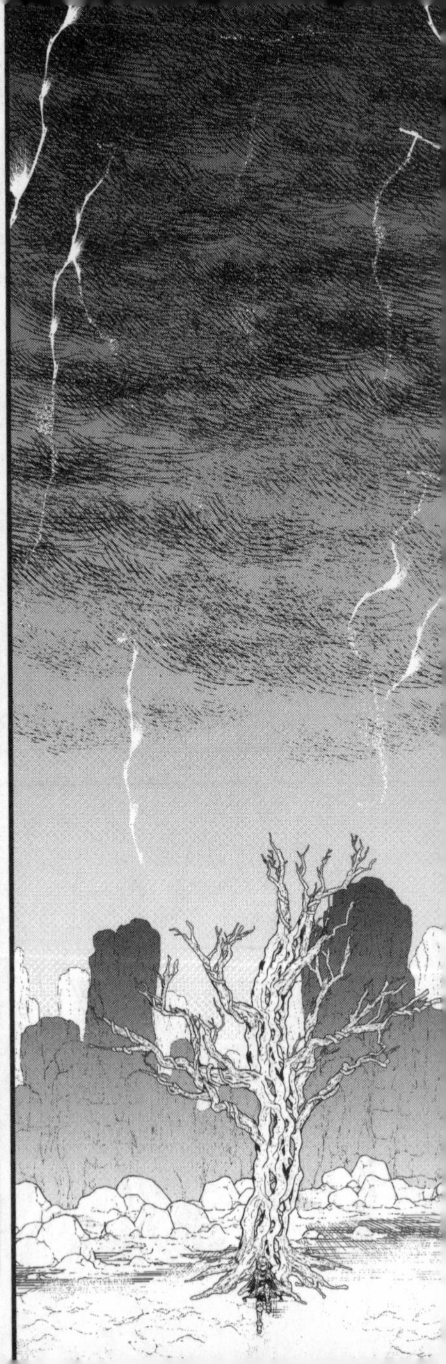
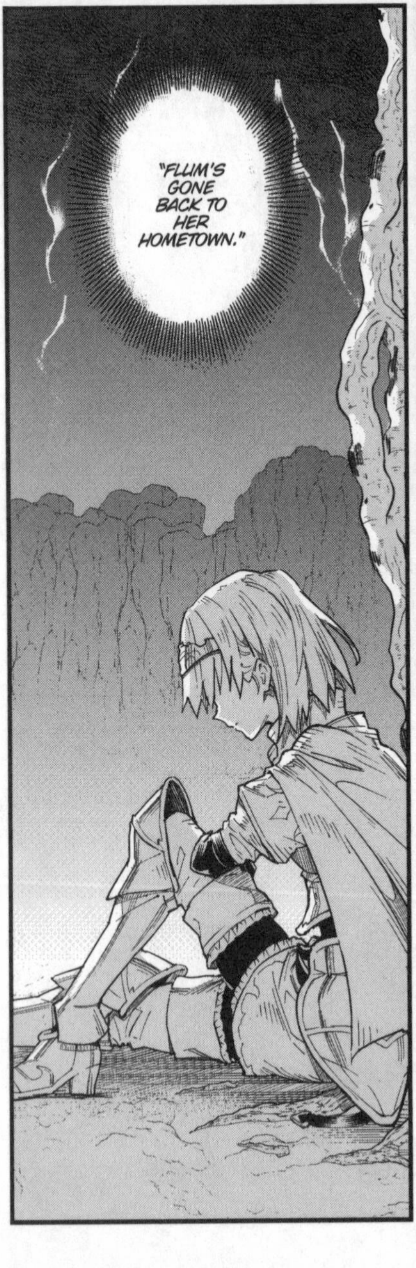
"FLUM'S GONE BACK TO HER HOMETOWN."

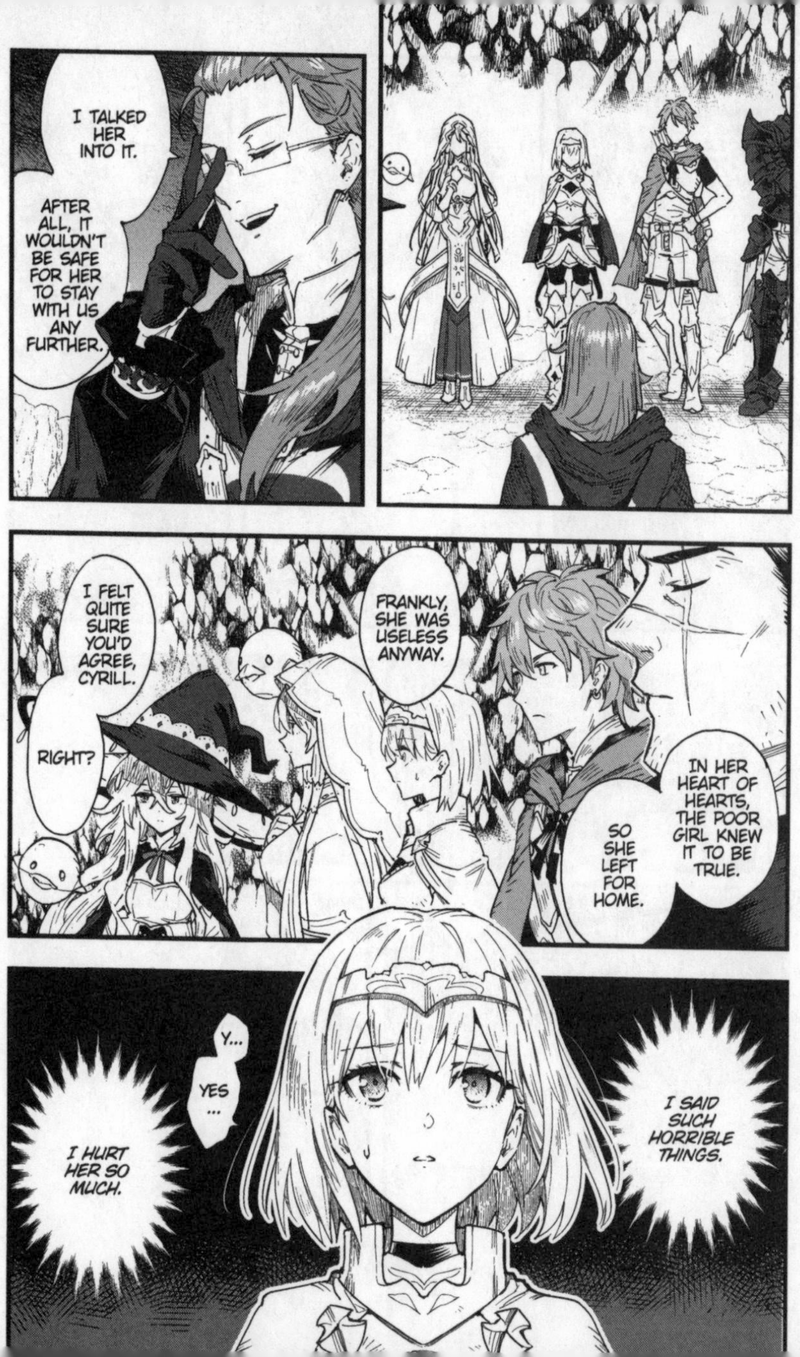
I TALKED HER INTO IT.
AFTER ALL, IT WOULDN'T BE SAFE FOR HER TO STAY WITH US ANY FURTHER.
FRANKLY, SHE WAS USELESS ANYWAY.
IN HER HEART OF HEARTS, THE POOR GIRL KNEW IT TO BE TRUE.
SO SHE LEFT FOR HOME.
I FELT QUITE SURE YOU'D AGREE, CYRILL.
RIGHT?
I SAID SUCH HORRIBLE THINGS.
Y... YES...
I HURT HER SO MUCH.

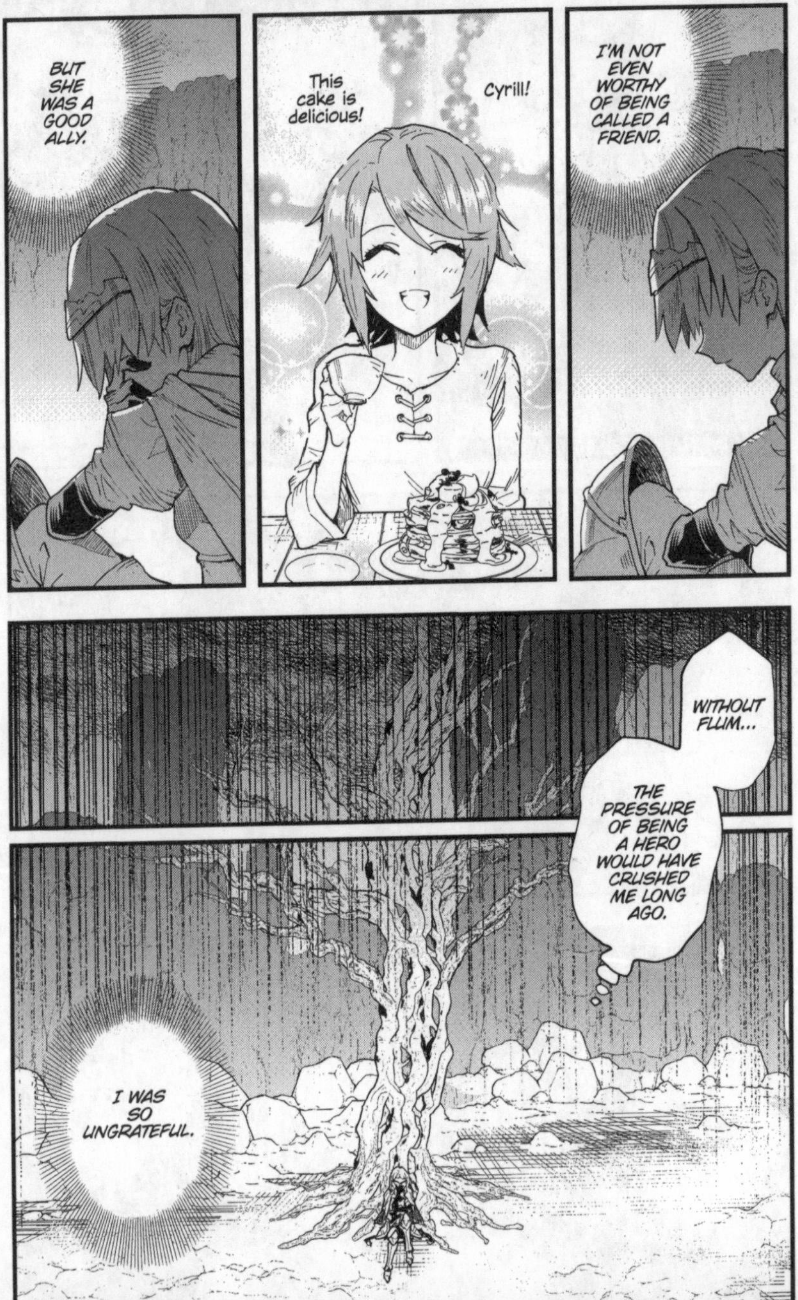

I'M NOT EVEN WORTHY OF BEING CALLED A FRIEND.
Cyrill!
This cake is delicious!
BUT SHE WAS A GOOD ALLY.
WITHOUT FLUM...
THE PRESSURE OF BEING A HERO WOULD HAVE CRUSHED ME LONG AGO.
I WAS SO UNGRATEFUL.

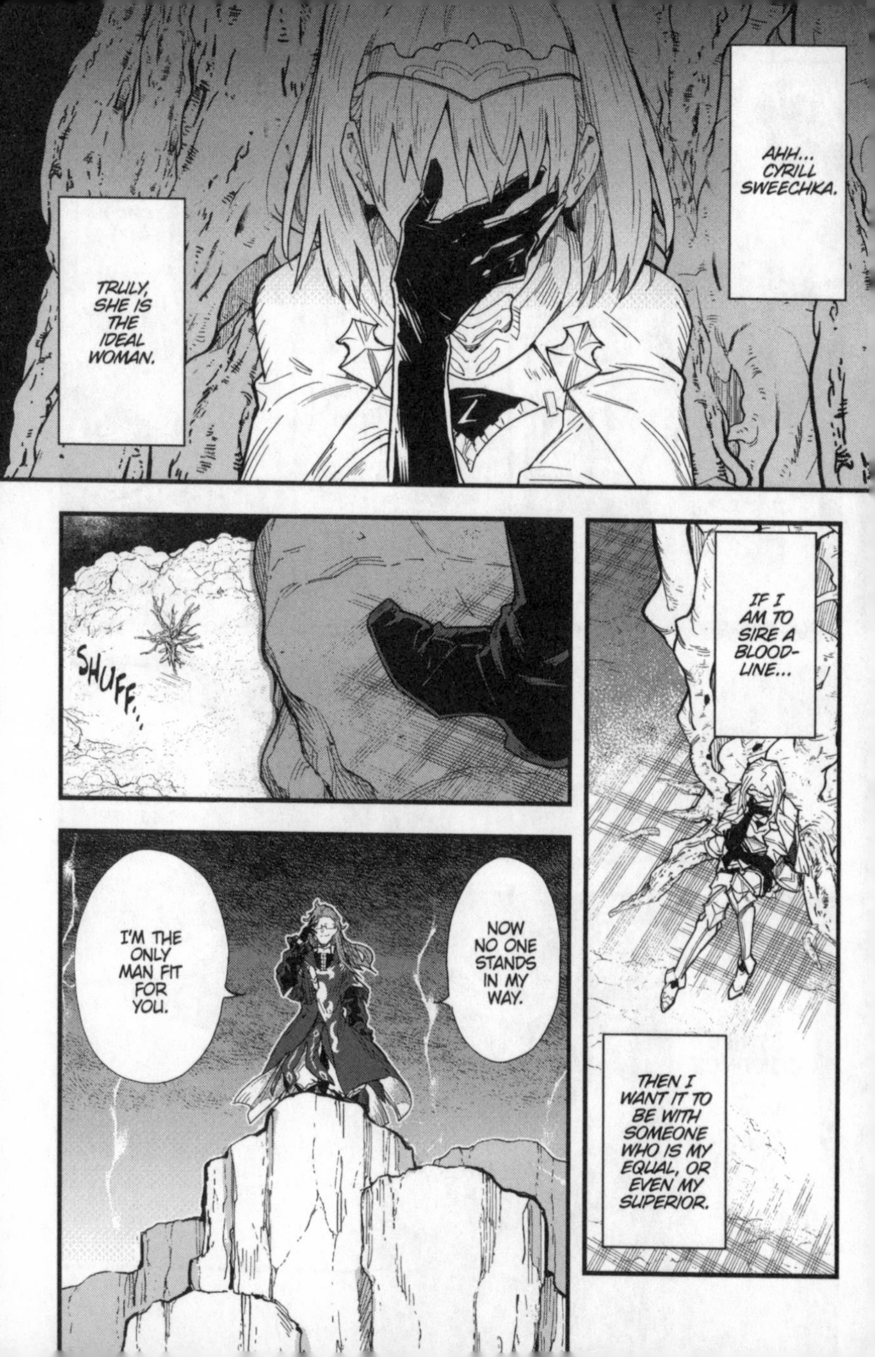
AHH... CYRILL SWEECHKA.
TRULY, SHE IS THE IDEAL WOMAN.
IF I AM TO SIRE A BLOOD-LINE...
THEN I WANT IT TO BE WITH SOMEONE WHO IS MY EQUAL, OR EVEN MY SUPERIOR.
SHUFF...
NOW NO ONE STANDS IN MY WAY.
I'M THE ONLY MAN FIT FOR YOU.

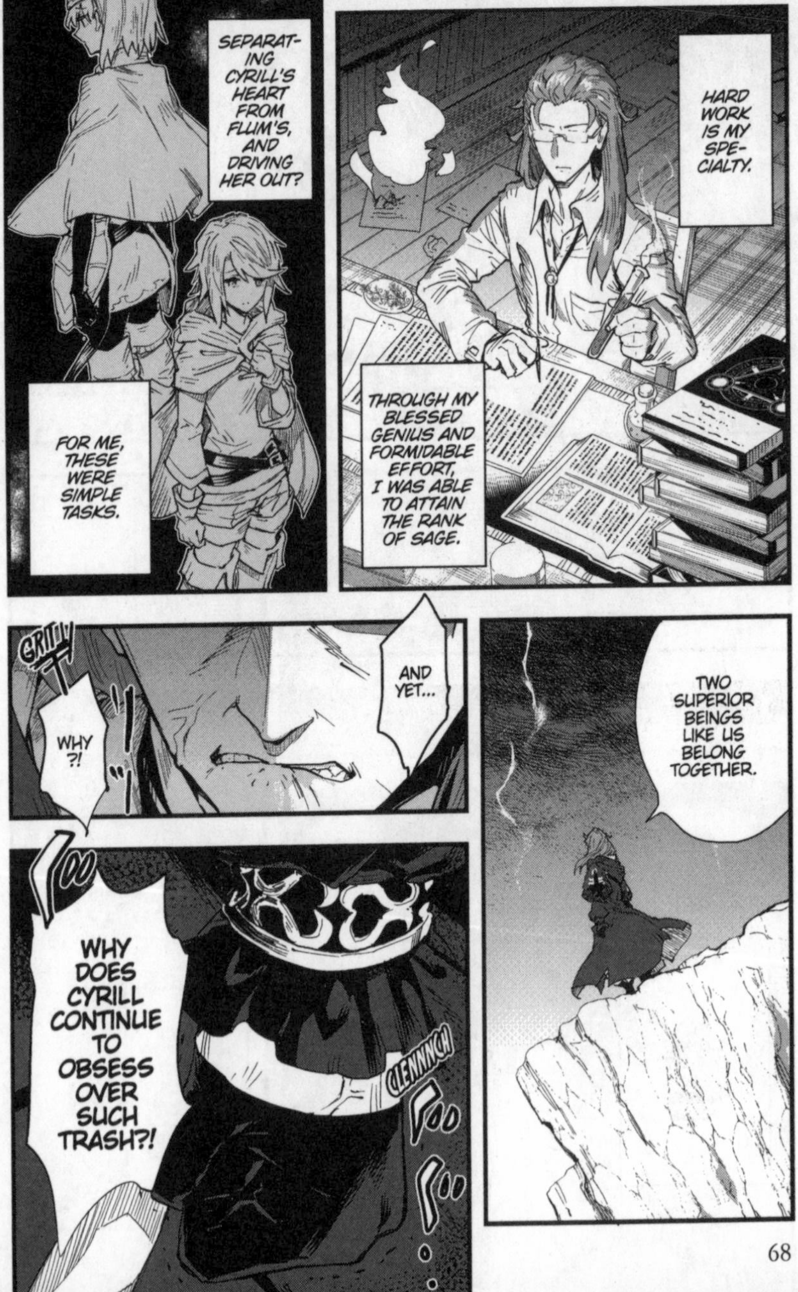

HARD WORK IS MY SPECIALTY.
THROUGH MY BLESSED GENIUS AND FORMIDABLE EFFORT, I WAS ABLE TO ATTAIN THE RANK OF SAGE.
SEPARATING CYRILL'S HEART FROM FLUM'S, AND DRIVING HER OUT?
FOR ME, THESE WERE SIMPLE TASKS.
TWO SUPERIOR BEINGS LIKE US BELONG TOGETHER.
AND YET...
GRIT
WHY?!
WHY DOES CYRILL CONTINUE TO OBSESS OVER SUCH TRASH?!
CLENNNCH

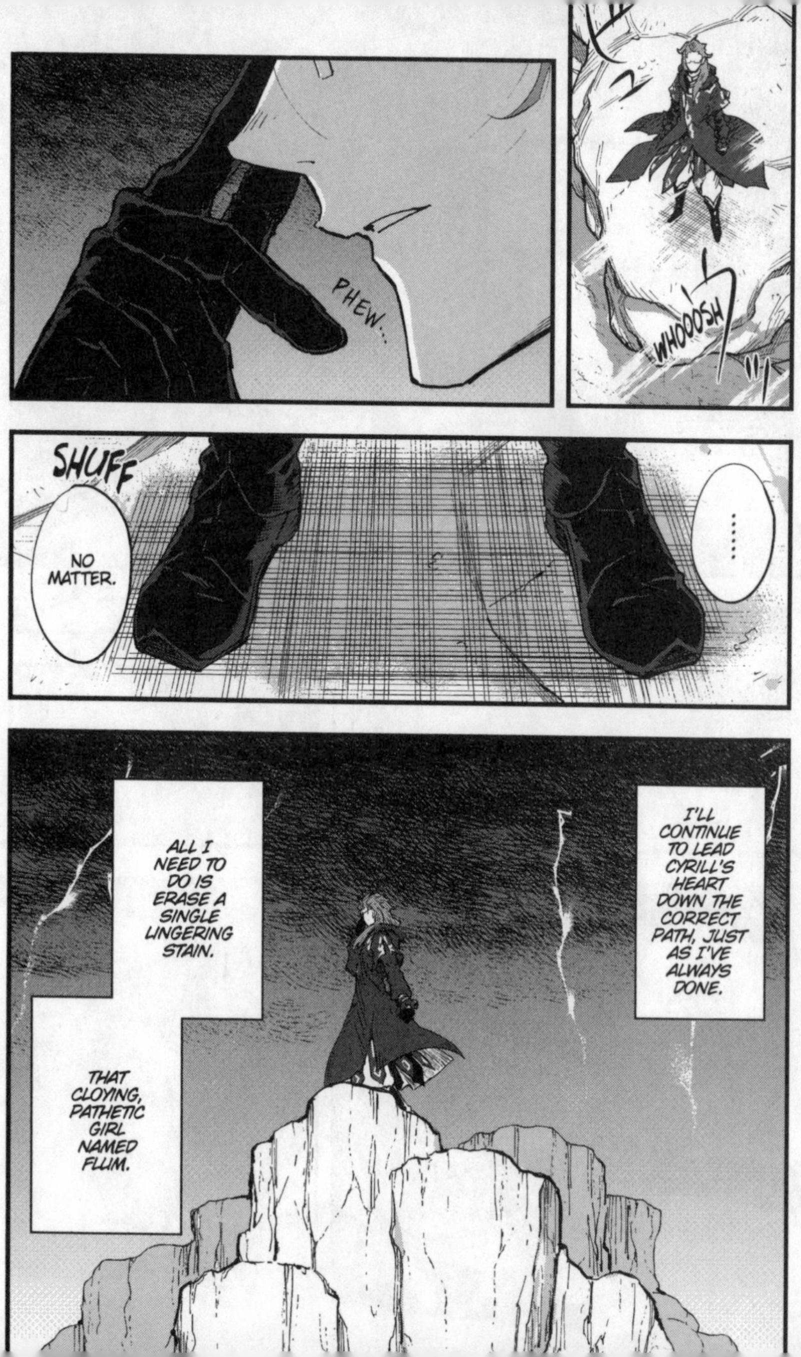
WHOOOSH
PHEW...
......
SHUFF
NO MATTER.
I'LL CONTINUE TO LEAD CYRILL'S HEART DOWN THE CORRECT PATH, JUST AS I'VE ALWAYS DONE.
ALL I NEED TO DO IS ERASE A SINGLE LINGERING STAIN.
THAT CLOYING, PATHETIC GIRL NAMED FLUM.

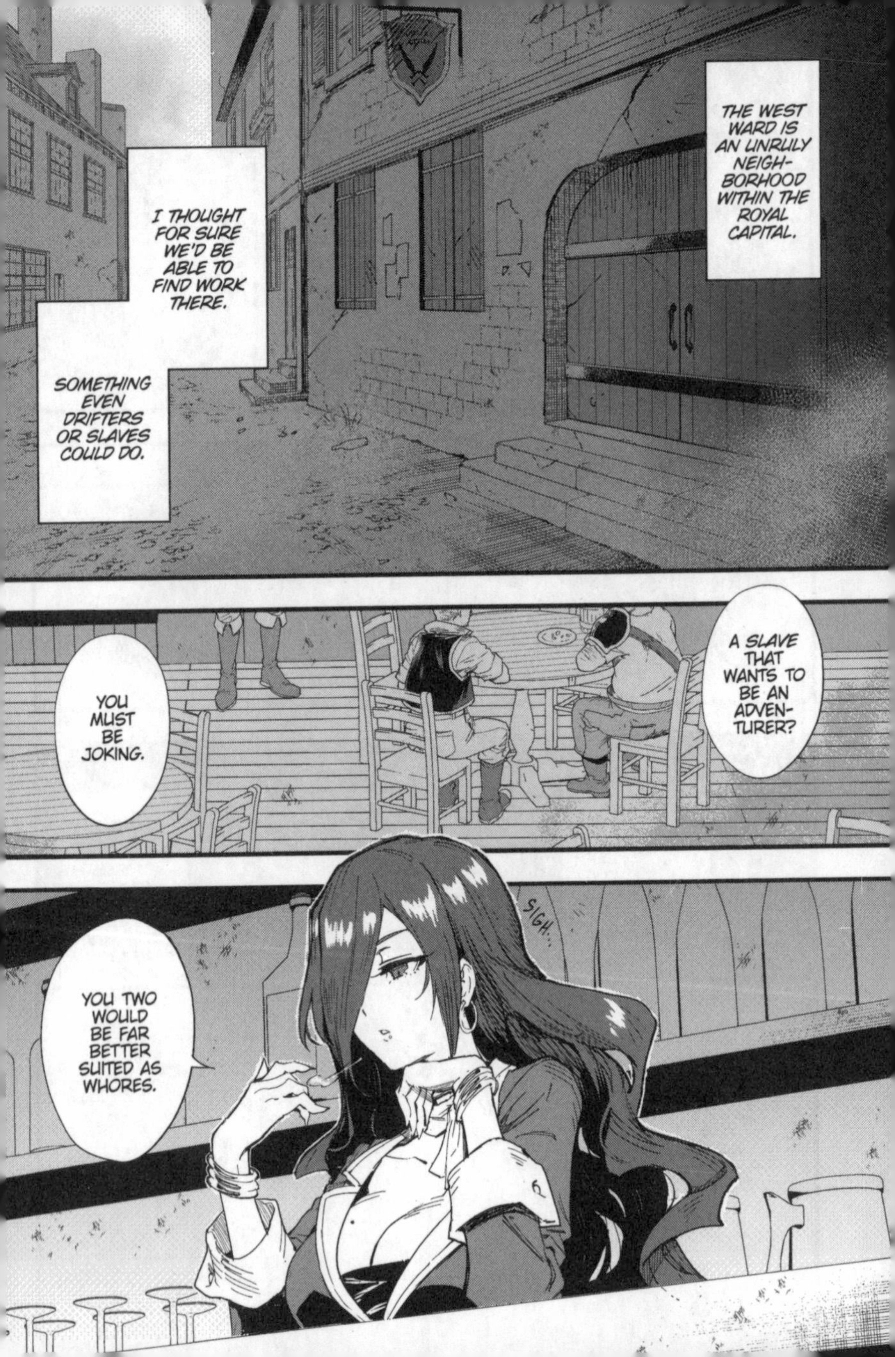
THE WEST WARD IS AN UNRULY NEIGH-BORHOOD WITHIN THE ROYAL CAPITAL.
I THOUGHT FOR SURE WE'D BE ABLE TO FIND WORK THERE.
SOMETHING EVEN DRIFTERS OR SLAVES COULD DO.
A SLAVE THAT WANTS TO BE AN ADVEN-TURER?
YOU MUST BE JOKING.
SIGH...
YOU TWO WOULD BE FAR BETTER SUITED AS WHORES.

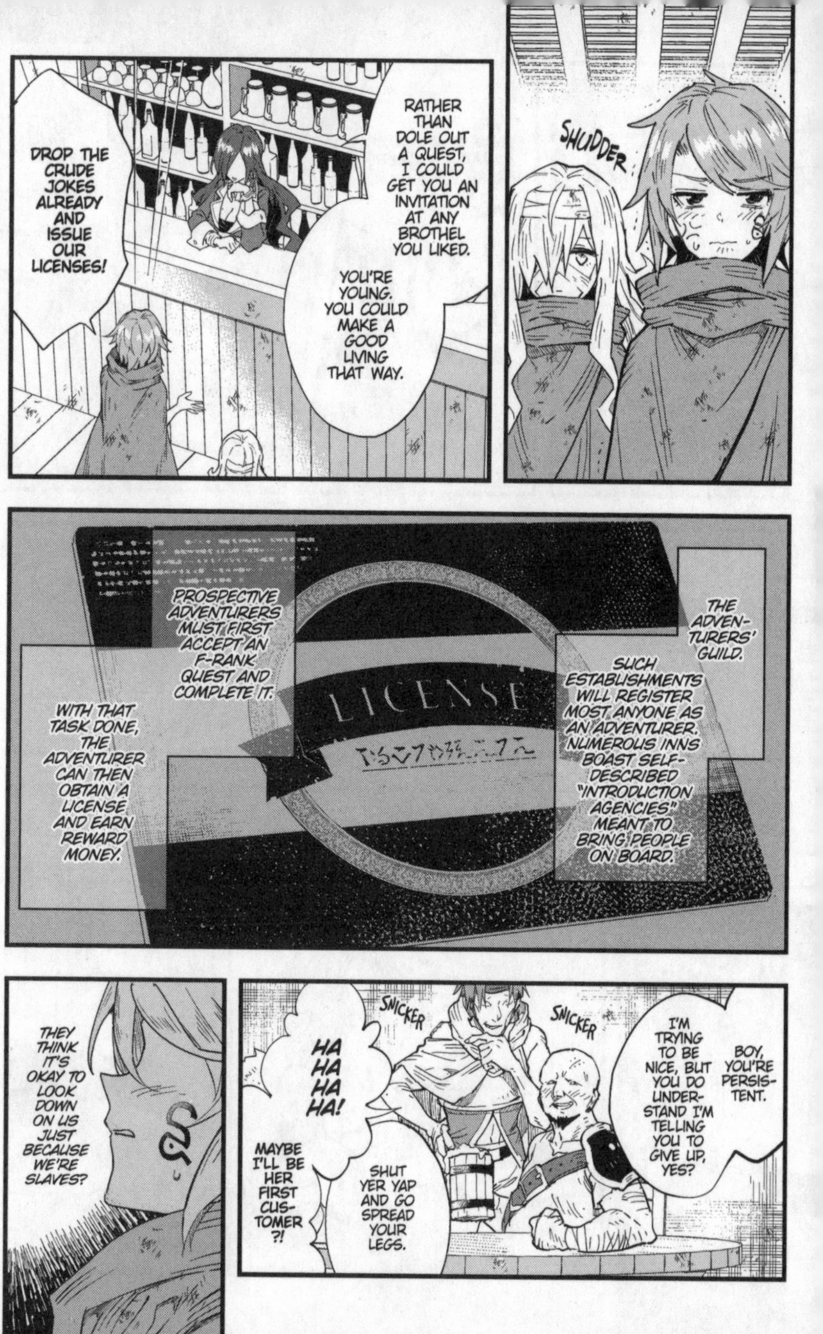
SHUDDER
RATHER THAN DOLE OUT A QUEST, I COULD GET YOU AN INVITATION AT ANY BROTHEL YOU LIKED.
YOU'RE YOUNG. YOU COULD MAKE A GOOD LIVING THAT WAY.
DROP THE CRUDE JOKES ALREADY AND ISSUE OUR LICENSES!
THE ADVENTURERS' GUILD.
SUCH ESTABLISHMENTS WILL REGISTER MOST ANYONE AS AN ADVENTURER. NUMEROUS INNS BOAST SELF-DESCRIBED "INTRODUCTION AGENCIES" MEANT TO BRING PEOPLE ON BOARD.
LICENSE
PROSPECTIVE ADVENTURERS MUST FIRST ACCEPT AN F-RANK QUEST AND COMPLETE IT.
WITH THAT TASK DONE, THE ADVENTURER CAN THEN OBTAIN A LICENSE AND EARN REWARD MONEY.
BOY, YOU'RE PERSISTENT.
I'M TRYING TO BE NICE, BUT YOU DO UNDERSTAND I'M TELLING YOU TO GIVE UP, YES?
SNICKER
SNICKER
HA HA HA HA!
SHUT YER YAP AND GO SPREAD YOUR LEGS.
MAYBE I'LL BE HER FIRST CUSTOMER?!
THEY THINK IT'S OKAY TO LOOK DOWN ON US JUST BECAUSE WE'RE SLAVES?

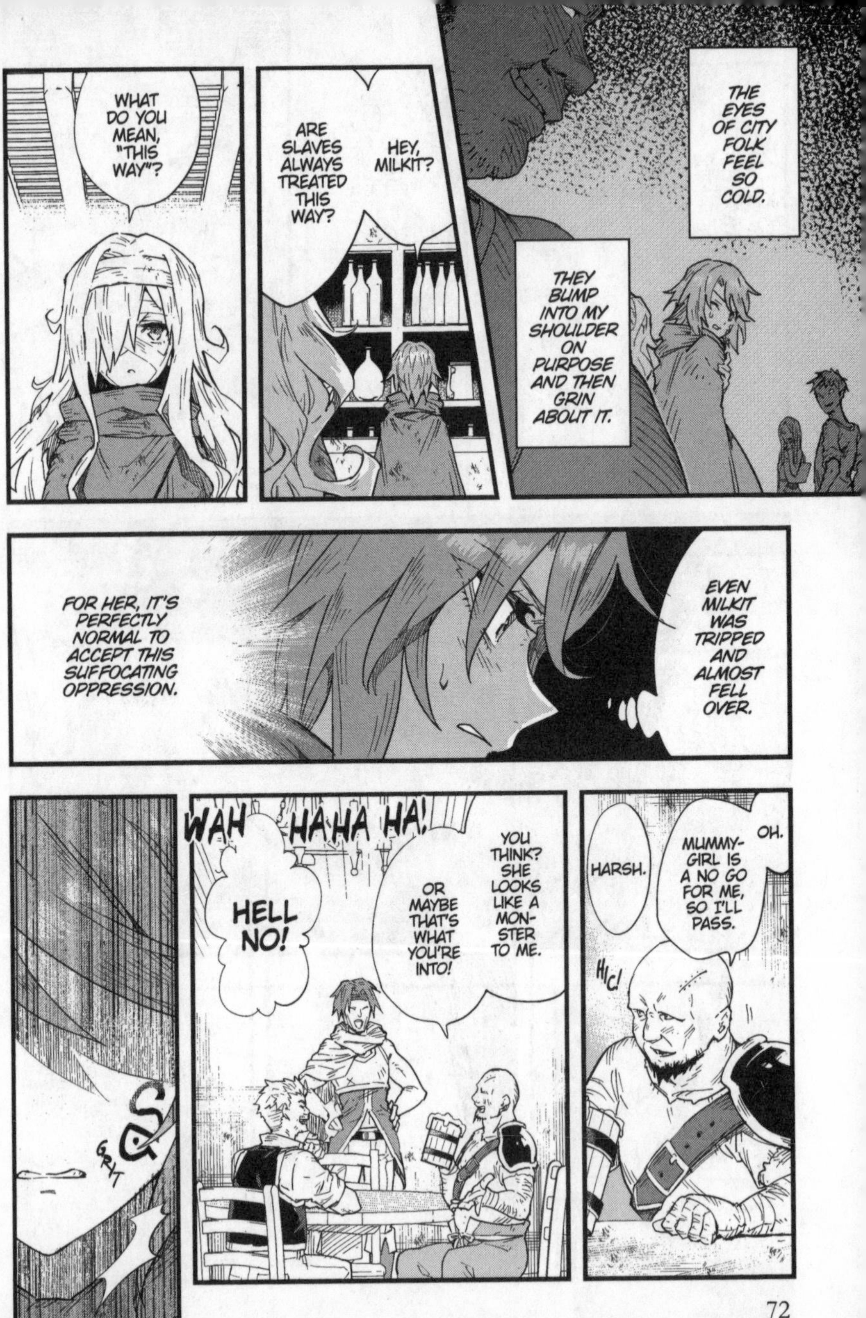
THE EYES OF CITY FOLK FEEL SO COLD.
THEY BUMP INTO MY SHOULDER ON PURPOSE AND THEN GRIN ABOUT IT.
HEY, MILKIT?
ARE SLAVES ALWAYS TREATED THIS WAY?
WHAT DO YOU MEAN, "THIS WAY"?
EVEN MILKIT WAS TRIPPED AND ALMOST FELL OVER.
FOR HER, IT'S PERFECTLY NORMAL TO ACCEPT THIS SUFFOCATING OPPRESSION.
OH.
MUMMY-GIRL IS A NO GO FOR ME, SO I'LL PASS.
HARSH.
HIC!
YOU THINK? SHE LOOKS LIKE A MON-STER TO ME.
OR MAYBE THAT'S WHAT YOU'RE INTO!
WAH HA HA HA!
HELL NO!
GRIT

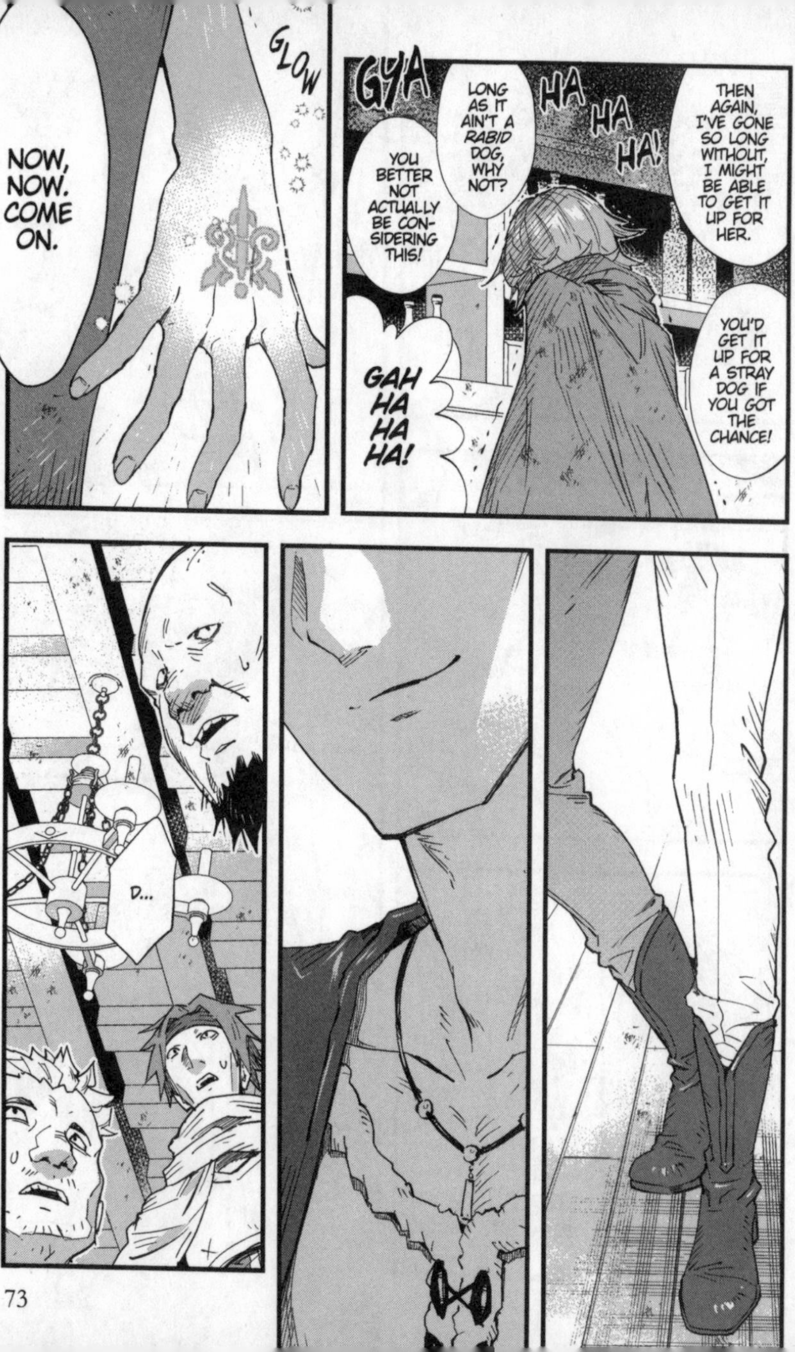
THEN AGAIN, I'VE GONE SO LONG WITHOUT, I MIGHT BE ABLE TO GET IT UP FOR HER.
HA HA HA!
LONG AS IT AIN'T A RABID DOG, WHY NOT?
GYA
YOU'D GET IT UP FOR A STRAY DOG IF YOU GOT THE CHANCE!
YOU BETTER NOT ACTUALLY BE CON-SIDERING THIS!
GAH HA HA HA!
GLOW
NOW, NOW. COME ON.
D...

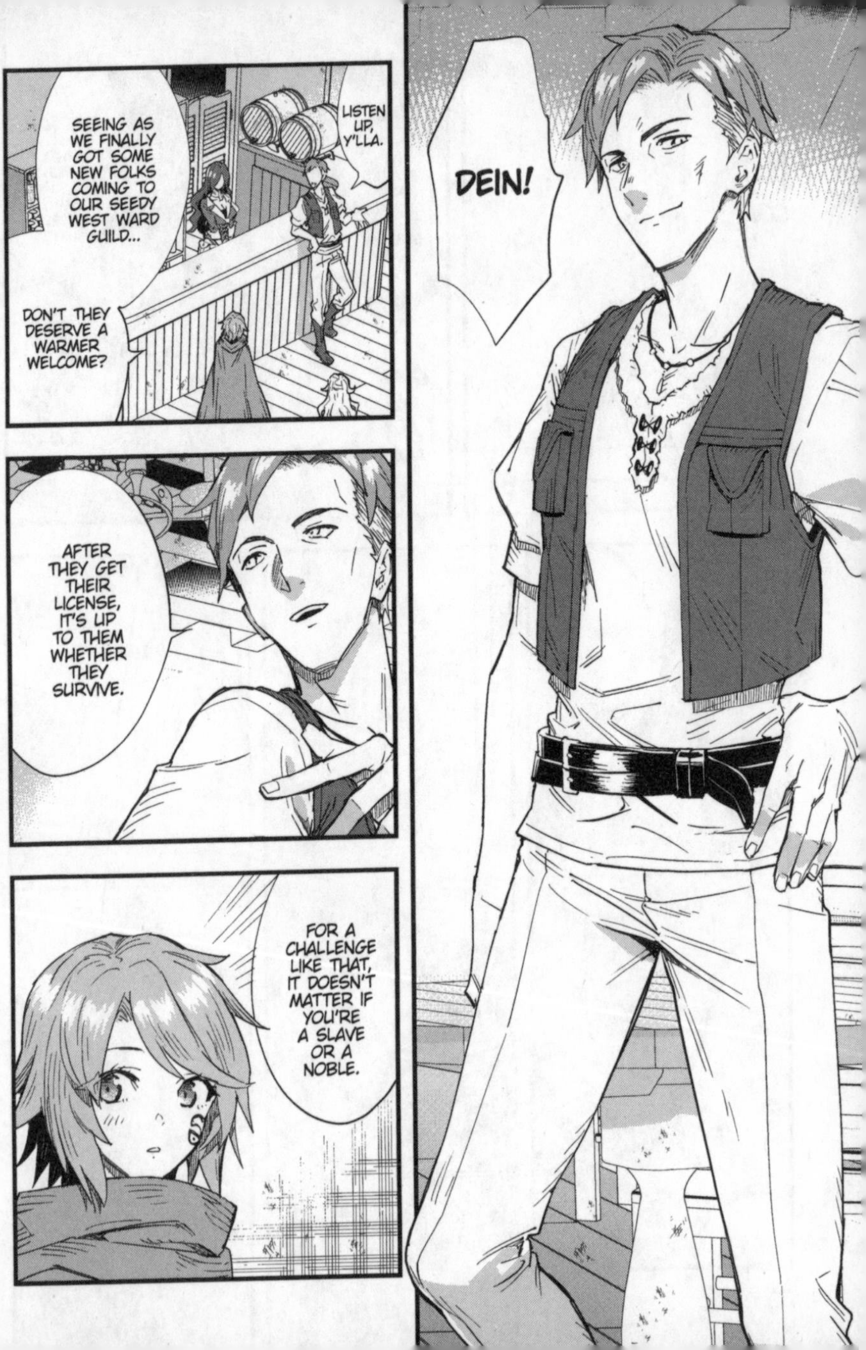
DEIN!
LISTEN UP, Y'LLA.
SEEING AS WE FINALLY GOT SOME NEW FOLKS COMING TO OUR SEEDY WEST WARD GUILD...
DON'T THEY DESERVE A WARMER WELCOME?
AFTER THEY GET THEIR LICENSE, IT'S UP TO THEM WHETHER THEY SURVIVE.
FOR A CHALLENGE LIKE THAT, IT DOESN'T MATTER IF YOU'RE A SLAVE OR A NOBLE.

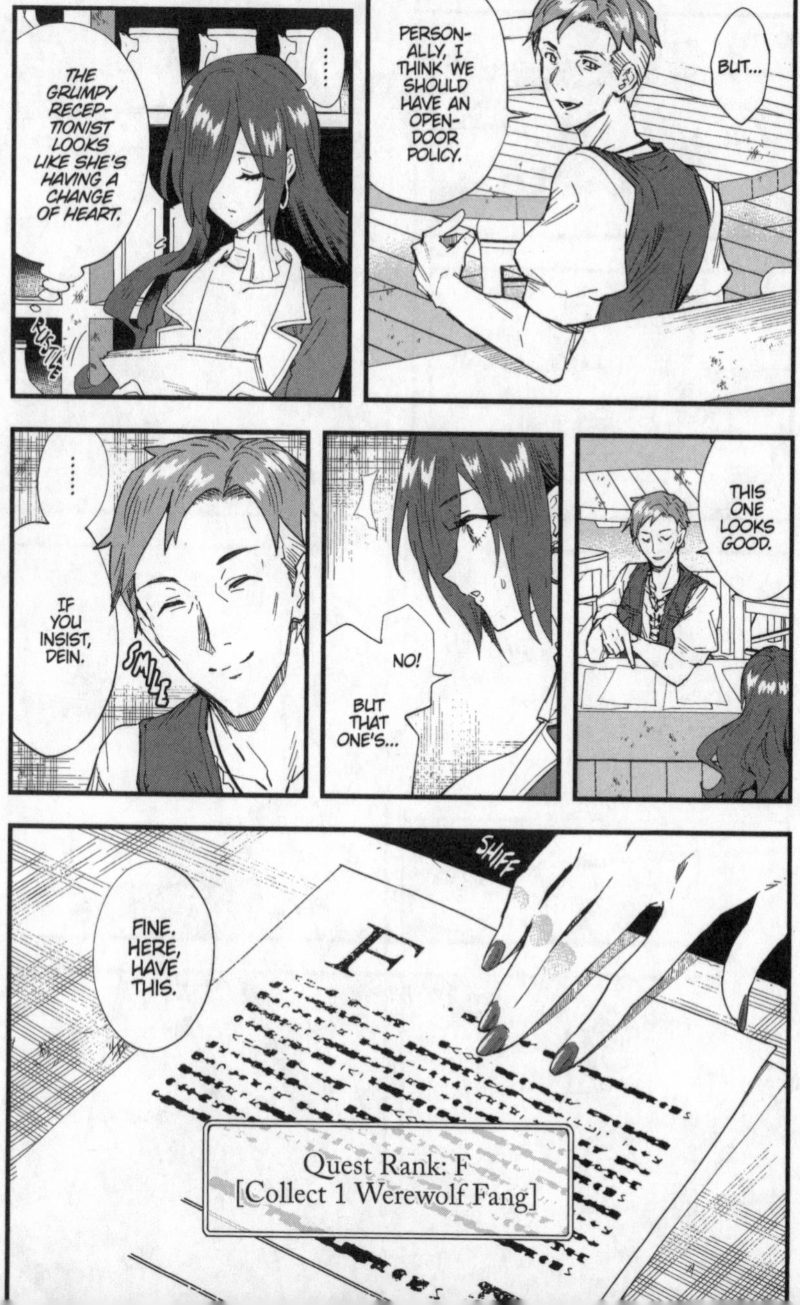
BUT...
PERSONALLY, I THINK WE SHOULD HAVE AN OPEN-DOOR POLICY.
......
THE GRUMPY RECEPTIONIST LOOKS LIKE SHE'S HAVING A CHANGE OF HEART.
RUSTLE
THIS ONE LOOKS GOOD.
NO!
BUT THAT ONE'S...
......
IF YOU INSIST, DEIN.
SMILE
SHIFF
FINE. HERE, HAVE THIS.
F
Quest Rank: F
[Collect 1 Werewolf Fang]

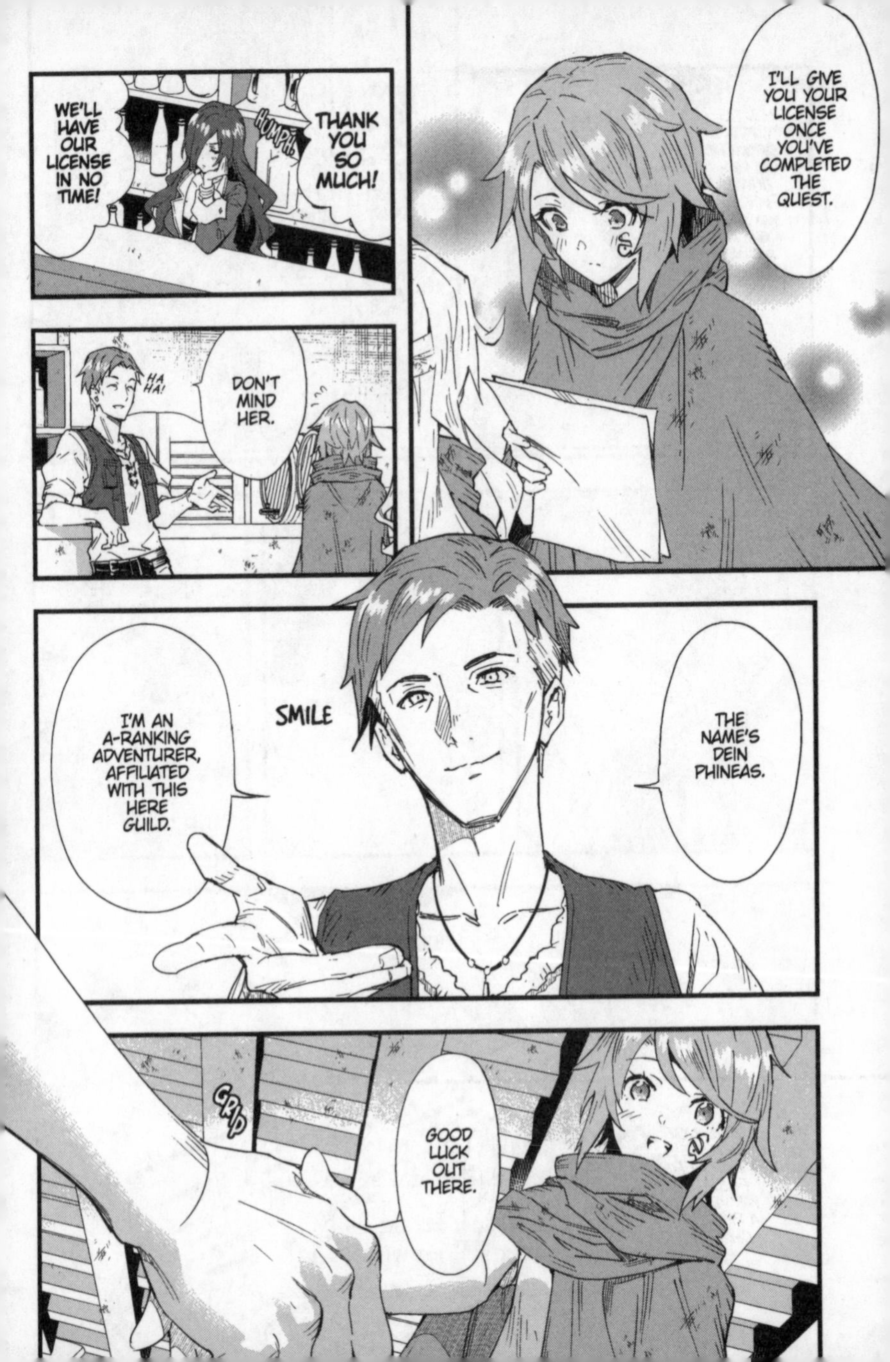
I'LL GIVE YOU YOUR LICENSE ONCE YOU'VE COMPLETED THE QUEST.
THANK YOU SO MUCH!
HUMPH
WE'LL HAVE OUR LICENSE IN NO TIME!
DON'T MIND HER.
HA HA!
THE NAME'S DEIN PHINEAS.
SMILE
I'M AN A-RANKING ADVENTURER, AFFILIATED WITH THIS HERE GUILD.
GOOD LUCK OUT THERE.
GRIP

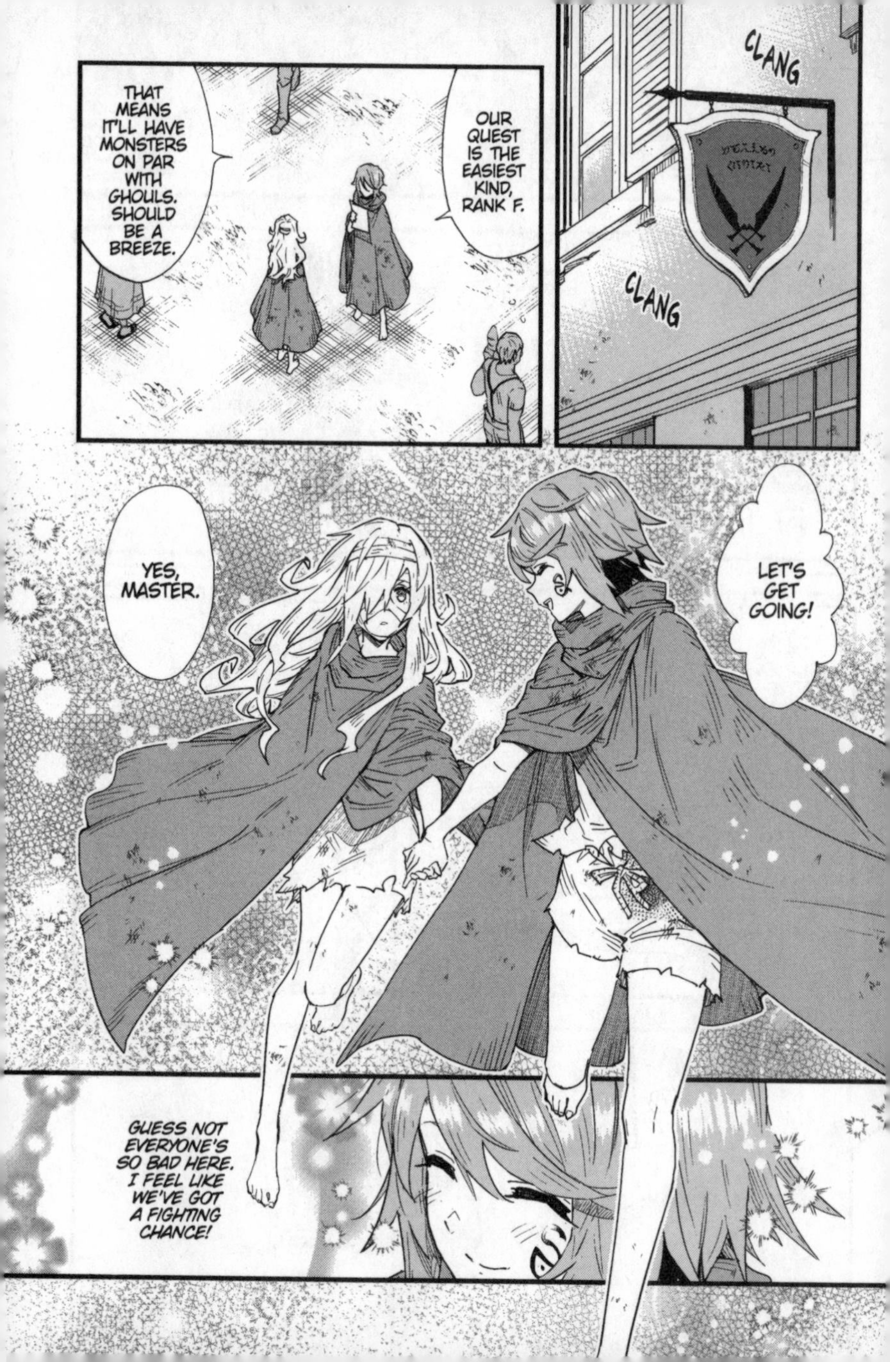
CLANG
CLANG
OUR QUEST IS THE EASIEST KIND, RANK F.
THAT MEANS IT'LL HAVE MONSTERS ON PAR WITH GHOULS. SHOULD BE A BREEZE.
LET'S GET GOING!
YES, MASTER.
GUESS NOT EVERYONE'S SO BAD HERE. I FEEL LIKE WE'VE GOT A FIGHTING CHANCE!

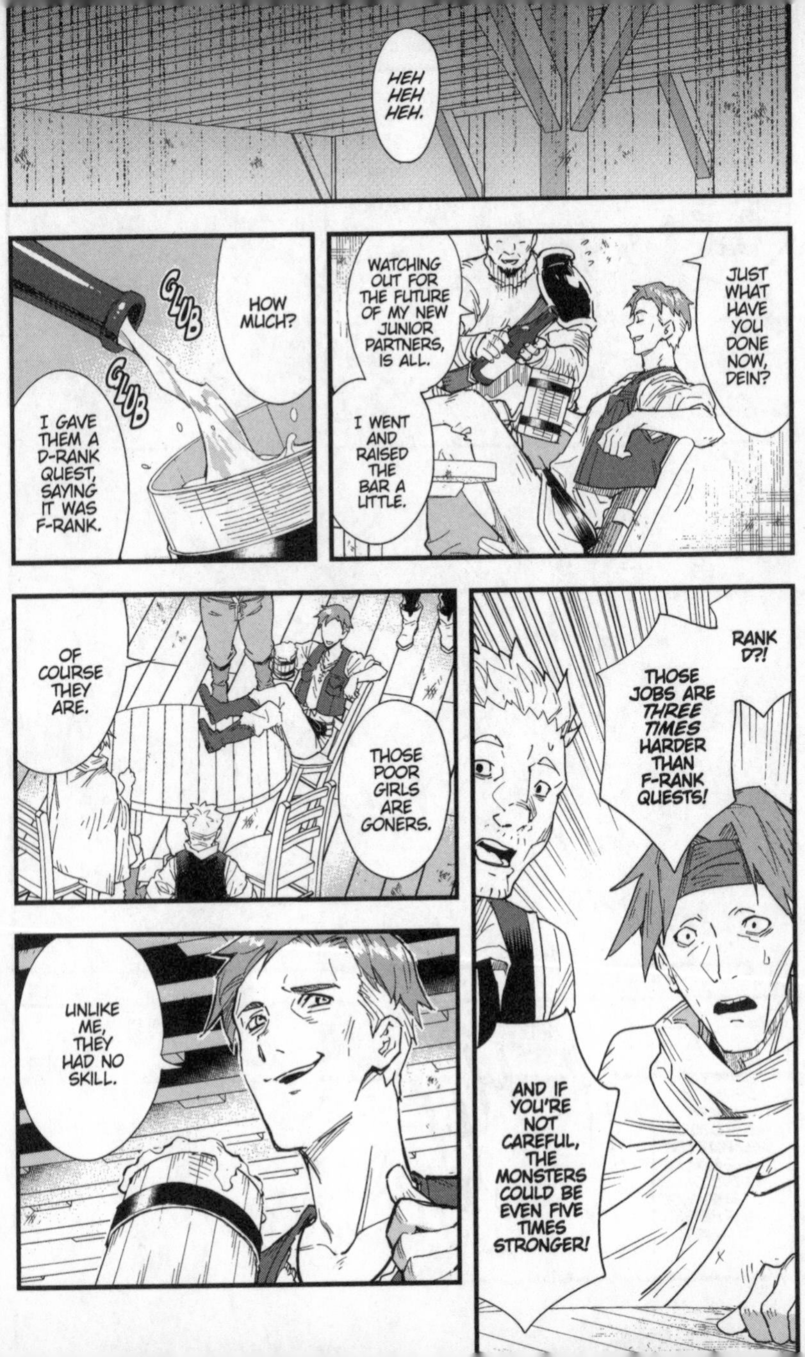
HEH HEH HEH.
JUST WHAT HAVE YOU DONE NOW, DEIN?
WATCHING OUT FOR THE FUTURE OF MY NEW JUNIOR PARTNERS, IS ALL.
I WENT AND RAISED THE BAR A LITTLE.
HOW MUCH?
GLUB
GLUB
I GAVE THEM A D-RANK QUEST, SAYING IT WAS F-RANK.
RANK D?!
THOSE JOBS ARE *THREE TIMES* HARDER THAN F-RANK QUESTS!
AND IF YOU'RE NOT CAREFUL, THE MONSTERS COULD BE EVEN FIVE TIMES STRONGER!
THOSE POOR GIRLS ARE GONERS.
OF COURSE THEY ARE.
UNLIKE ME, THEY HAD NO SKILL.

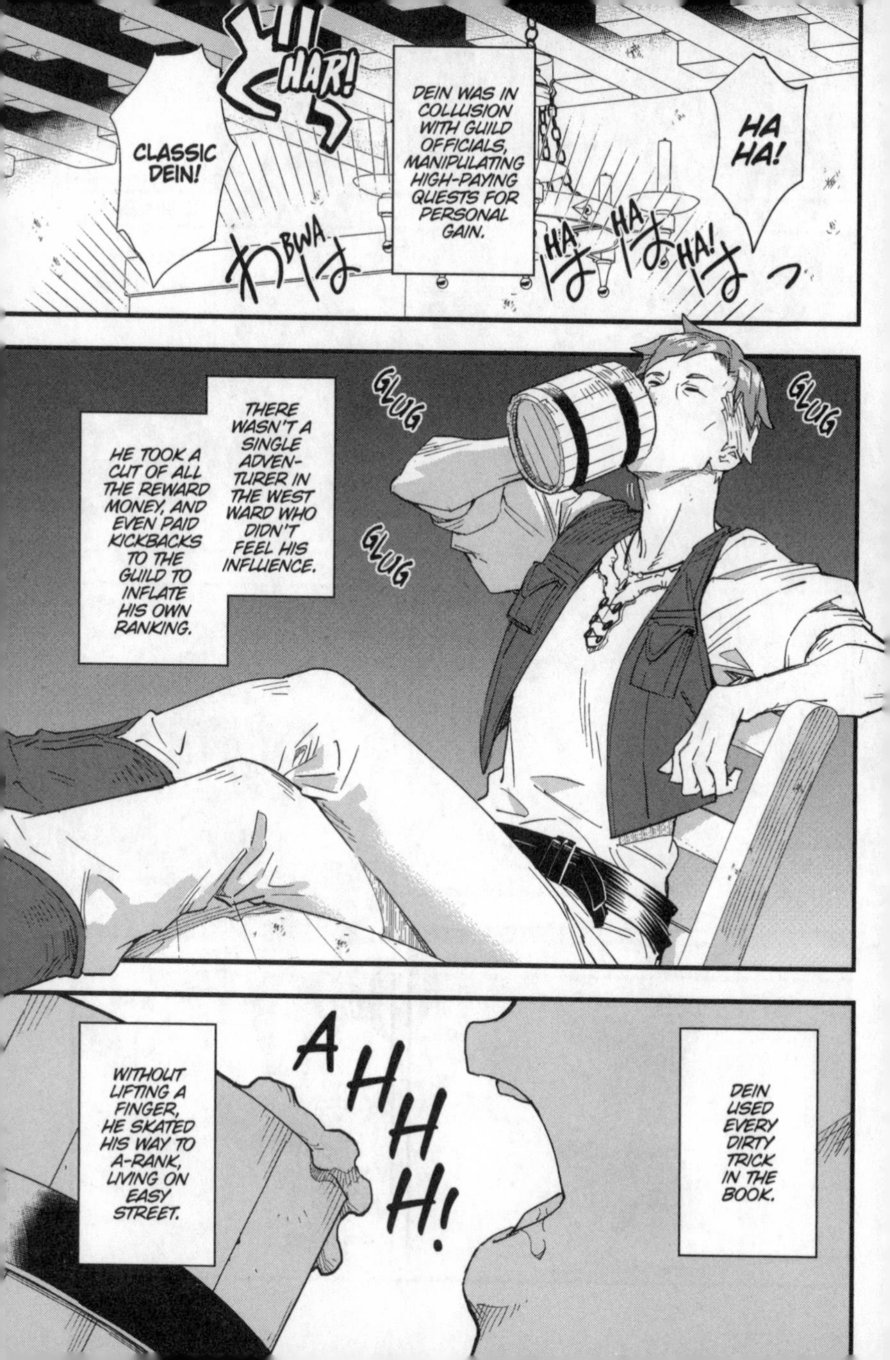
HA HA!
DEIN WAS IN COLLUSION WITH GUILD OFFICIALS, MANIPULATING HIGH-PAYING QUESTS FOR PERSONAL GAIN.
HAR!
CLASSIC DEIN!
BWA HA HA HA!
GLUG
THERE WASN'T A SINGLE ADVEN-TURER IN THE WEST WARD WHO DIDN'T FEEL HIS INFLUENCE.
HE TOOK A CUT OF ALL THE REWARD MONEY, AND EVEN PAID KICKBACKS TO THE GUILD TO INFLATE HIS OWN RANKING.
GLUG
GLUG
DEIN USED EVERY DIRTY TRICK IN THE BOOK.
AHHHH!
WITHOUT LIFTING A FINGER, HE SKATED HIS WAY TO A-RANK, LIVING ON EASY STREET.

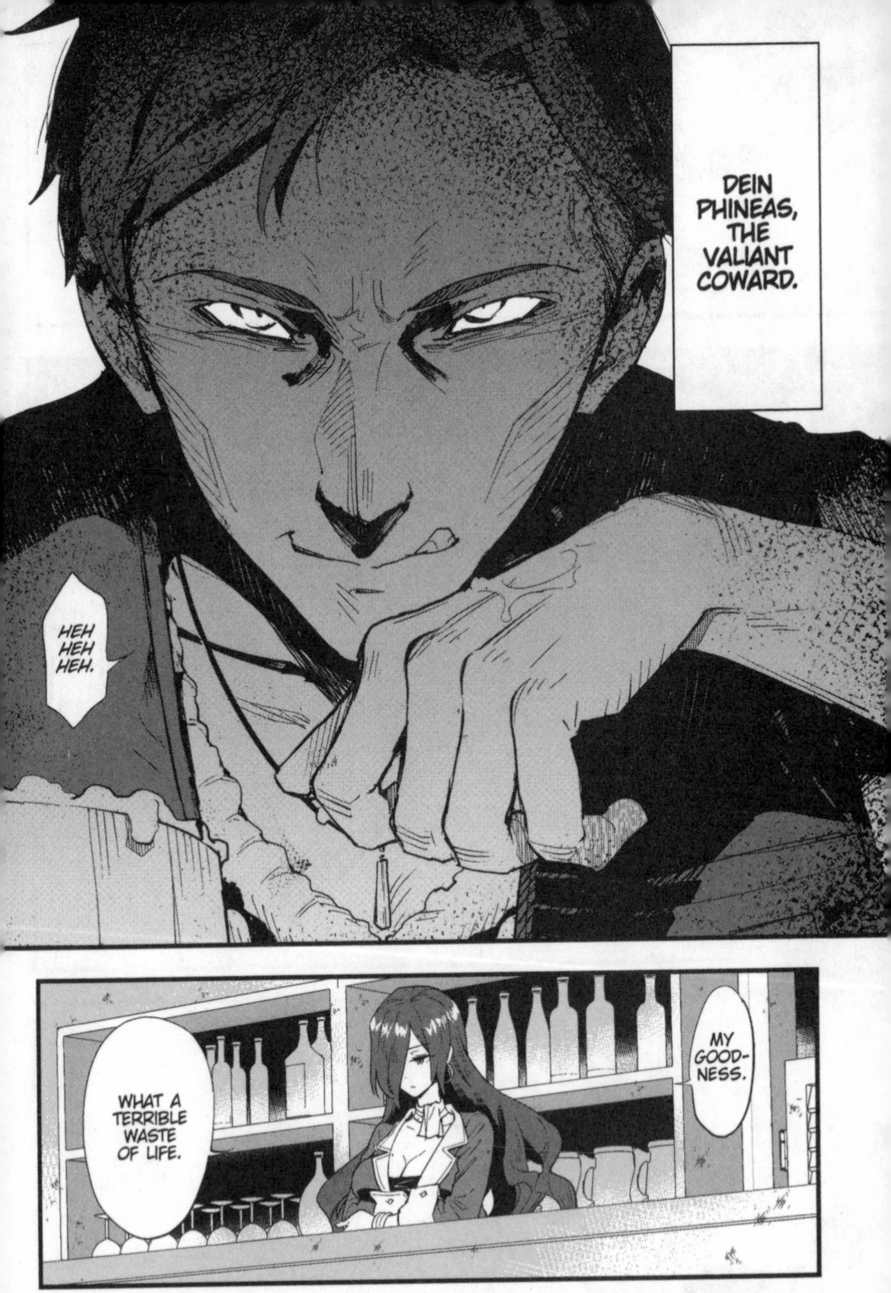
DEIN PHINEAS, THE VALIANT COWARD.
HEH HEH HEH.
MY GOODNESS.
WHAT A TERRIBLE WASTE OF LIFE.

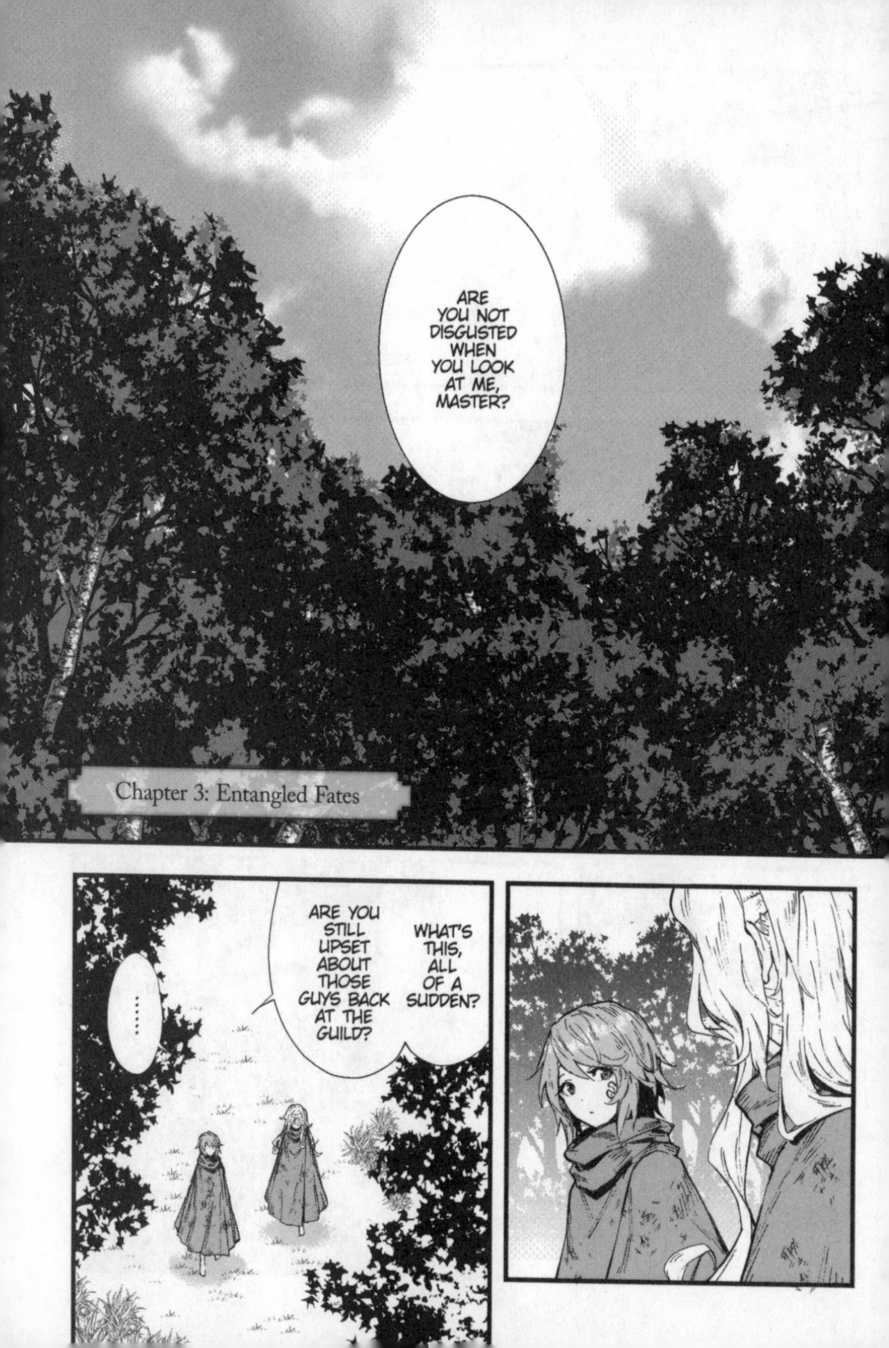
ARE YOU NOT DISGUSTED WHEN YOU LOOK AT ME, MASTER?
Chapter 3: Entangled Fates
WHAT'S THIS, ALL OF A SUDDEN? ARE YOU STILL UPSET ABOUT THOSE GUYS BACK AT THE GUILD?
......

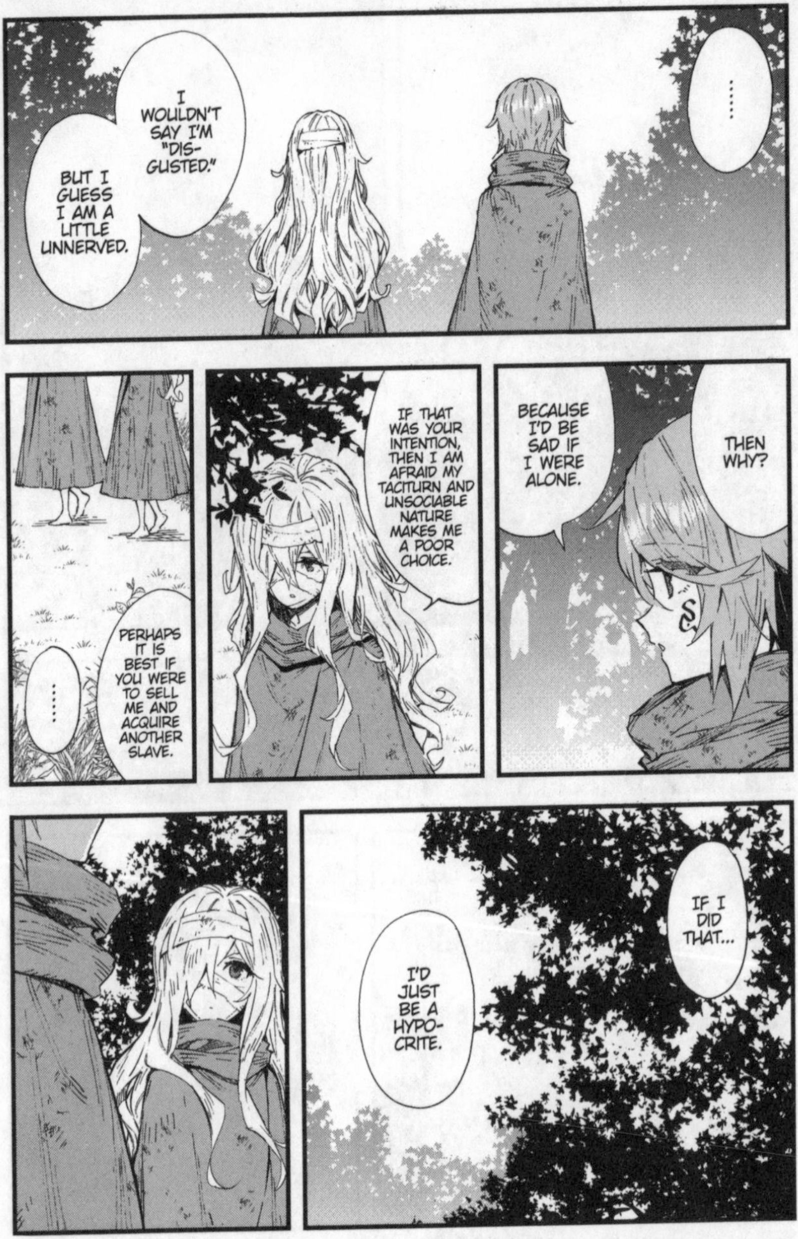
......
I WOULDN'T SAY I'M "DIS-GUSTED."
BUT I GUESS I AM A LITTLE UNNERVED.
THEN WHY?
BECAUSE I'D BE SAD IF I WERE ALONE.
IF THAT WAS YOUR INTENTION, THEN I AM AFRAID MY TACITURN AND UNSOCIABLE NATURE MAKES ME A POOR CHOICE.
PERHAPS IT IS BEST IF YOU WERE TO SELL ME AND ACQUIRE ANOTHER SLAVE.
......
IF I DID THAT...
I'D JUST BE A HYPOCRITE.

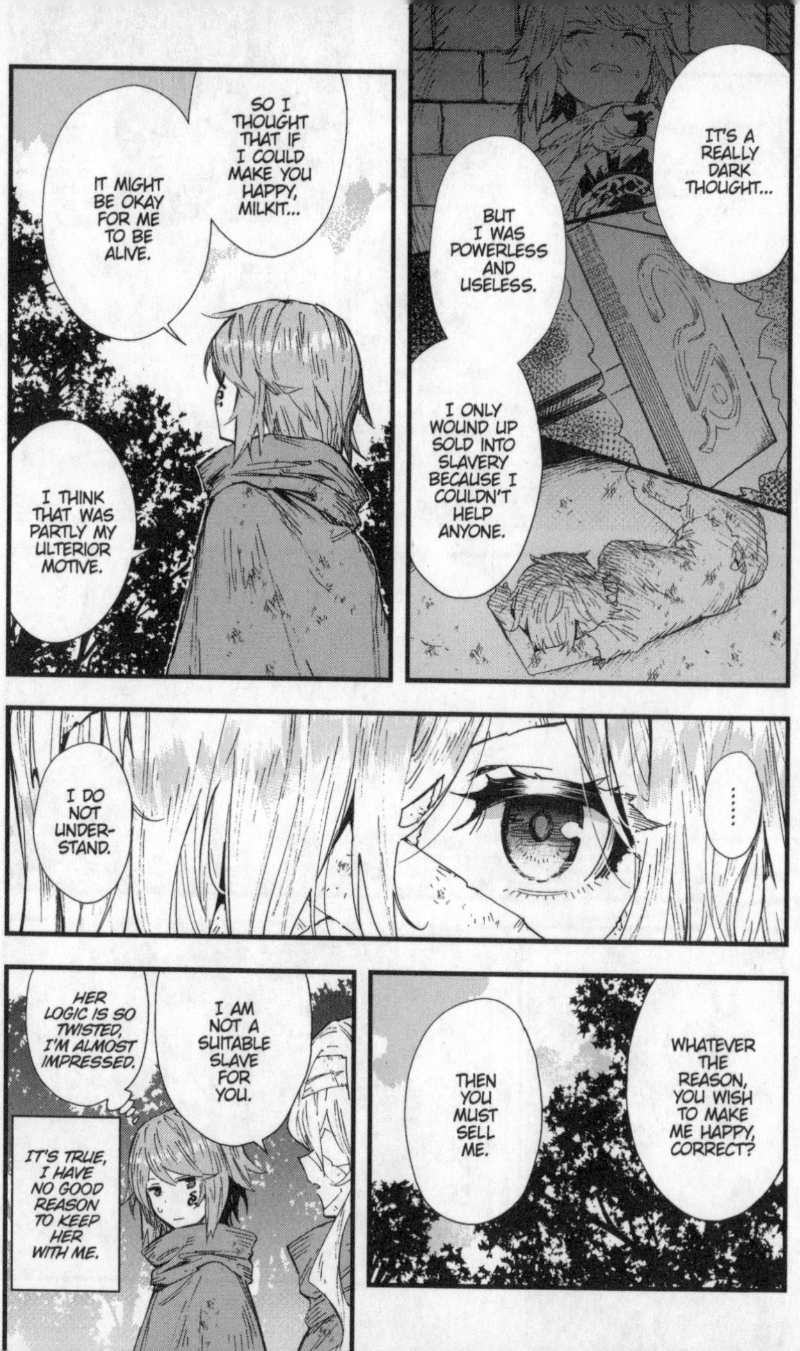
IT'S A REALLY DARK THOUGHT...
BUT I WAS POWERLESS AND USELESS.
I ONLY WOUND UP SOLD INTO SLAVERY BECAUSE I COULDN'T HELP ANYONE.
SO I THOUGHT THAT IF I COULD MAKE YOU HAPPY, MILKIT...
IT MIGHT BE OKAY FOR ME TO BE ALIVE.
I THINK THAT WAS PARTLY MY ULTERIOR MOTIVE.
......
I DO NOT UNDER-STAND.
WHATEVER THE REASON, YOU WISH TO MAKE ME HAPPY, CORRECT?
THEN YOU MUST SELL ME.
I AM NOT A SUITABLE SLAVE FOR YOU.
HER LOGIC IS SO TWISTED, I'M ALMOST IMPRESSED.
IT'S TRUE, I HAVE NO GOOD REASON TO KEEP HER WITH ME.

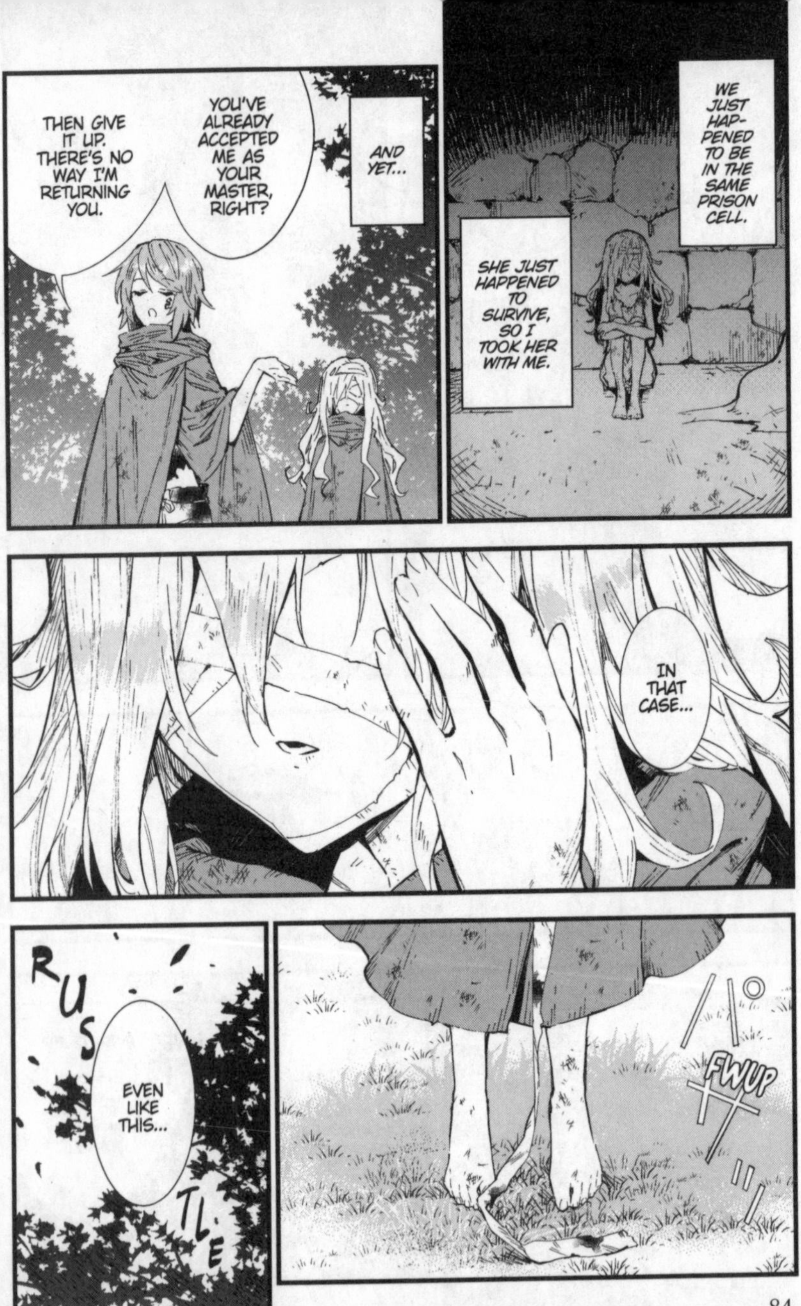
WE JUST HAPPENED TO BE IN THE SAME PRISON CELL.
SHE JUST HAPPENED TO SURVIVE, SO I TOOK HER WITH ME.
AND YET...
YOU'VE ALREADY ACCEPTED ME AS YOUR MASTER, RIGHT?
THEN GIVE IT UP. THERE'S NO WAY I'M RETURNING YOU.
IN THAT CASE...
FWUP
RUSTLE
EVEN LIKE THIS...

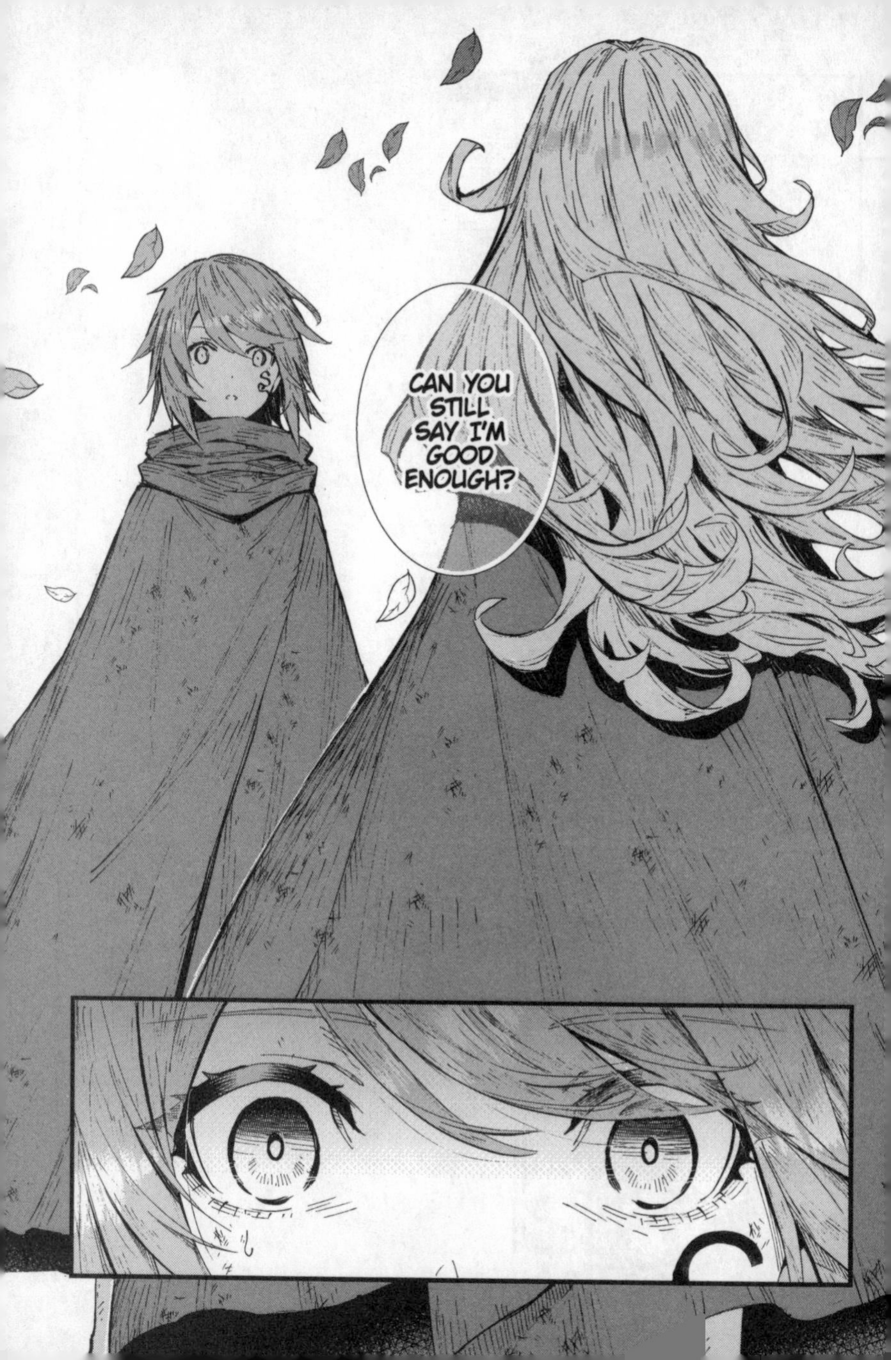
CAN YOU STILL SAY I'M GOOD ENOUGH?

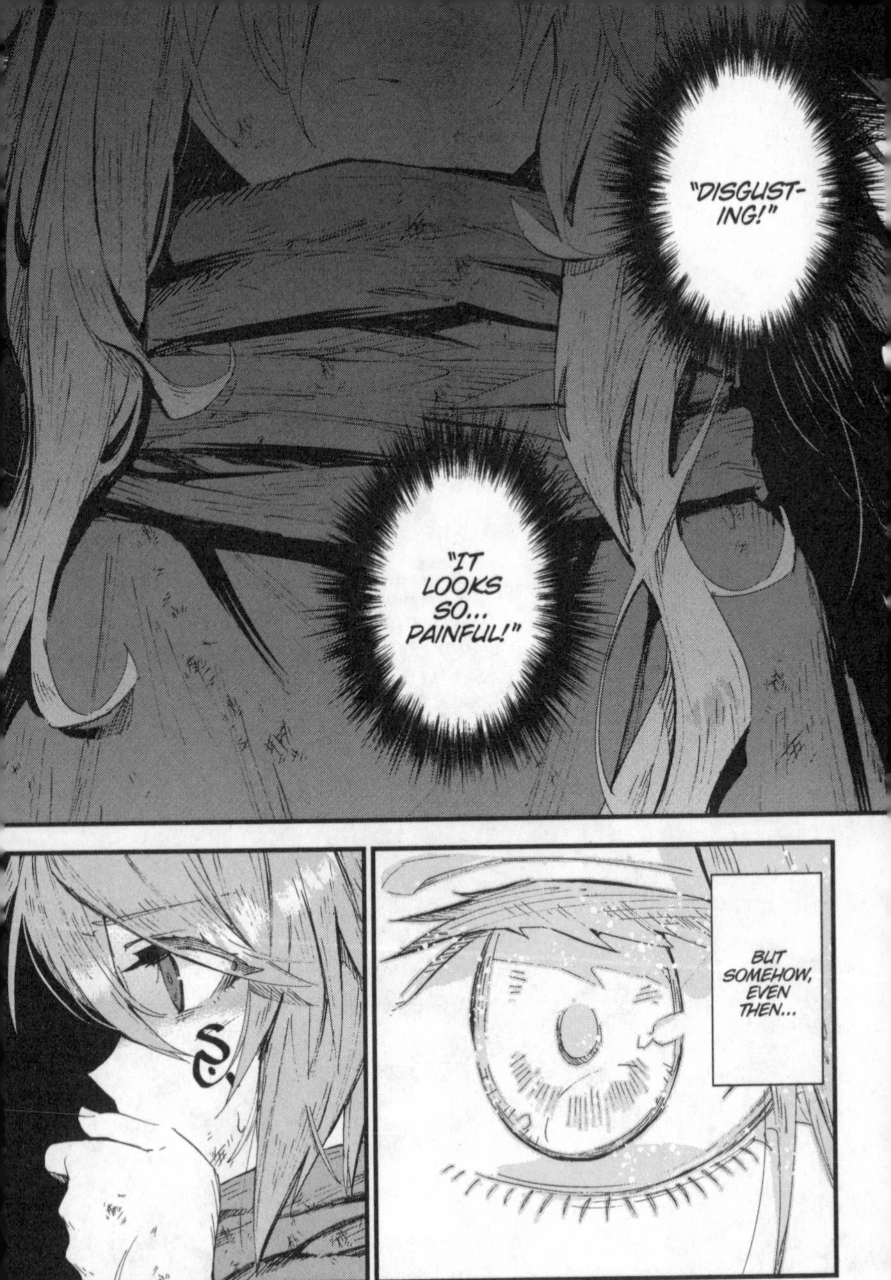
"DISGUST-ING!"
"IT LOOKS SO... PAINFUL!"
BUT SOMEHOW, EVEN THEN...

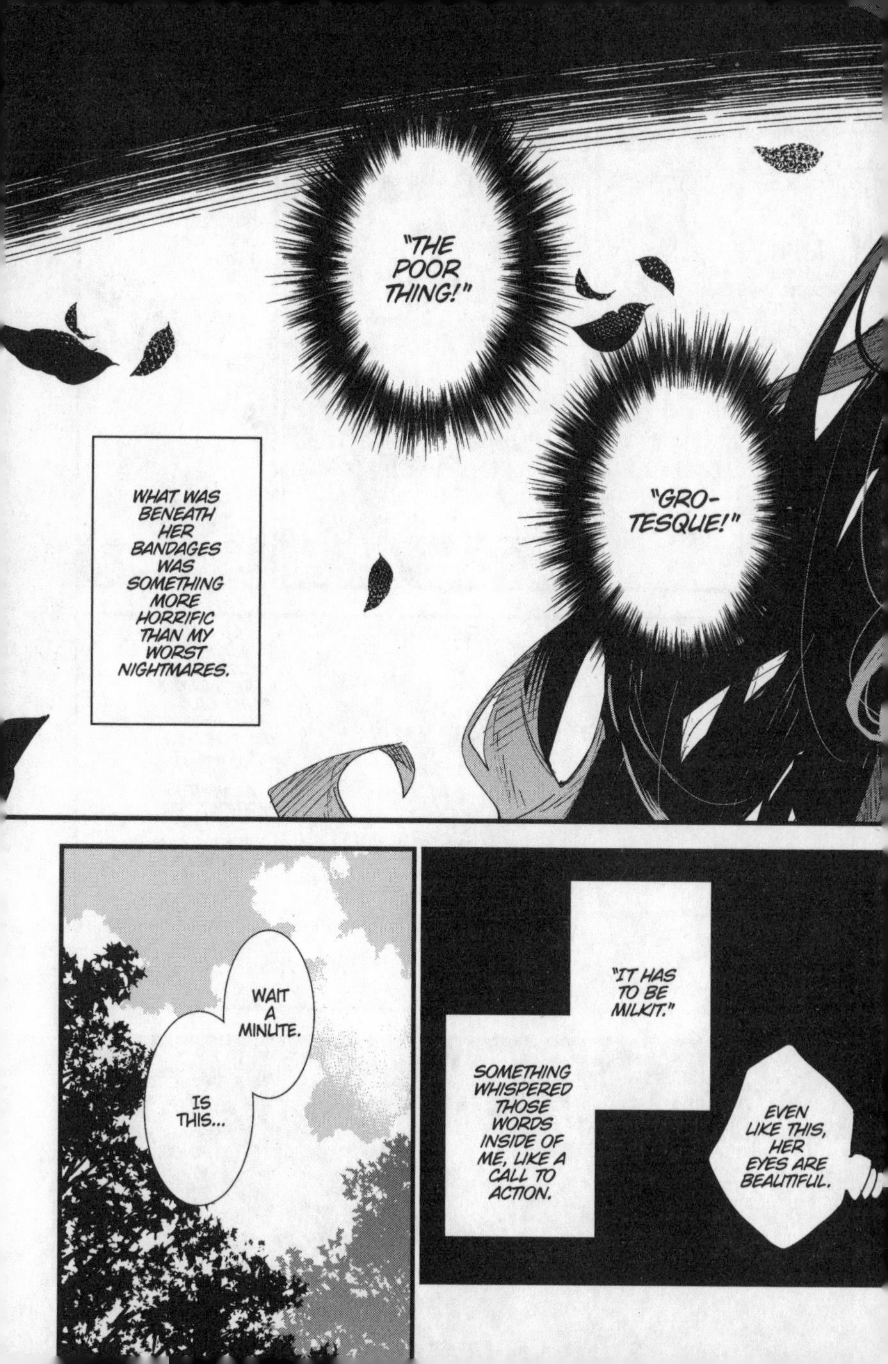
"THE POOR THING!"
"GRO-TESQUE!"
WHAT WAS BENEATH HER BANDAGES WAS SOMETHING MORE HORRIFIC THAN MY WORST NIGHTMARES.
"IT HAS TO BE MILKIT."
EVEN LIKE THIS, HER EYES ARE BEAUTIFUL.
SOMETHING WHISPERED THOSE WORDS INSIDE OF ME, LIKE A CALL TO ACTION.
WAIT A MINUTE.
IS THIS...

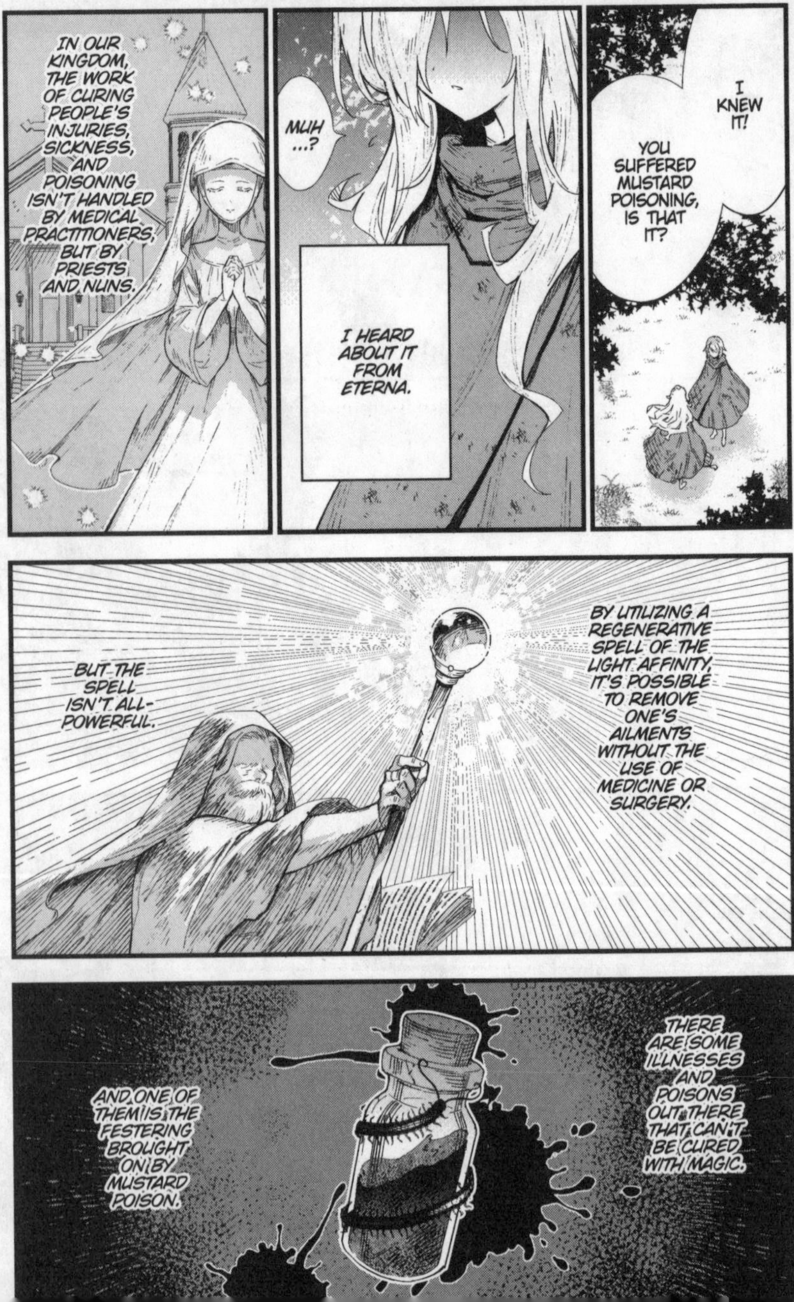
I KNEW IT!
YOU SUFFERED MUSTARD POISONING, IS THAT IT?
MUH ...?
I HEARD ABOUT IT FROM ETERNA.
IN OUR KINGDOM, THE WORK OF CURING PEOPLE'S INJURIES, SICKNESS, AND POISONING ISN'T HANDLED BY MEDICAL PRACTITIONERS, BUT BY PRIESTS AND NUNS.
BY UTILIZING A REGENERATIVE SPELL OF THE LIGHT AFFINITY, IT'S POSSIBLE TO REMOVE ONE'S AILMENTS WITHOUT THE USE OF MEDICINE OR SURGERY.
BUT THE SPELL ISN'T ALL-POWERFUL.
THERE ARE SOME ILLNESSES AND POISONS OUT THERE THAT CAN'T BE CURED WITH MAGIC.
AND ONE OF THEM IS THE FESTERING BROUGHT ON BY MUSTARD POISON.

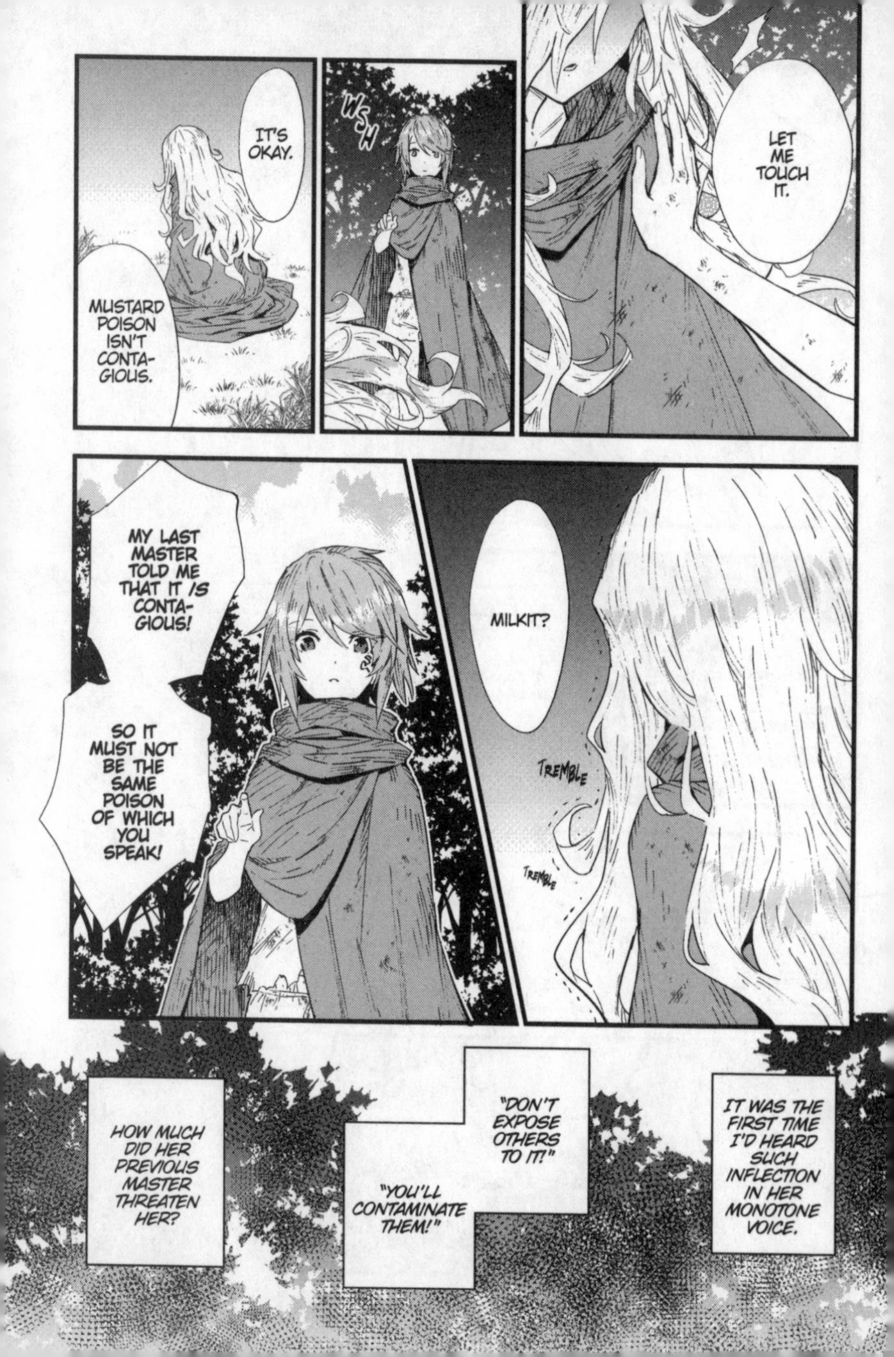
LET ME TOUCH IT.
WSH
IT'S OKAY.
MUSTARD POISON ISN'T CONTAGIOUS.
MILKIT?
TREMBLE
TREMBLE
MY LAST MASTER TOLD ME THAT IT IS CONTAGIOUS!
SO IT MUST NOT BE THE SAME POISON OF WHICH YOU SPEAK!
IT WAS THE FIRST TIME I'D HEARD SUCH INFLECTION IN HER MONOTONE VOICE.
"DON'T EXPOSE OTHERS TO IT!"
"YOU'LL CONTAMINATE THEM!"
HOW MUCH DID HER PREVIOUS MASTER THREATEN HER?

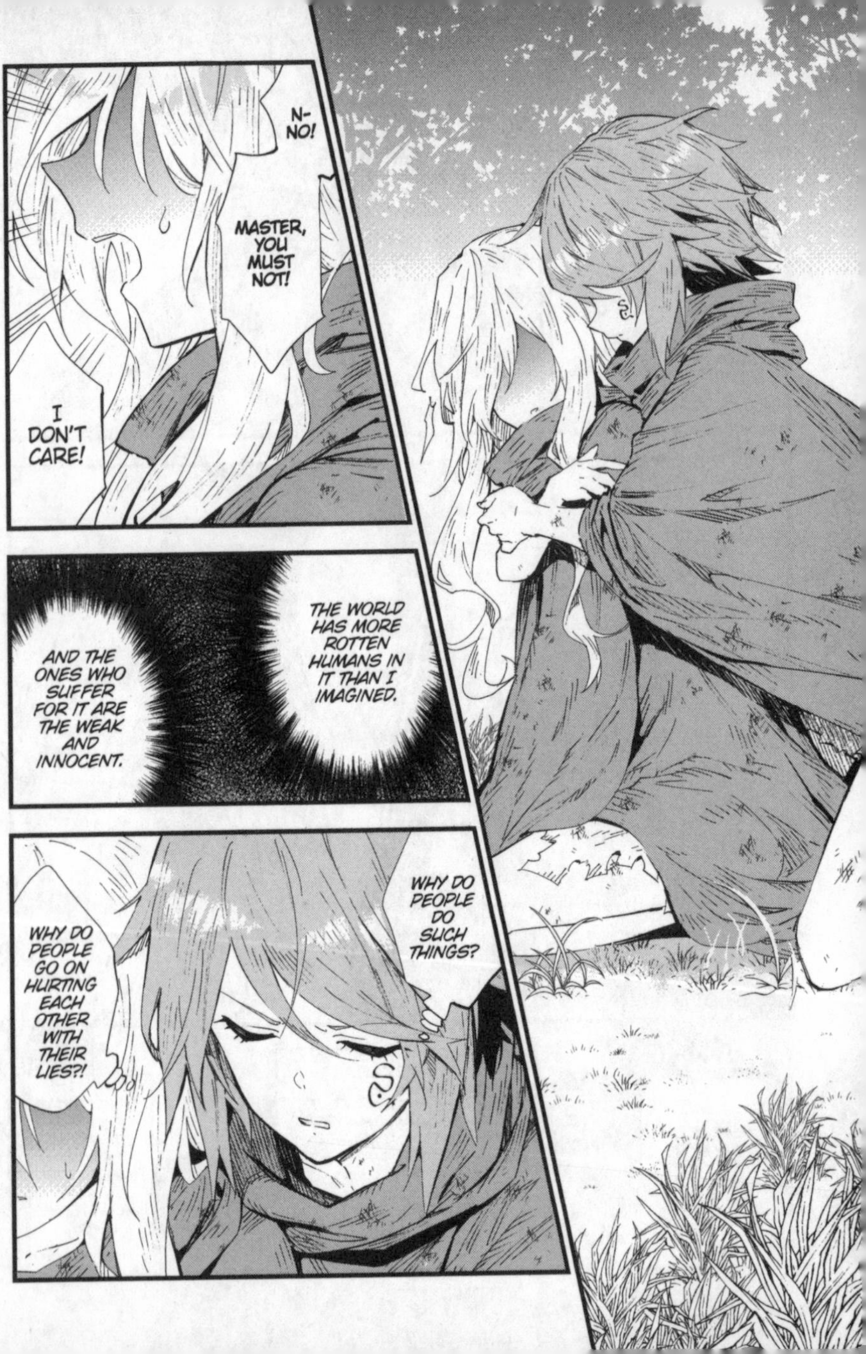
N- NO!
MASTER, YOU MUST NOT!
I DON'T CARE!
THE WORLD HAS MORE ROTTEN HUMANS IN IT THAN I IMAGINED.
AND THE ONES WHO SUFFER FOR IT ARE THE WEAK AND INNOCENT.
WHY DO PEOPLE DO SUCH THINGS?
WHY DO PEOPLE GO ON HURTING EACH OTHER WITH THEIR LIES?!

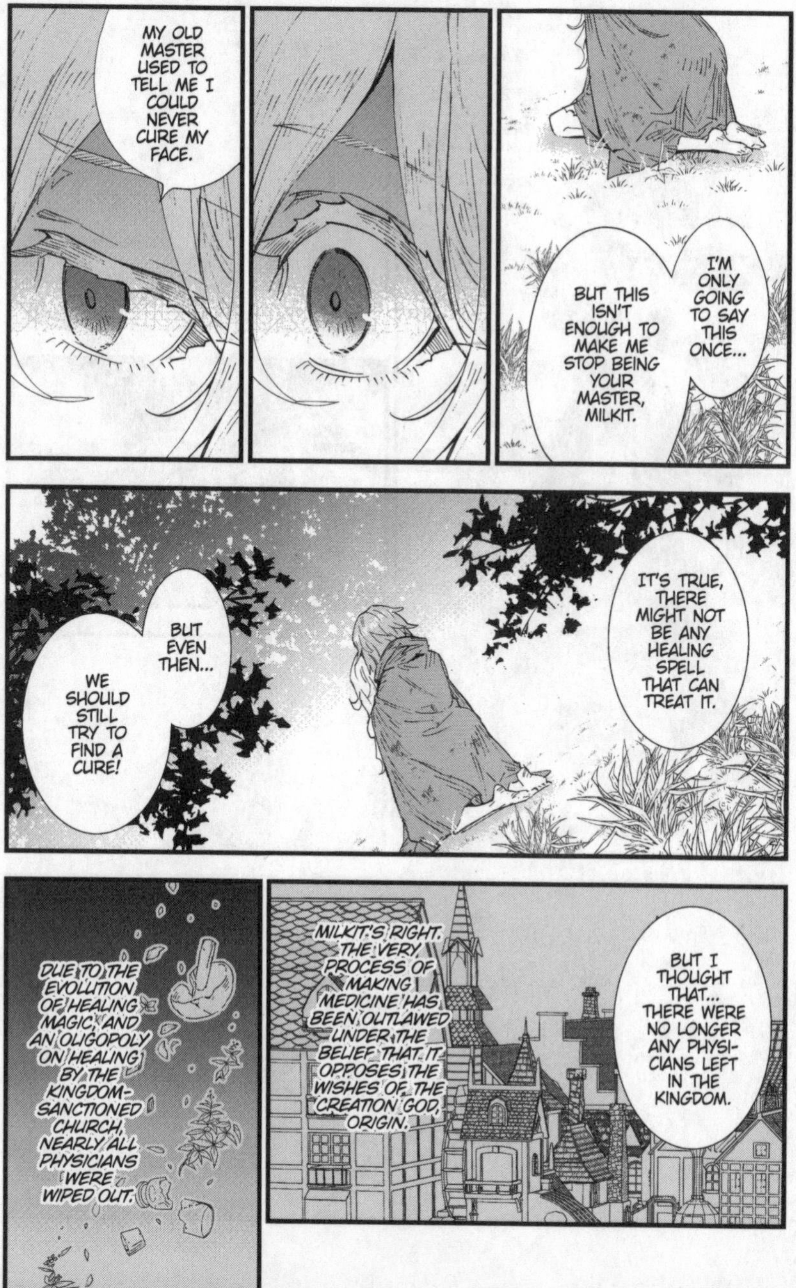
I'M ONLY GOING TO SAY THIS ONCE...
BUT THIS ISN'T ENOUGH TO MAKE ME STOP BEING YOUR MASTER, MILKIT.
MY OLD MASTER USED TO TELL ME I COULD NEVER CURE MY FACE.
IT'S TRUE, THERE MIGHT NOT BE ANY HEALING SPELL THAT CAN TREAT IT.
BUT EVEN THEN...
WE SHOULD STILL TRY TO FIND A CURE!
BUT I THOUGHT THAT... THERE WERE NO LONGER ANY PHYSICIANS LEFT IN THE KINGDOM.
MILKIT'S RIGHT. THE VERY PROCESS OF MAKING MEDICINE HAS BEEN OUTLAWED UNDER THE BELIEF THAT IT OPPOSES THE WISHES OF THE CREATION GOD, ORIGIN.
DUE TO THE EVOLUTION OF HEALING MAGIC, AND AN OLIGOPOLY ON HEALING BY THE KINGDOM-SANCTIONED CHURCH, NEARLY ALL PHYSICIANS WERE WIPED OUT.

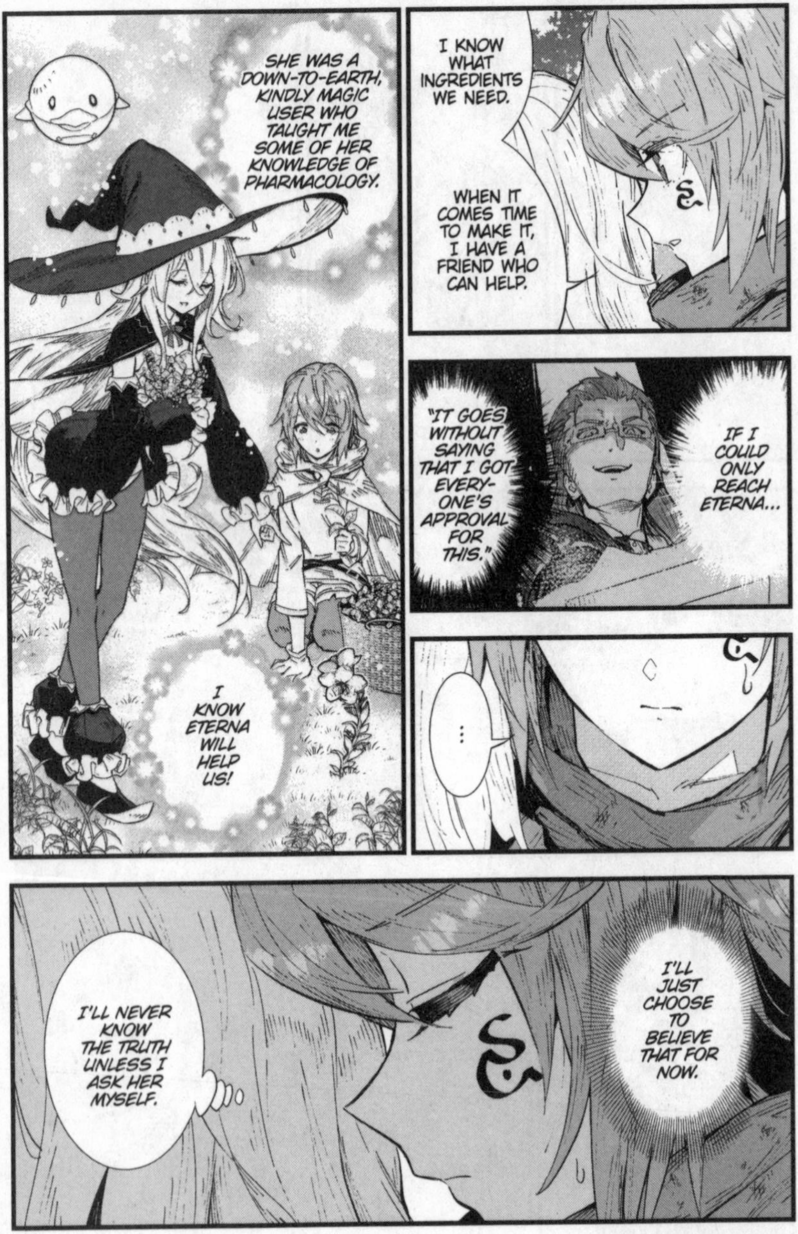

I KNOW WHAT INGREDIENTS WE NEED.
WHEN IT COMES TIME TO MAKE IT, I HAVE A FRIEND WHO CAN HELP.
IF I COULD ONLY REACH ETERNA...
"IT GOES WITHOUT SAYING THAT I GOT EVERY-ONE'S APPROVAL FOR THIS."
...
SHE WAS A DOWN-TO-EARTH, KINDLY MAGIC USER WHO TAUGHT ME SOME OF HER KNOWLEDGE OF PHARMACOLOGY.
I KNOW ETERNA WILL HELP US!
I'LL JUST CHOOSE TO BELIEVE THAT FOR NOW.
I'LL NEVER KNOW THE TRUTH UNLESS I ASK HER MYSELF.

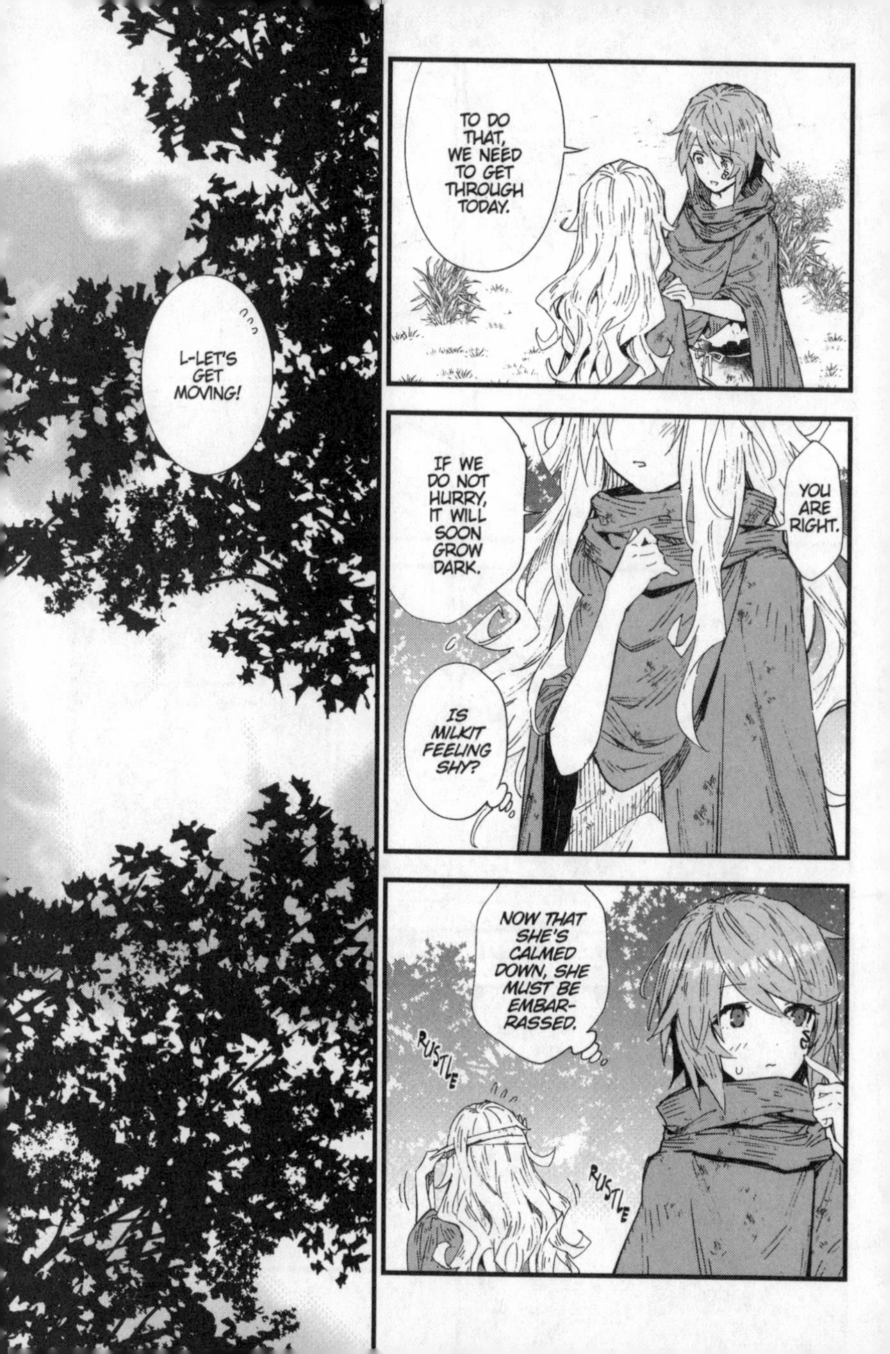
TO DO THAT, WE NEED TO GET THROUGH TODAY.
YOU ARE RIGHT.
IF WE DO NOT HURRY, IT WILL SOON GROW DARK.
IS MILKIT FEELING SHY?
NOW THAT SHE'S CALMED DOWN, SHE MUST BE EMBARRASSED.
RUSTLE
RUSTLE
L-LET'S GET MOVING!

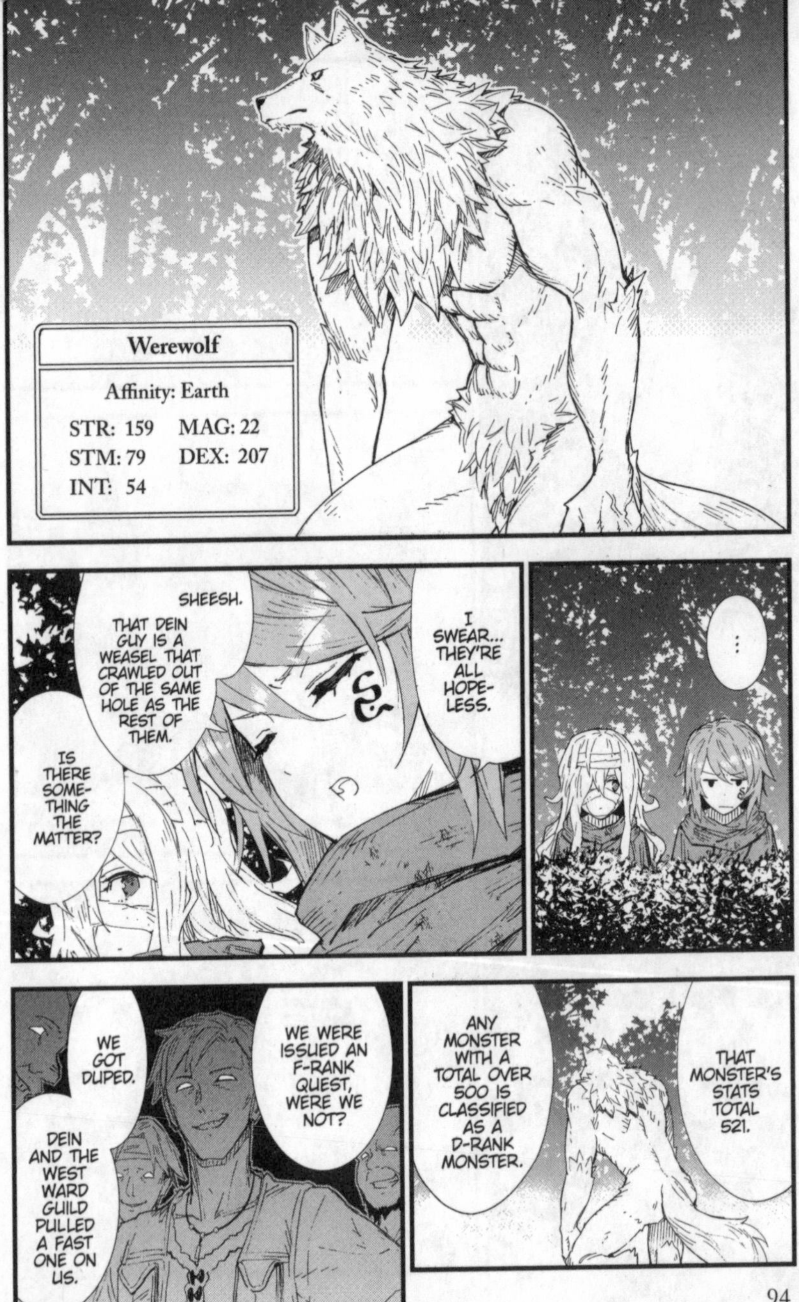
Werewolf
Affinity: Earth
STR: 159 MAG: 22
STM: 79 DEX: 207
INT: 54
...
I SWEAR... THEY'RE ALL HOPELESS.
SHEESH. THAT DEIN GUY IS A WEASEL THAT CRAWLED OUT OF THE SAME HOLE AS THE REST OF THEM.
IS THERE SOMETHING THE MATTER?
THAT MONSTER'S STATS TOTAL 521.
ANY MONSTER WITH A TOTAL OVER 500 IS CLASSIFIED AS A D-RANK MONSTER.
WE WERE ISSUED AN F-RANK QUEST, WERE WE NOT?
WE GOT DUPED.
DEIN AND THE WEST WARD GUILD PULLED A FAST ONE ON US.

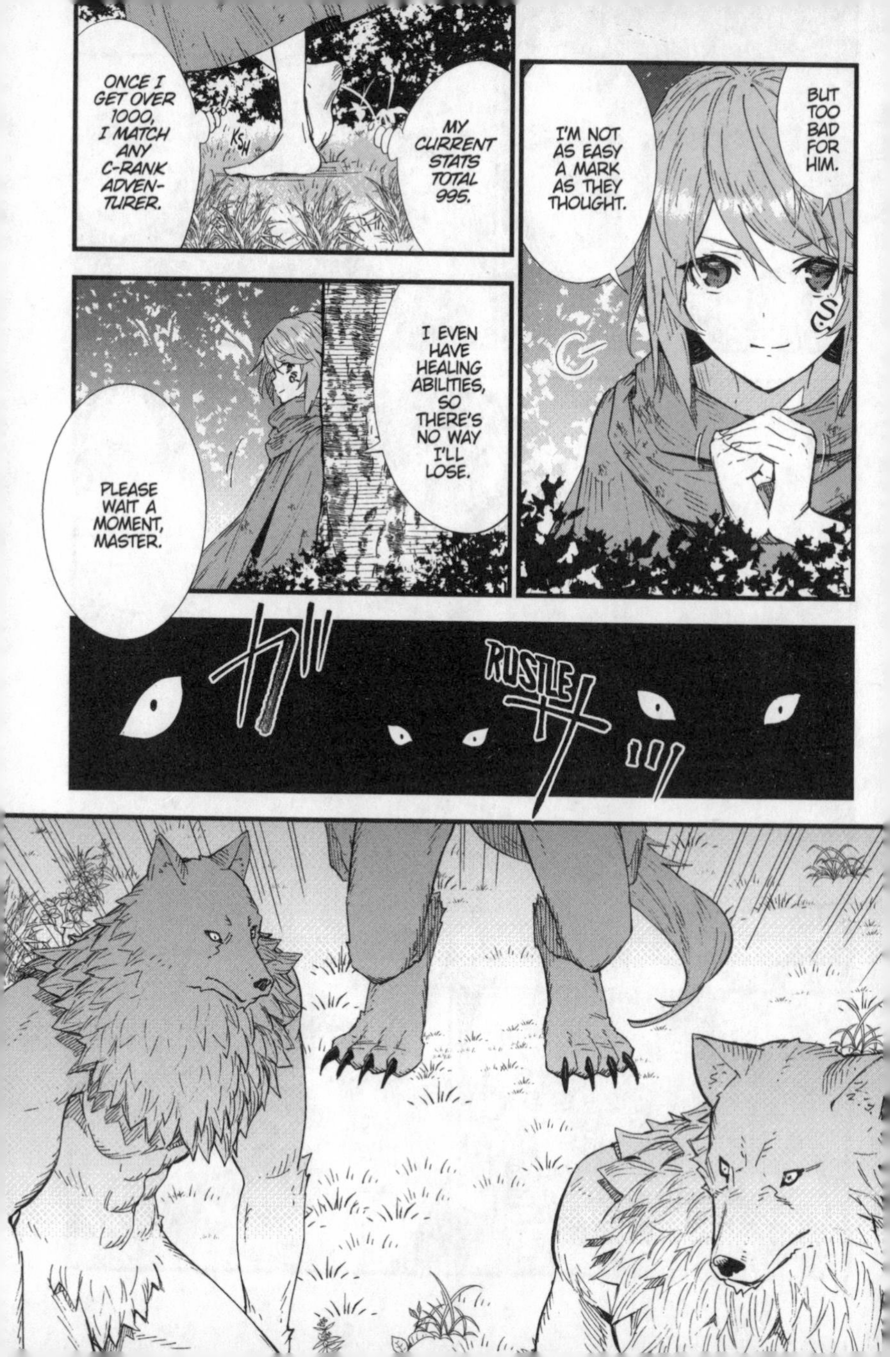
BUT TOO BAD FOR HIM.
I'M NOT AS EASY A MARK AS THEY THOUGHT.
MY CURRENT STATS TOTAL 995.
KSH
ONCE I GET OVER 1000, I MATCH ANY C-RANK ADVEN-TURER.
I EVEN HAVE HEALING ABILITIES, SO THERE'S NO WAY I'LL LOSE.
PLEASE WAIT A MOMENT, MASTER.
RUSTLE

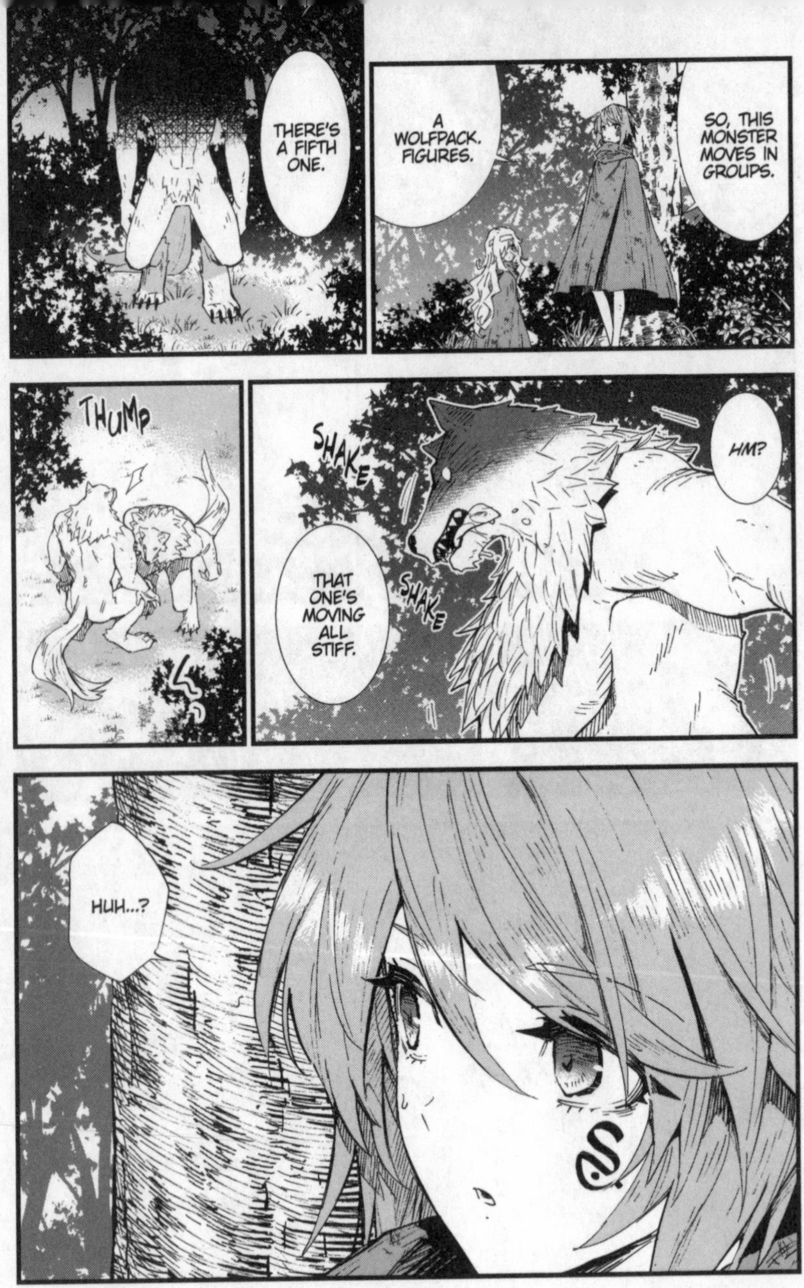
SO, THIS MONSTER MOVES IN GROUPS.
A WOLFPACK. FIGURES.
THERE'S A FIFTH ONE.
HM?
SHAKE
SHAKE
THAT ONE'S MOVING ALL STIFF.
THUMP
HUH...?

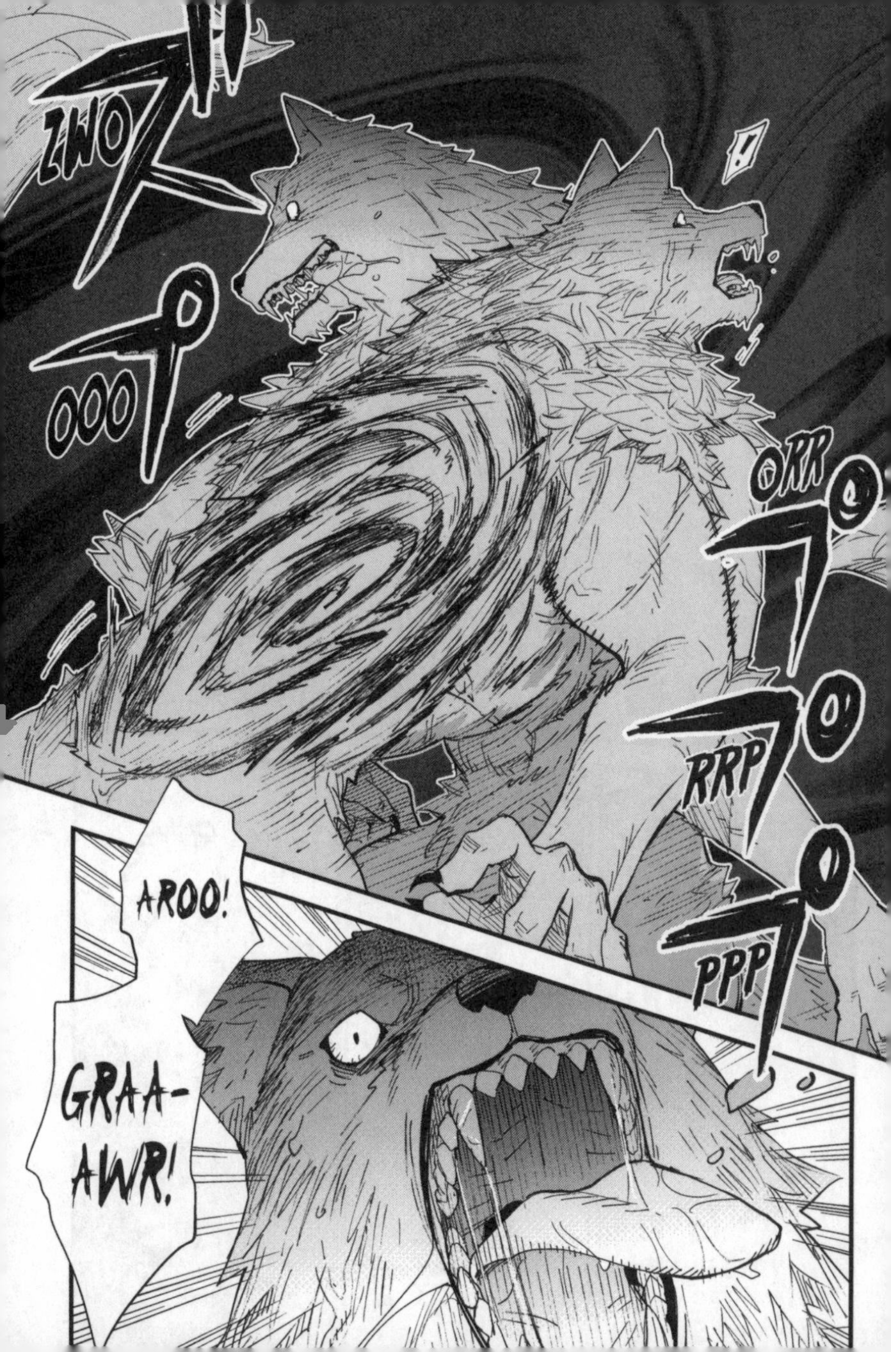
!
ORR
RRP
PPP
ZWO
OOO
AROO!
GRAA-
AWR!

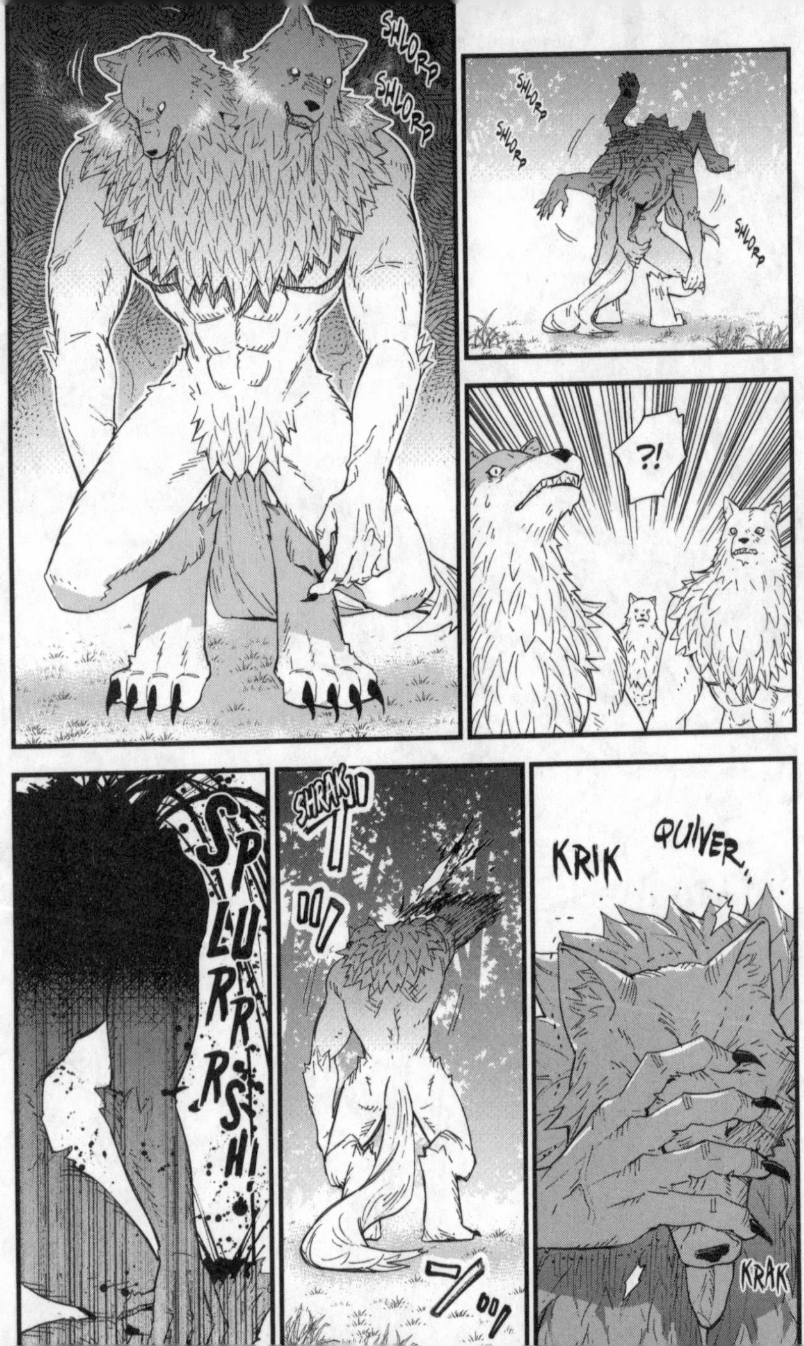
SHLORP
SHLORP
SHLORP
?!
SHLORP
SHLORP
KRIK
QUIVER...
KRAK
SHRAK
SPLURRRSH!

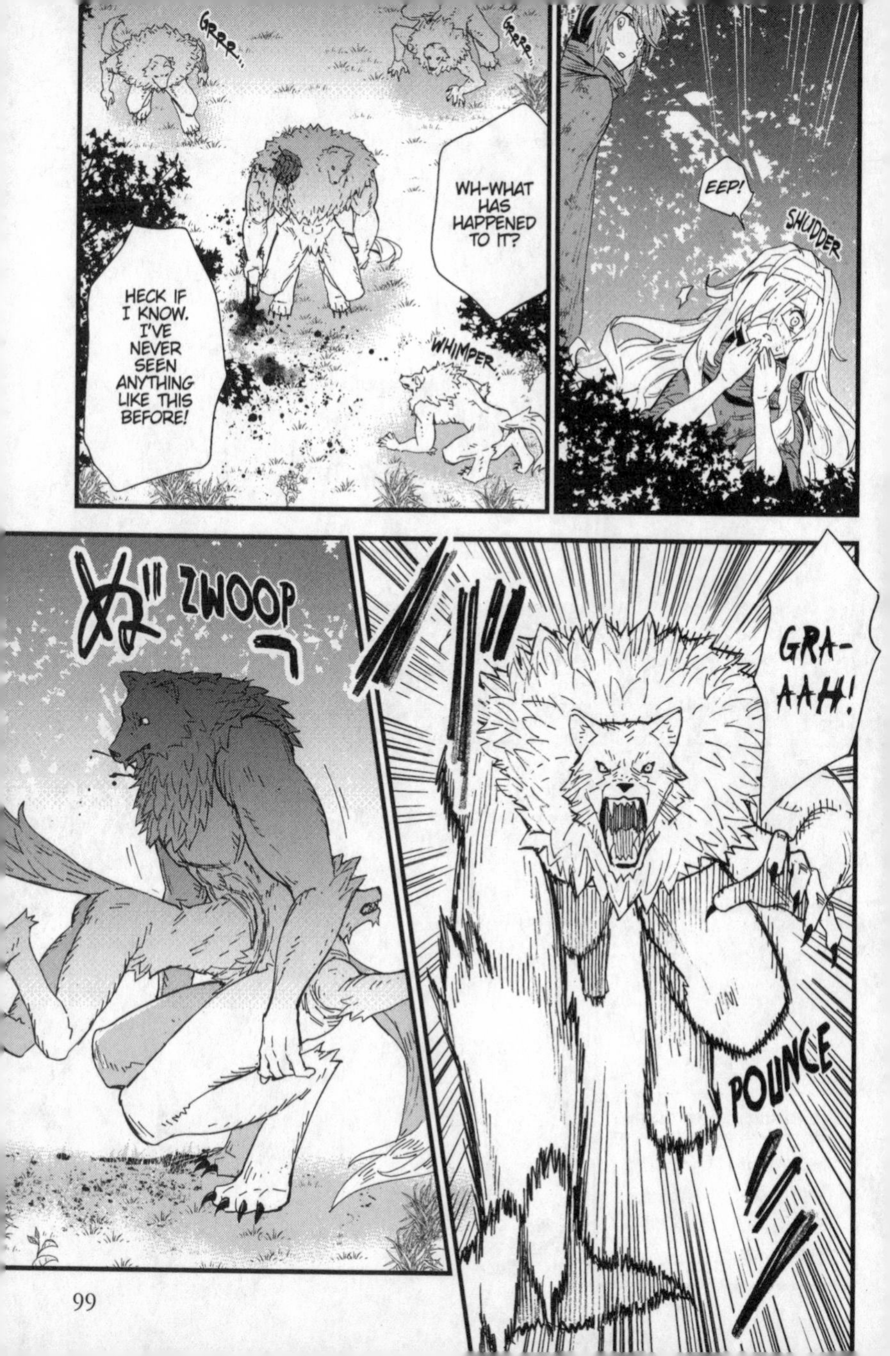
EEP!
SHUDDER
GRRR...
GRRR...
WH-WHAT HAS HAPPENED TO IT?
HECK IF I KNOW. I'VE NEVER SEEN ANYTHING LIKE THIS BEFORE!
WHIMPER...
GRA-AAH!
POUNCE
ぬ" ZWOOP

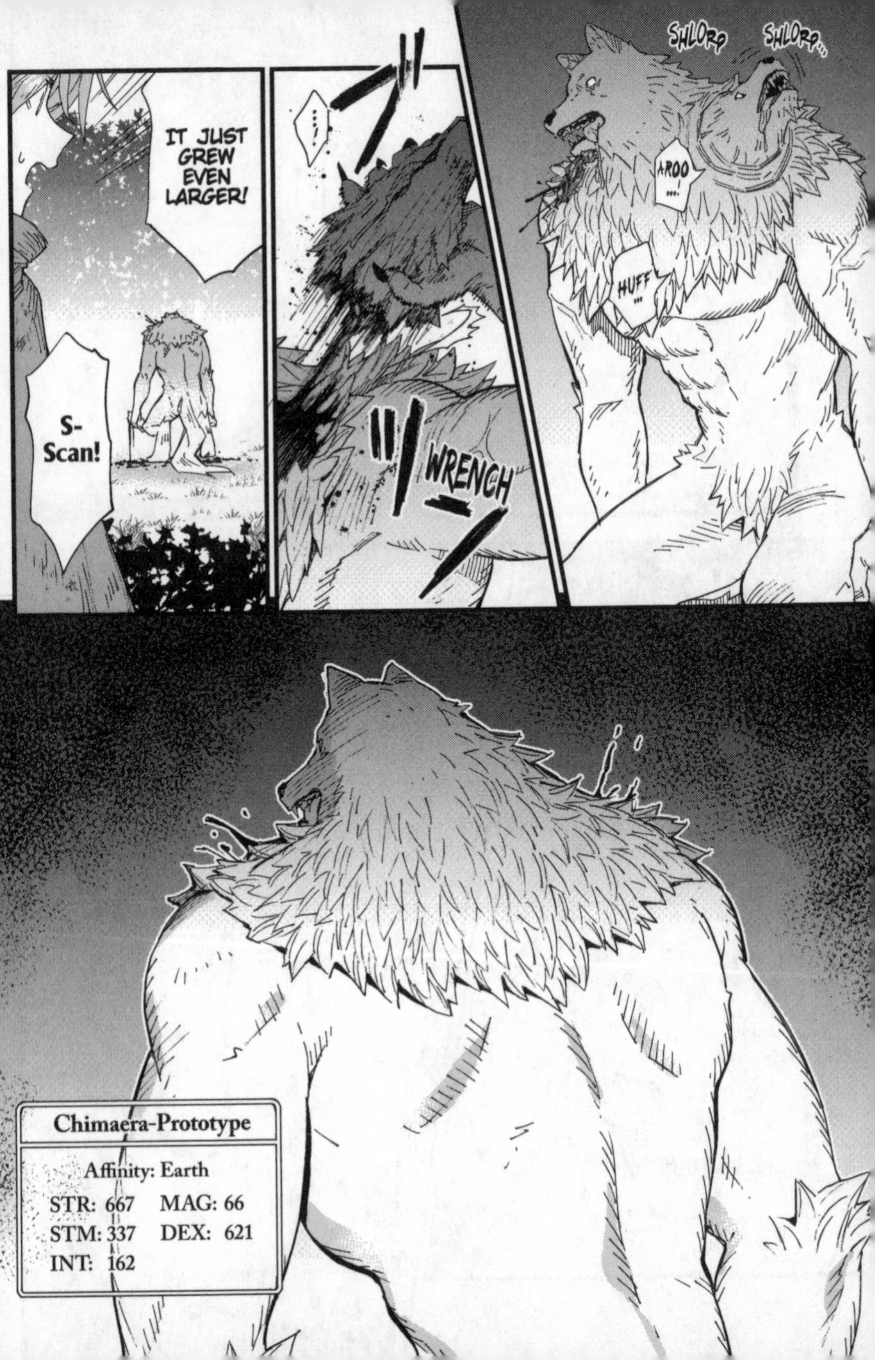
SHLORP SHLORP...
AROO...!
HUFF...
...!
WRENCH
IT JUST GREW EVEN LARGER!
S-Scan!
Chimaera-Prototype
Affinity: Earth
STR: 667 MAG: 66
STM: 337 DEX: 621
INT: 162

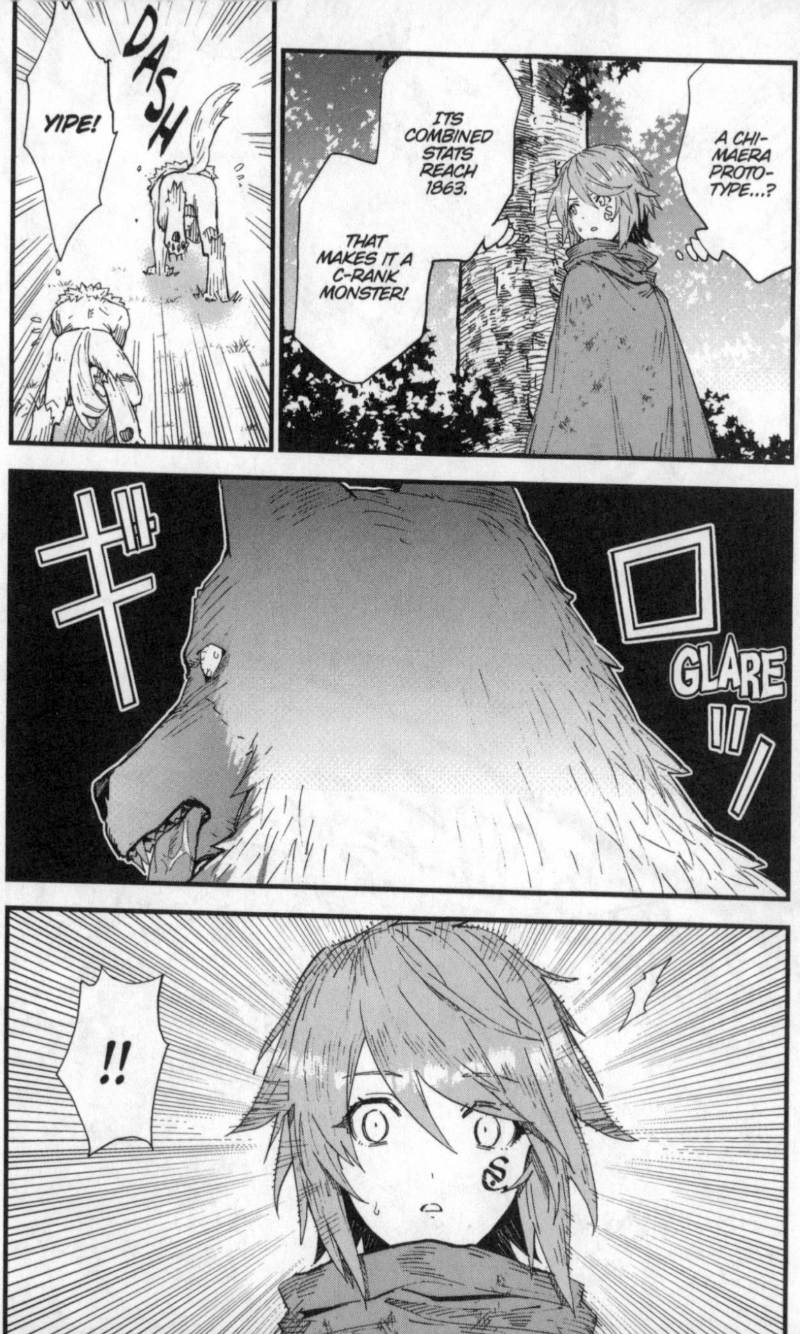
A CHI-MAERA PROTO-TYPE...?
ITS COMBINED STATS REACH 1863.
THAT MAKES IT A C-RANK MONSTER!
DASH
YIPE!
ギロ
GLARE
!!

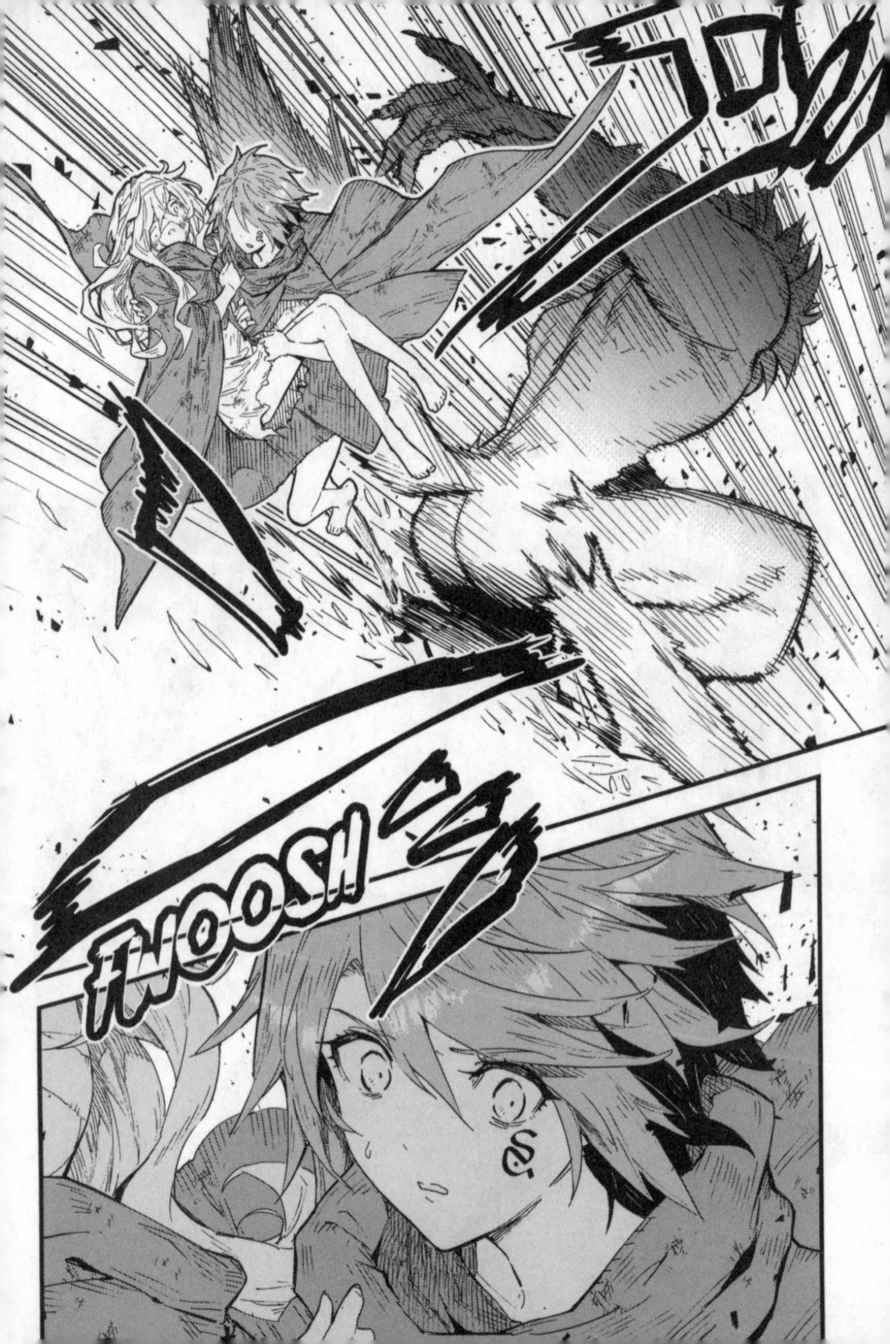
FWOOSH

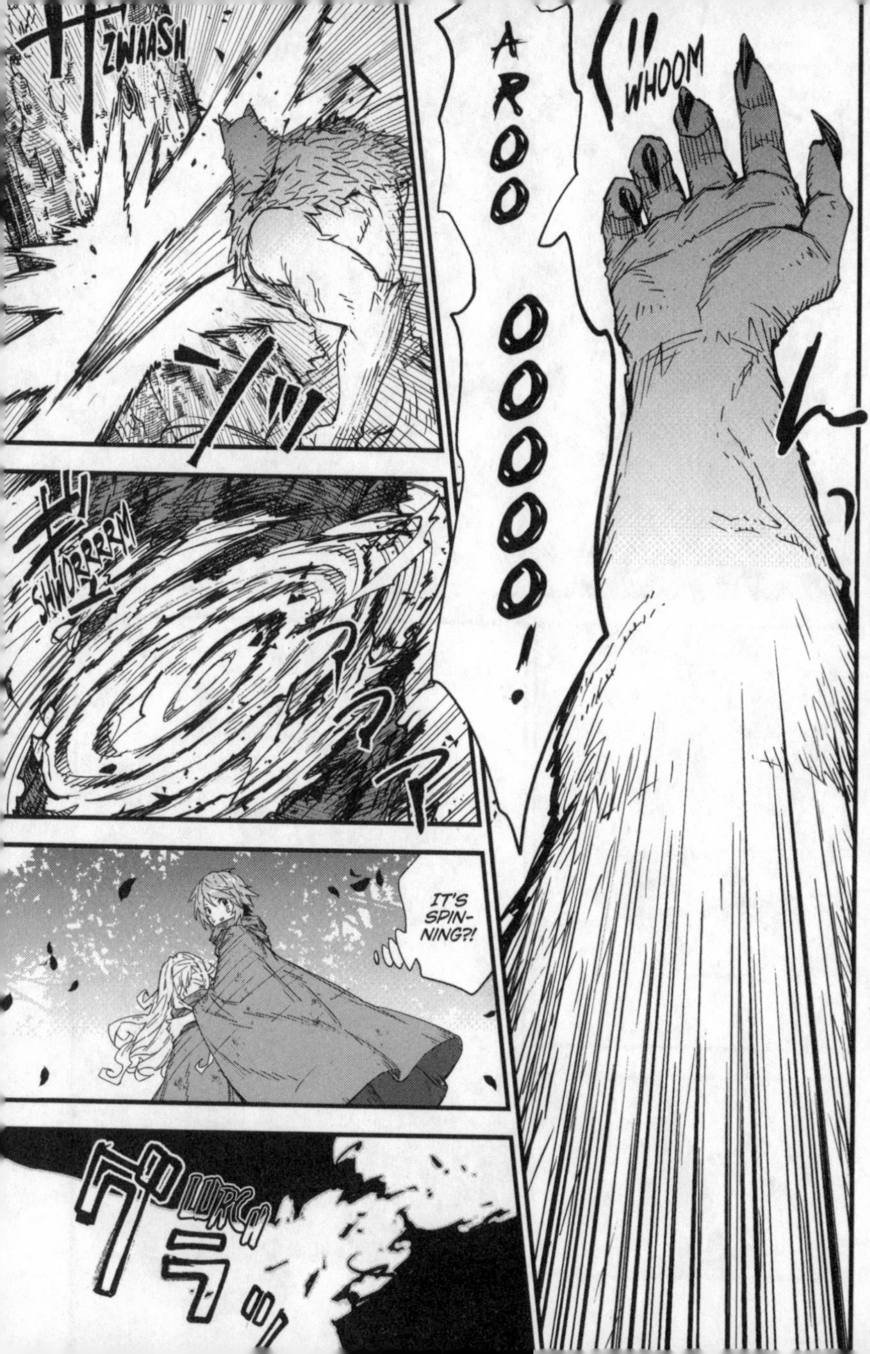
WHOOM
AROOOOOOOOO!
ZWAASH
SHWORRRRM
IT'S SPIN-NING?!
LURCH

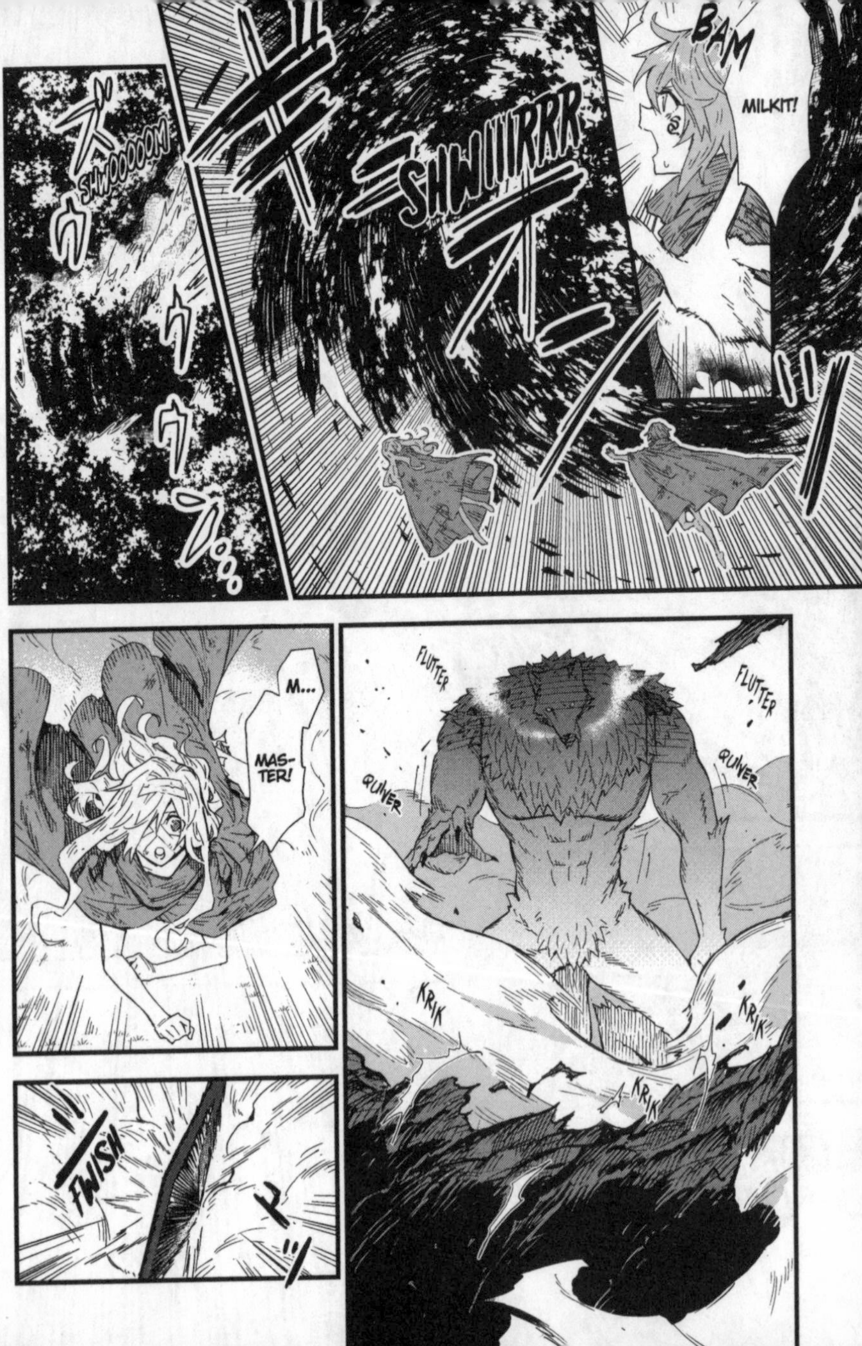
BAM
MILKIT!
SHWIIIRRR
SHWOOOOOM
FLUTTER
FLUTTER
QUIVER
QUIVER
KRIK
KRIK
KRIK
M...
MASTER!
FWISH

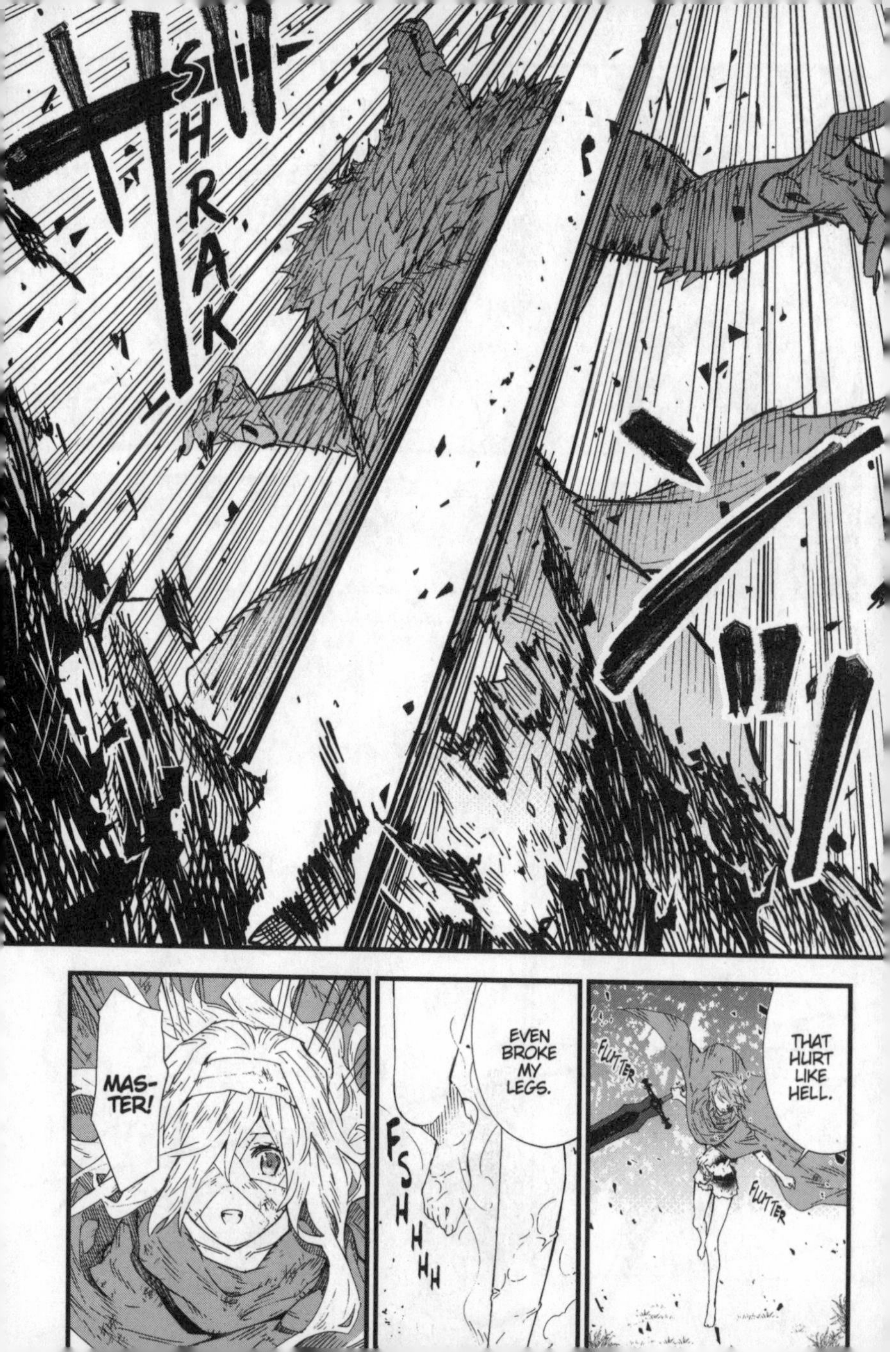
SHRAK
THAT HURT LIKE HELL.
FLUTTER
FLUTTER
EVEN BROKE MY LEGS.
FSHHHH
MAS-TER!

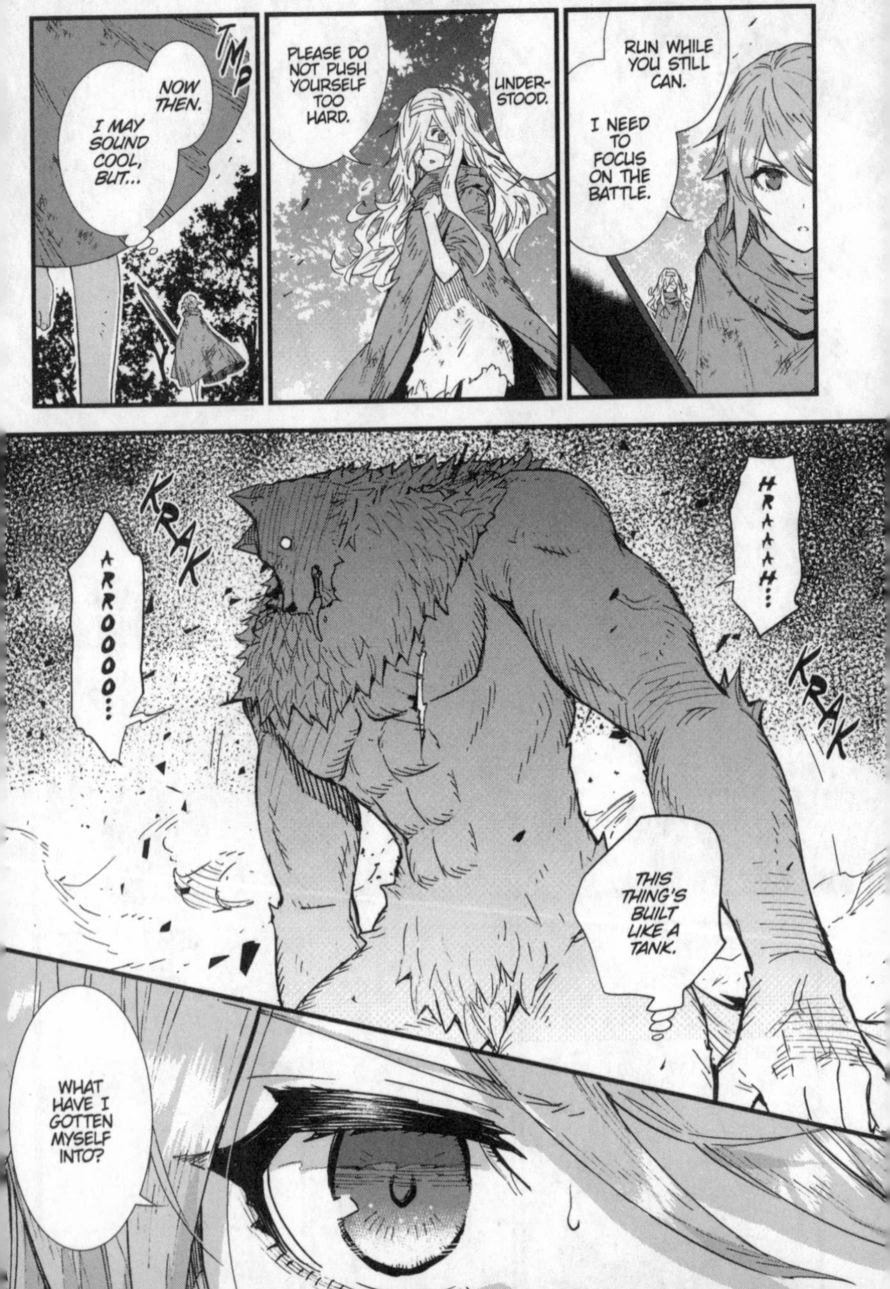
RUN WHILE YOU STILL CAN.
I NEED TO FOCUS ON THE BATTLE.
UNDER-STOOD.
PLEASE DO NOT PUSH YOURSELF TOO HARD.
TMP
NOW THEN.
I MAY SOUND COOL, BUT...
HRAAAAH...
KRAK
KRAK
ARROOOOO...
THIS THING'S BUILT LIKE A TANK.
WHAT HAVE I GOTTEN MYSELF INTO?

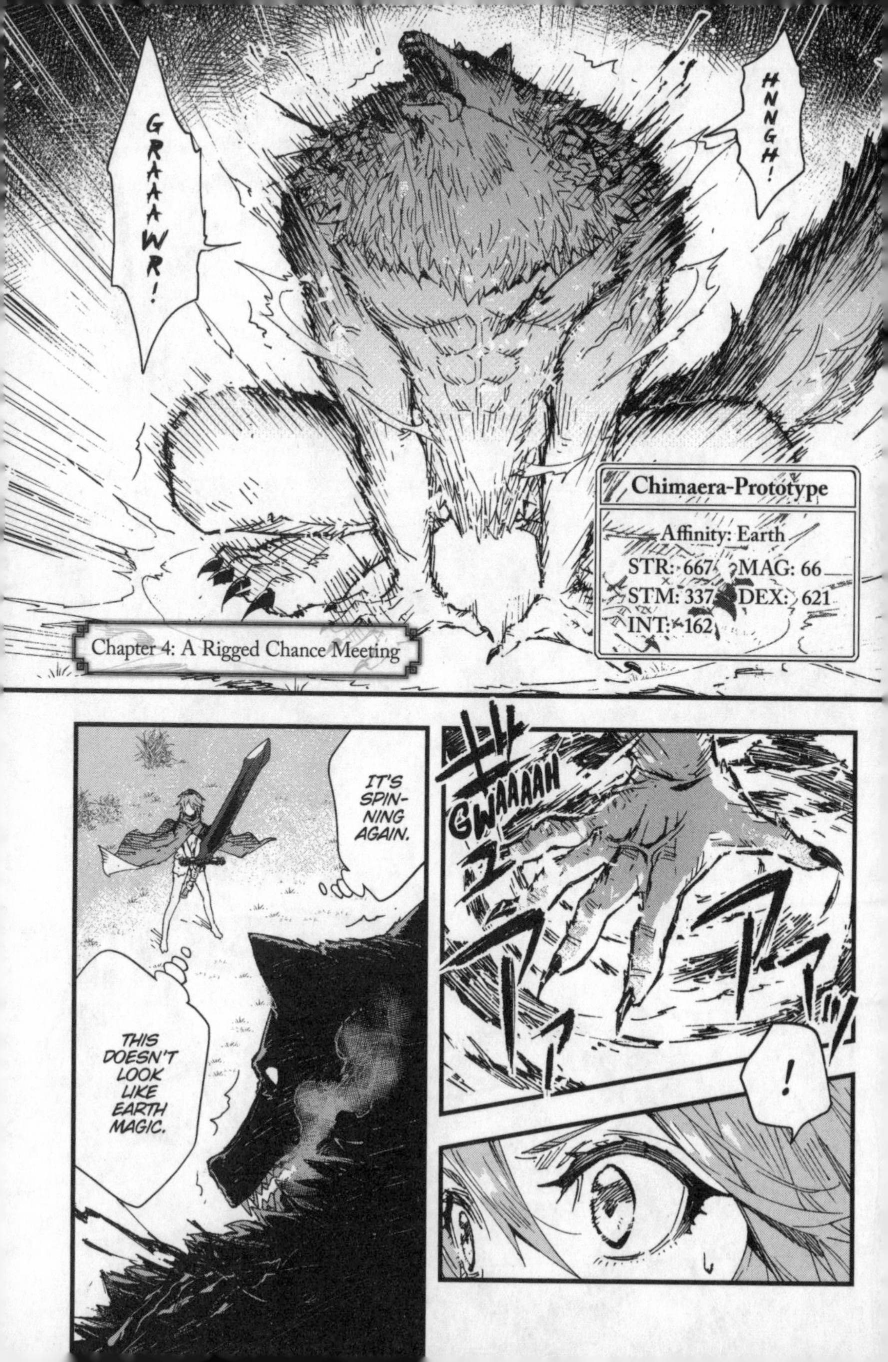
HNNGH!
GRAAAAWR!
Chimaera-Prototype
Affinity: Earth
STR: 667 MAG: 66
STM: 337 DEX: 621
INT: 162
Chapter 4: A Rigged Chance Meeting
GWAAAAH
!
IT'S SPINNING AGAIN.
THIS DOESN'T LOOK LIKE EARTH MAGIC.

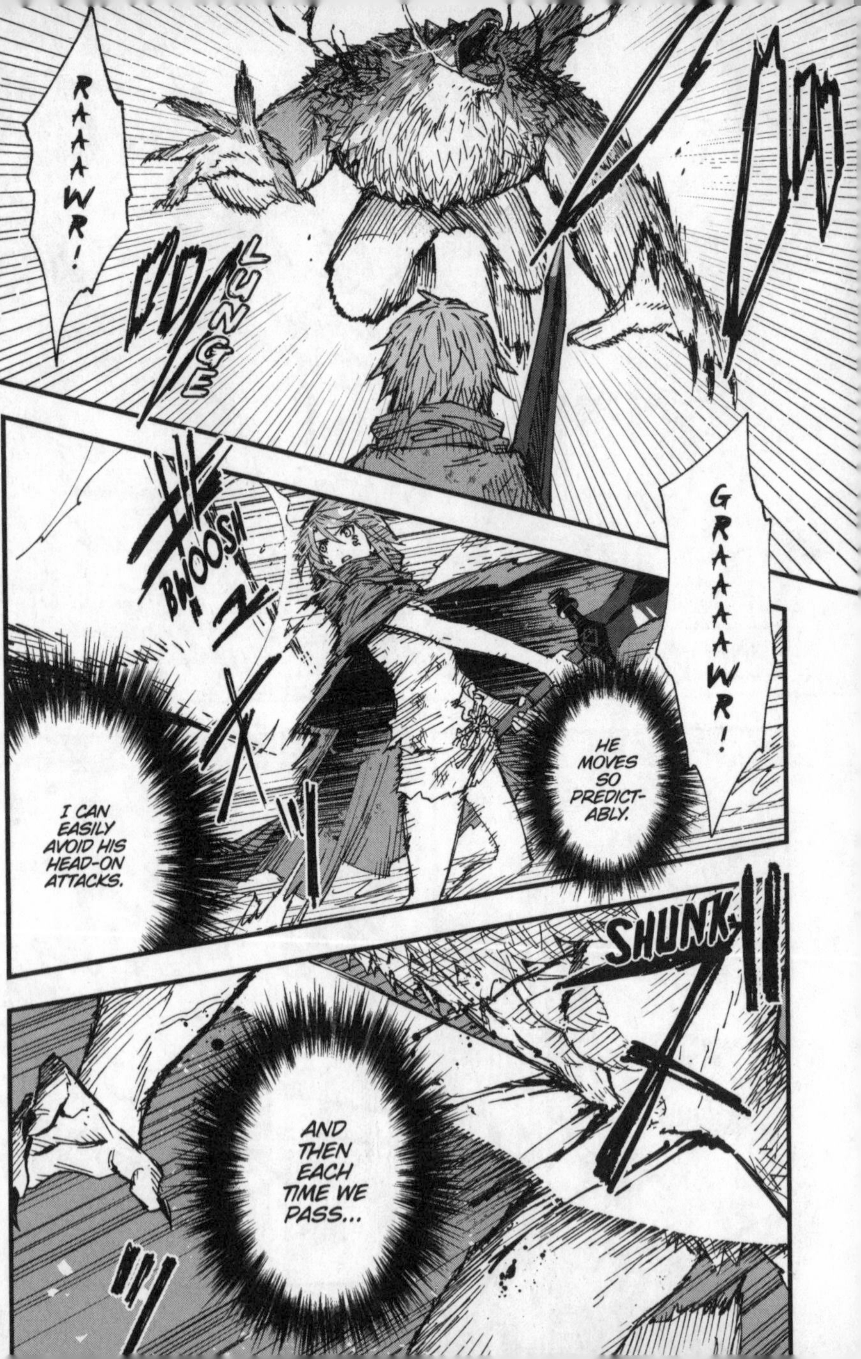
LUNGE
RAAAAWR!
GRAAAAAWR!
BWOOSH
HE MOVES SO PREDICTABLY.
I CAN EASILY AVOID HIS HEAD-ON ATTACKS.
SHUNK
AND THEN EACH TIME WE PASS...

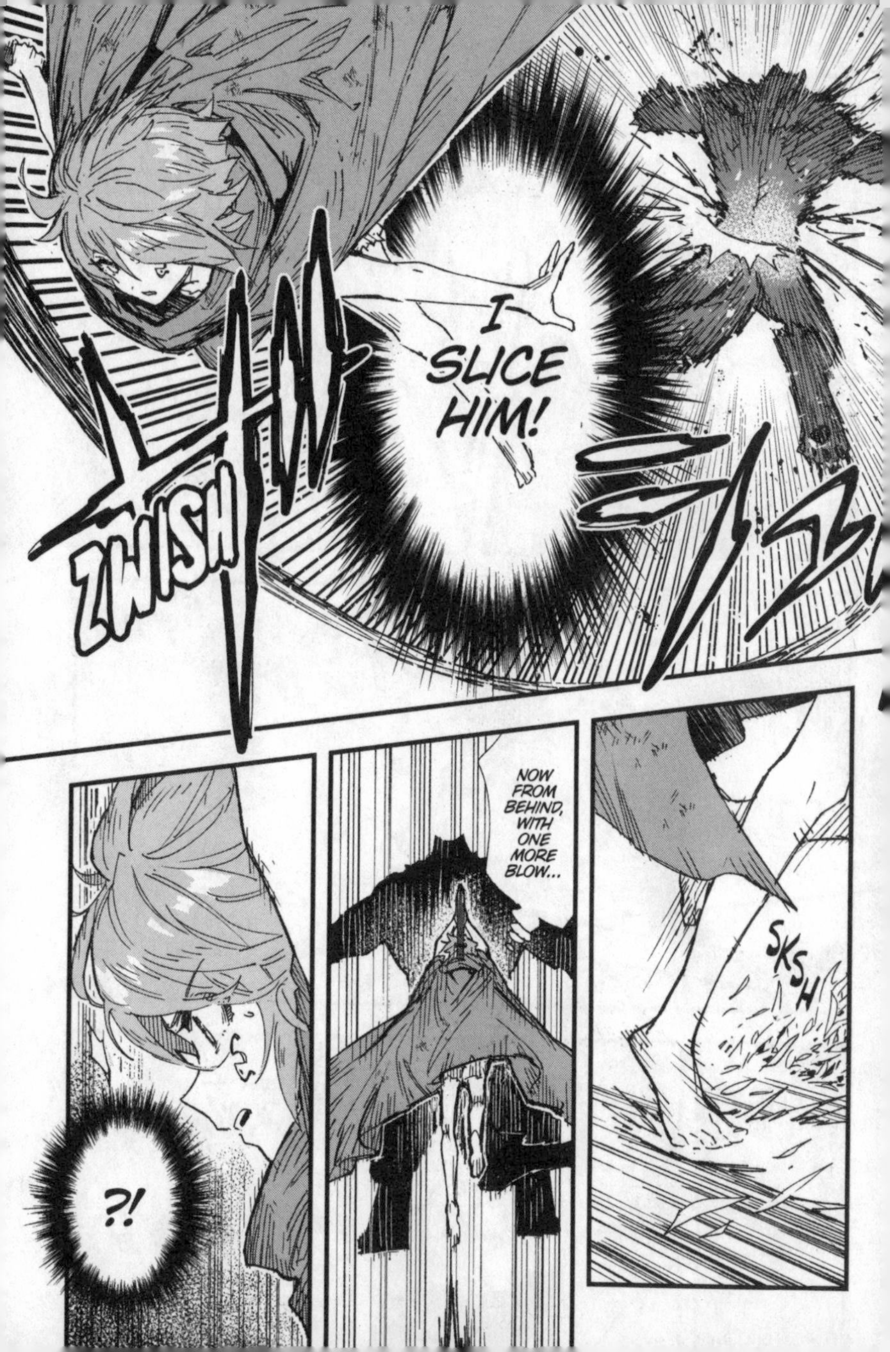
I SLICE HIM!
ZWISH
SKSH
NOW FROM BEHIND, WITH ONE MORE BLOW...
?!

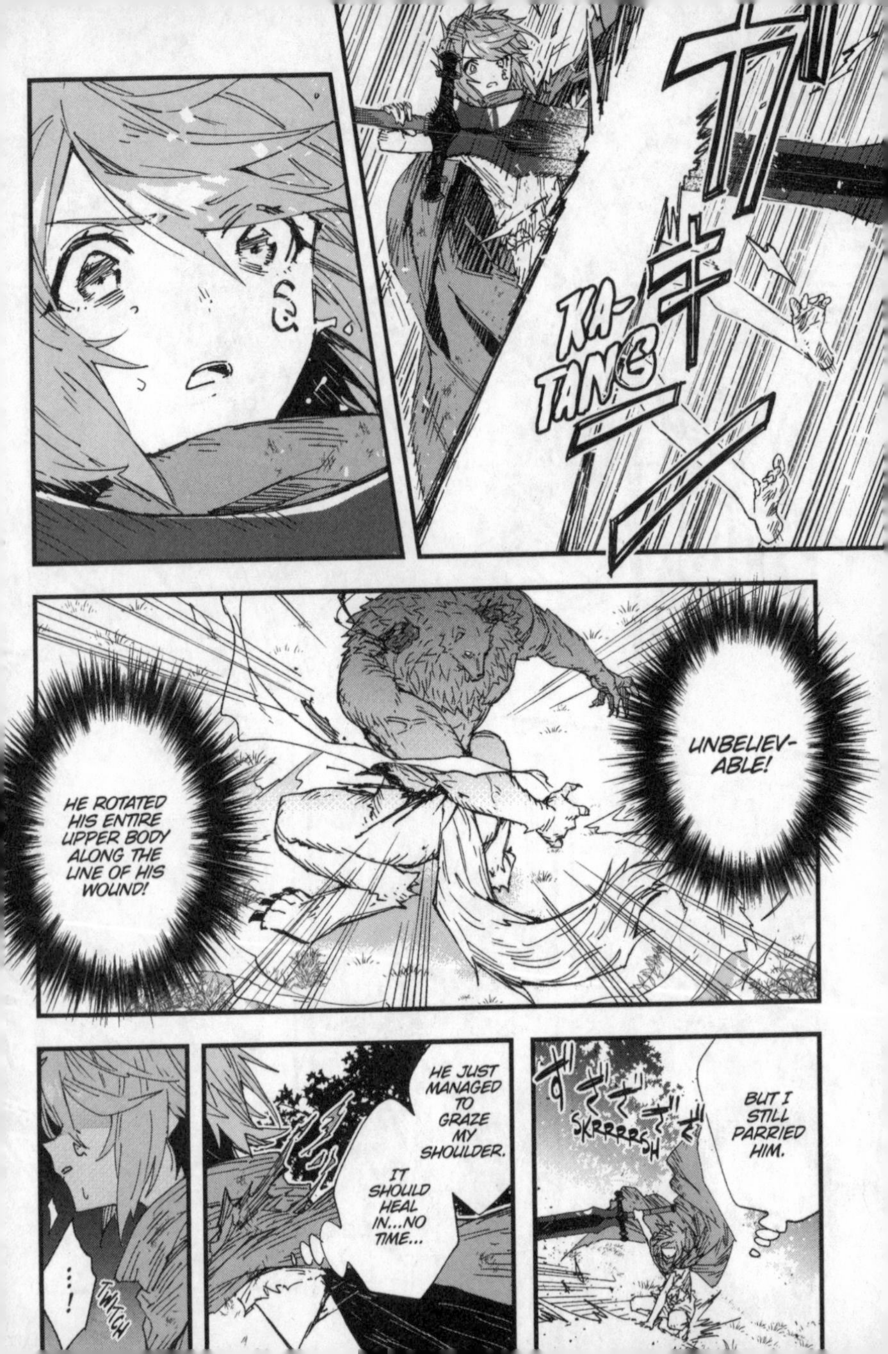

KA-TANG
UNBELIEV-ABLE!
HE ROTATED HIS ENTIRE UPPER BODY ALONG THE LINE OF HIS WOUND!
SKRRRRSH
BUT I STILL PARRIED HIM.
HE JUST MANAGED TO GRAZE MY SHOULDER.
IT SHOULD HEAL IN...NO TIME...
...!
TWITCH

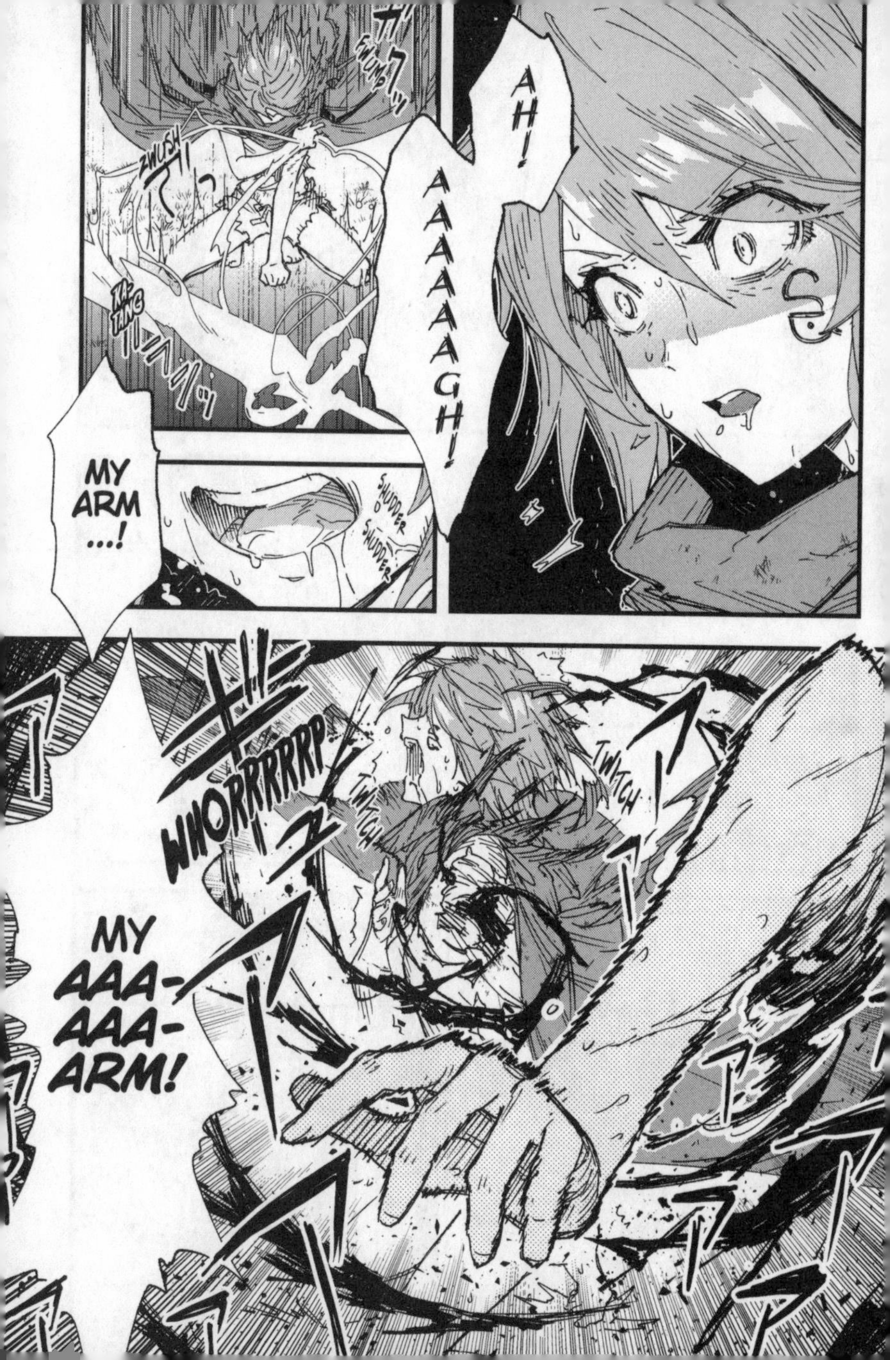
AH! AAAAAAAGH!
FWUMP
ZWUSH
KA-TANG
SHUDDER SHUDDER
MY ARM ...!
WHORRRRRP
TWITCH
TWITCH
MY AAA-AAA-ARM!

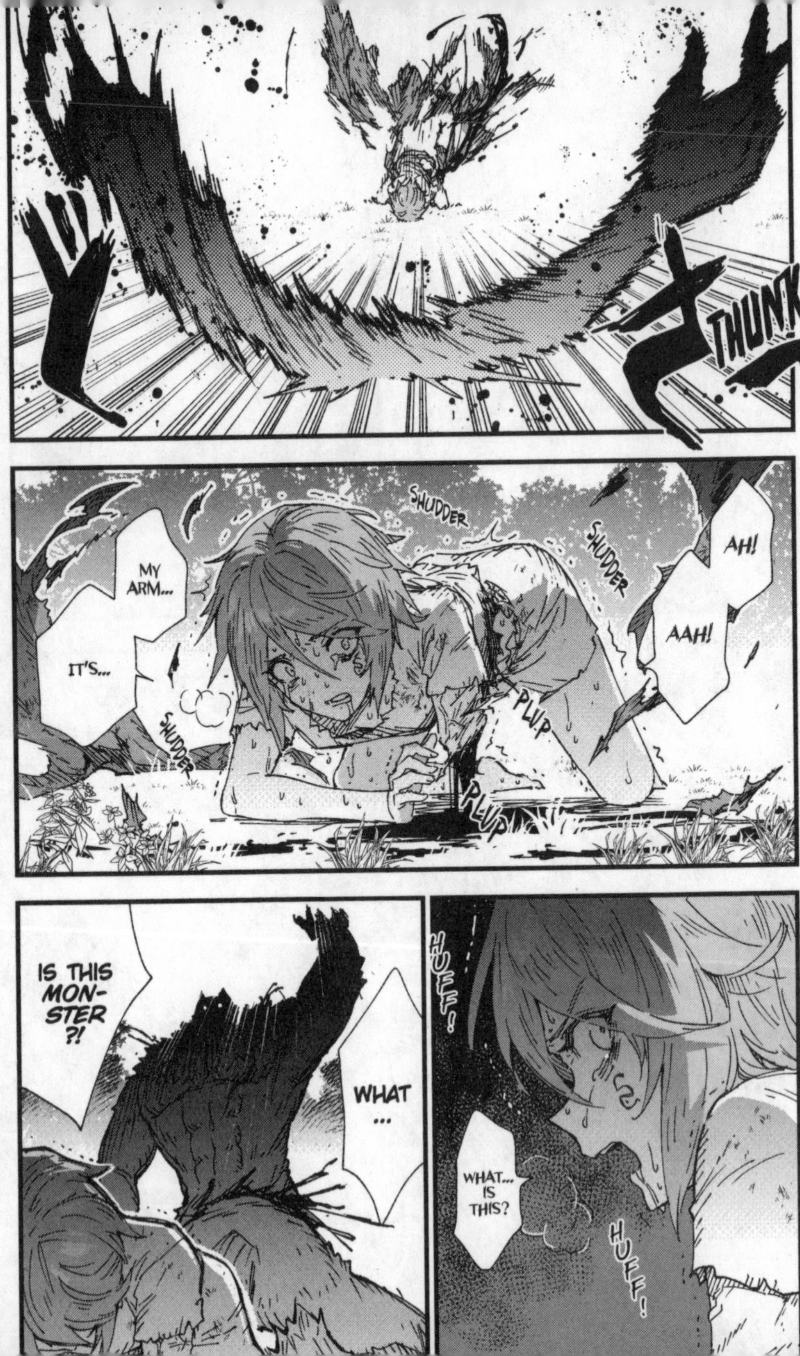
THUNK
SHUDDER
SHUDDER
AH! AAH!
MY ARM... IT'S...
PLUP
SHUDDER
PLUP
HUFF!
WHAT... IS THIS?
HUFF!
WHAT...
IS THIS MONSTER?!

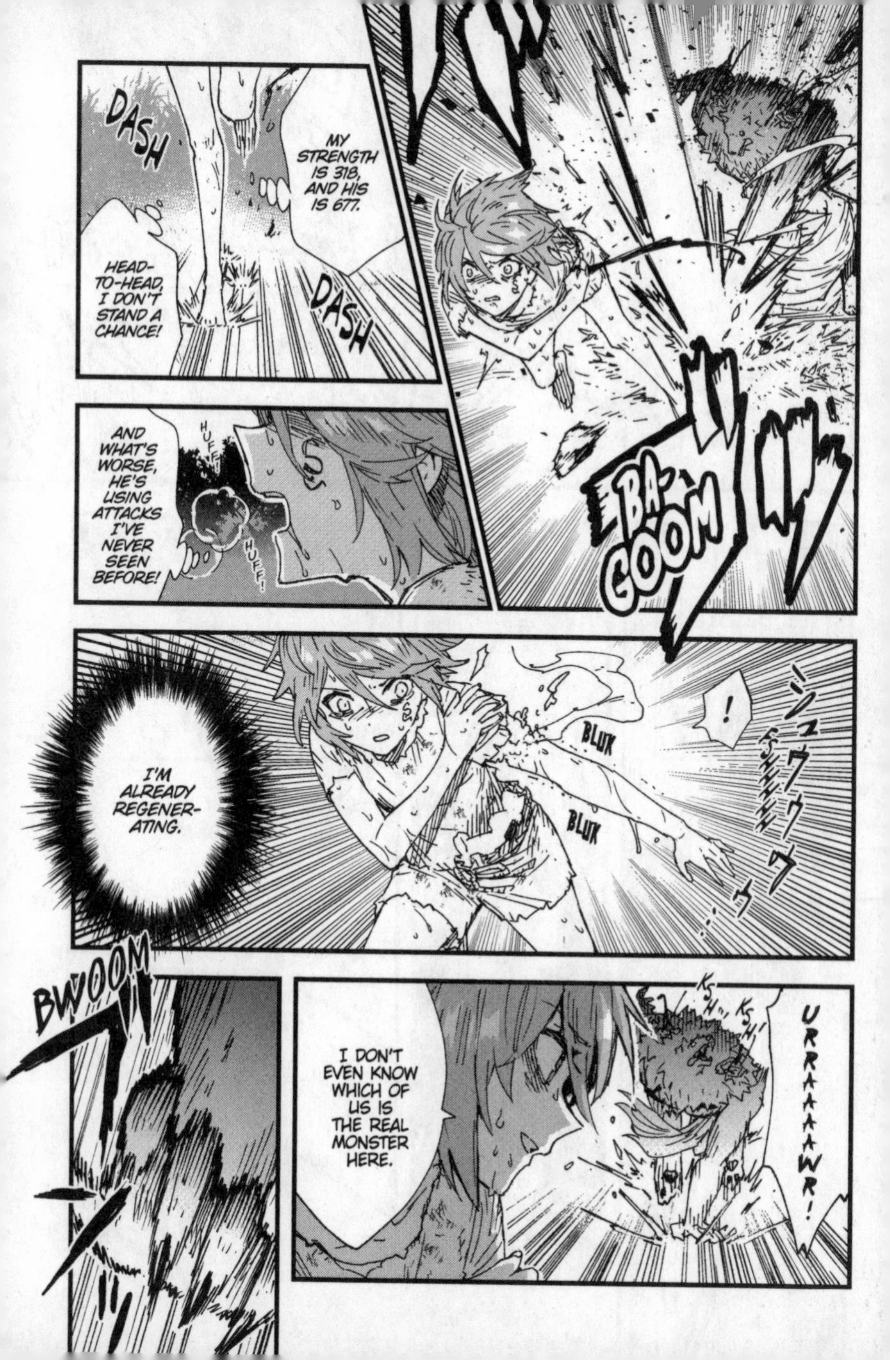
BA-GOOM
DASH
MY STRENGTH IS 318, AND HIS IS 677.
DASH
HEAD-TO-HEAD, I DON'T STAND A CHANCE!
HUFF
HUFF
AND WHAT'S WORSE, HE'S USING ATTACKS I'VE NEVER SEEN BEFORE!
FSHHHHH
!
BLUK
BLUK
I'M ALREADY REGENER-ATING.
URRAAAAWR!
KSH KSH
I DON'T EVEN KNOW WHICH OF US IS THE REAL MONSTER HERE.
BWOOM

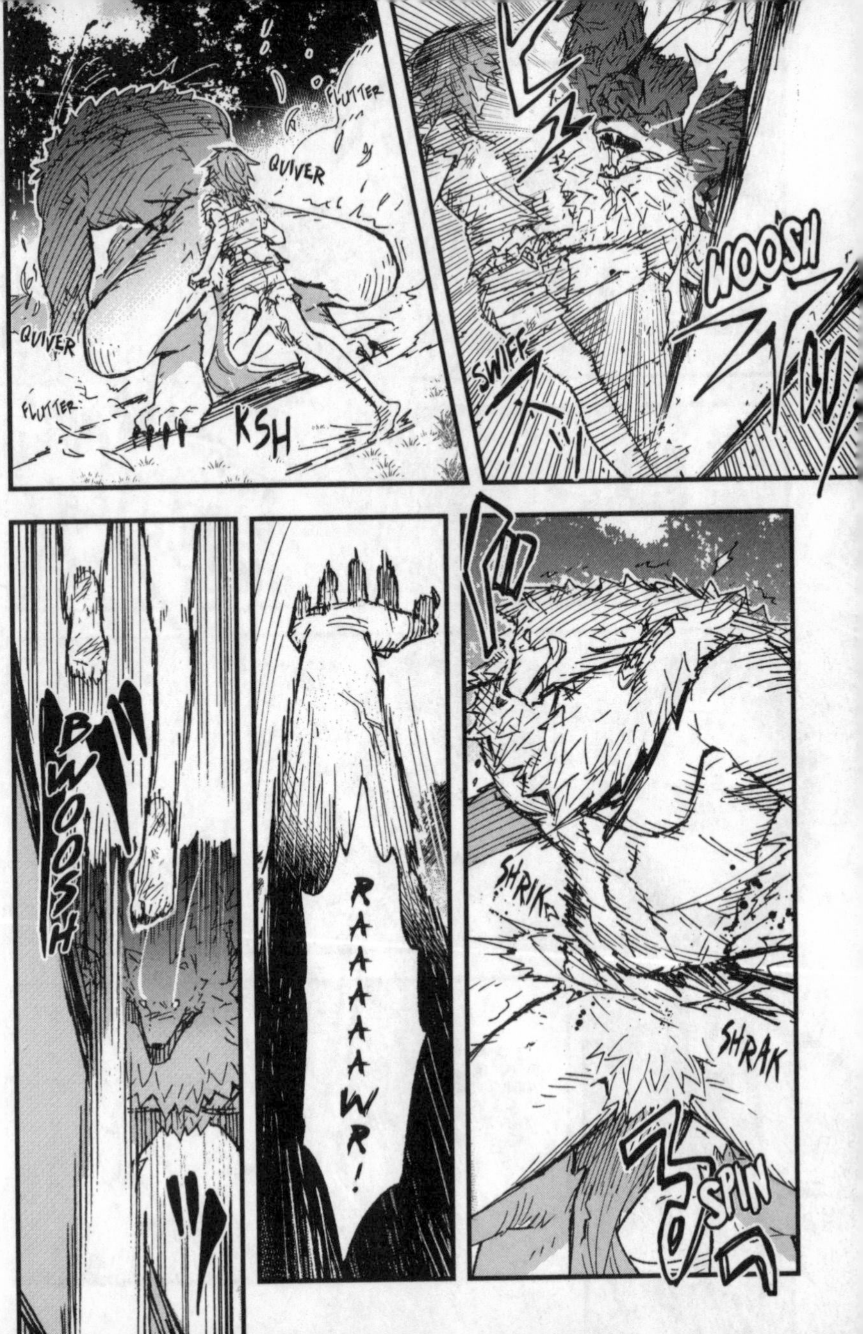
WOOSH
SWIFF
FLUTTER
QUIVER
QUIVER
FLUTTER
KSH
SHRIK
SHRAK
SPIN
RAAAAAAWR!
BWOOSH

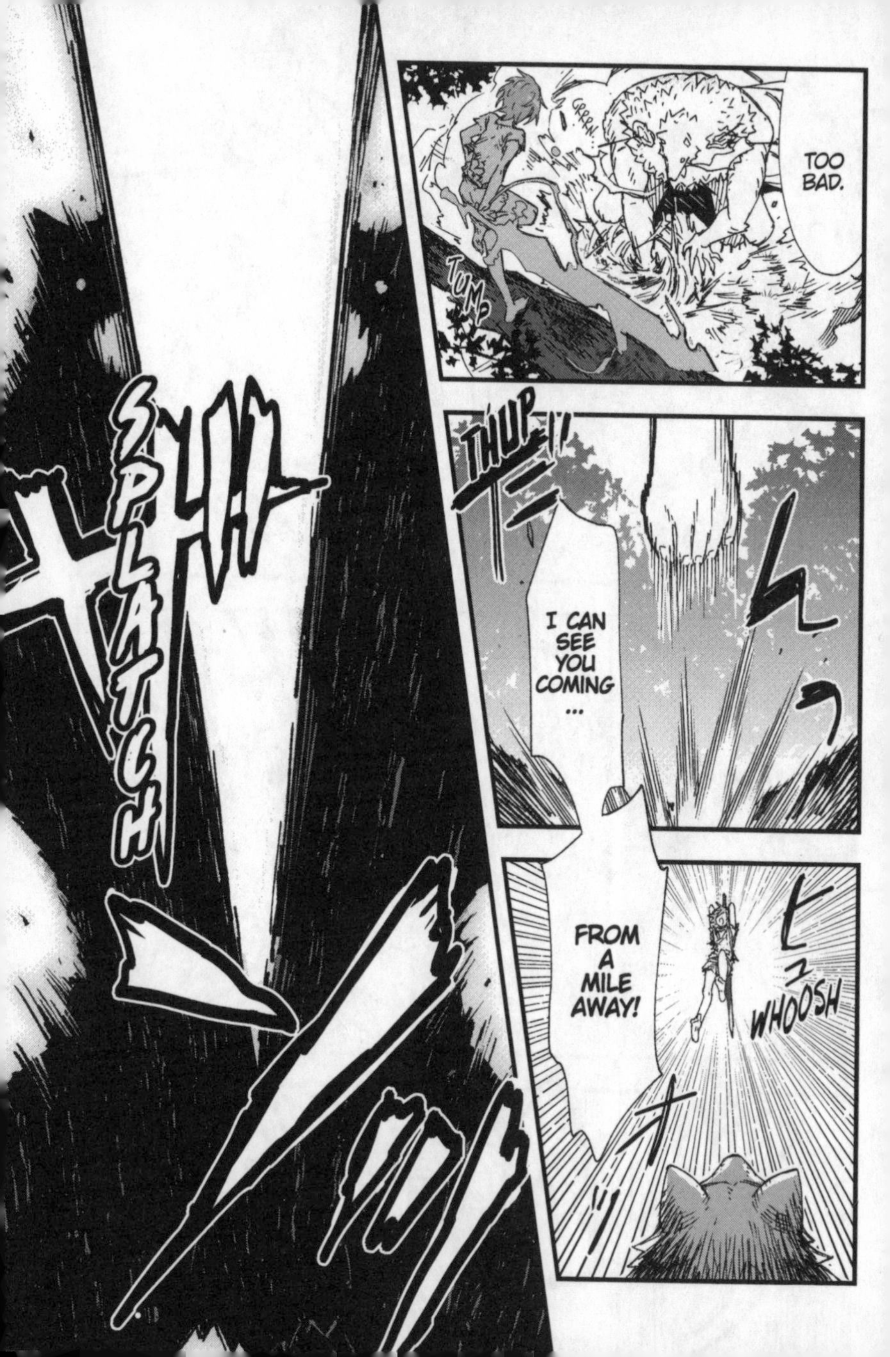
TOO BAD.
GRRRN...
TUMP
THUP
I CAN SEE YOU COMING ...
FROM A MILE AWAY!
WHOOSH
SPLATCH

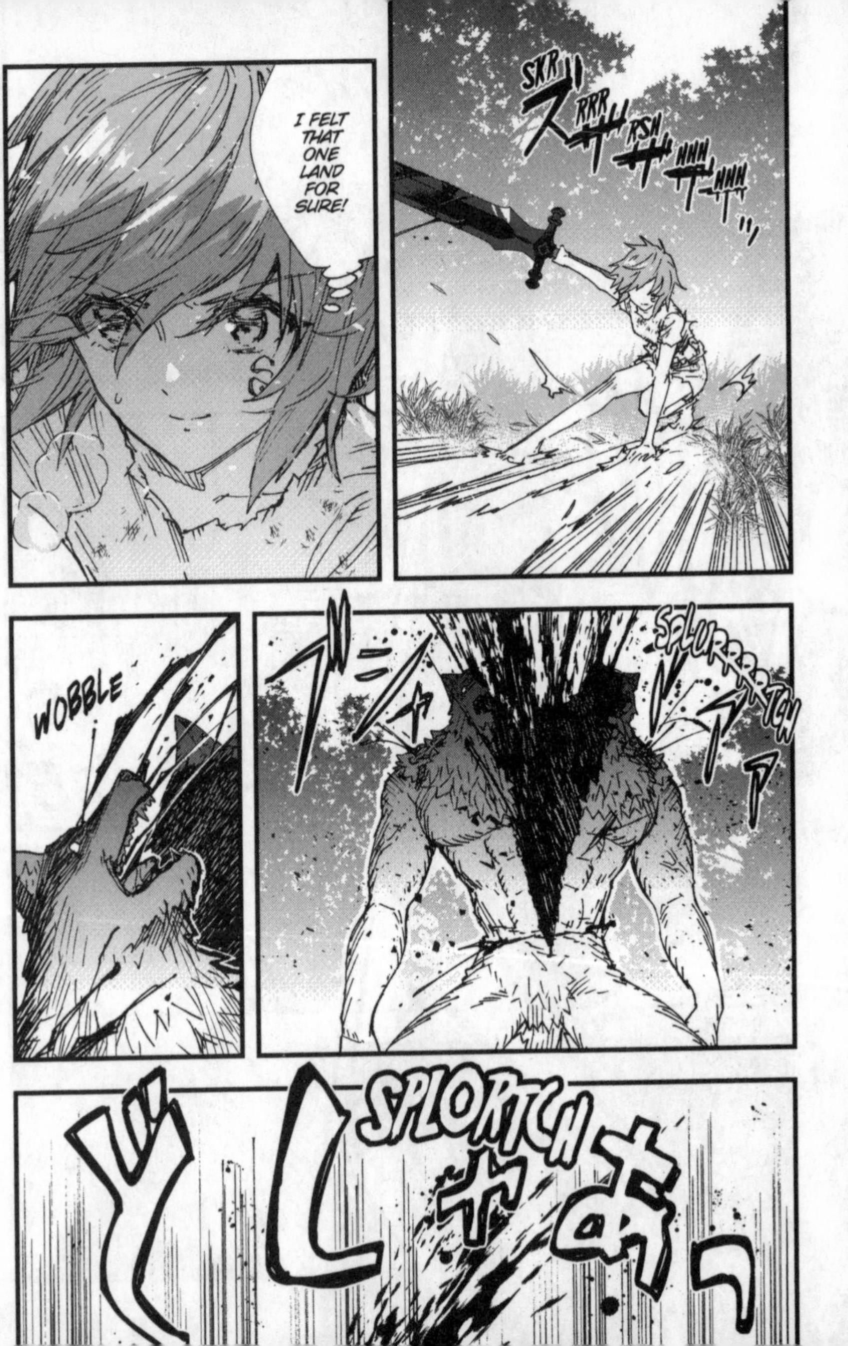

SKR RRR RSH HHH HHH
I FELT THAT ONE LAND FOR SURE!
SPLURRRRTCH
WOBBLE
SPLORTCH

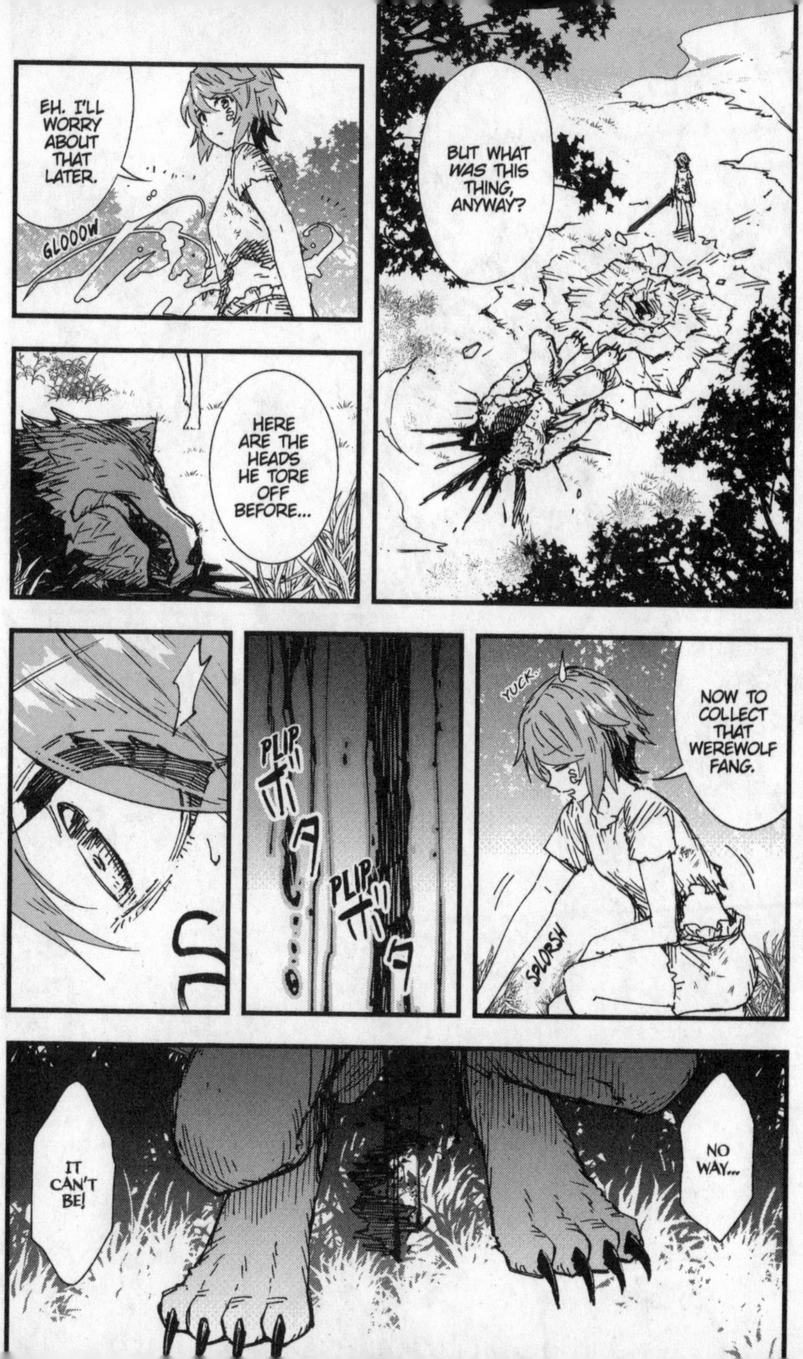
BUT WHAT WAS THIS THING, ANYWAY?
EH. I'LL WORRY ABOUT THAT LATER.
GLOOOW
HERE ARE THE HEADS HE TORE OFF BEFORE...
NOW TO COLLECT THAT WEREWOLF FANG.
YUCK.
SPLORSH
PLIP
PLIP
NO WAY...
IT CAN'T BE!

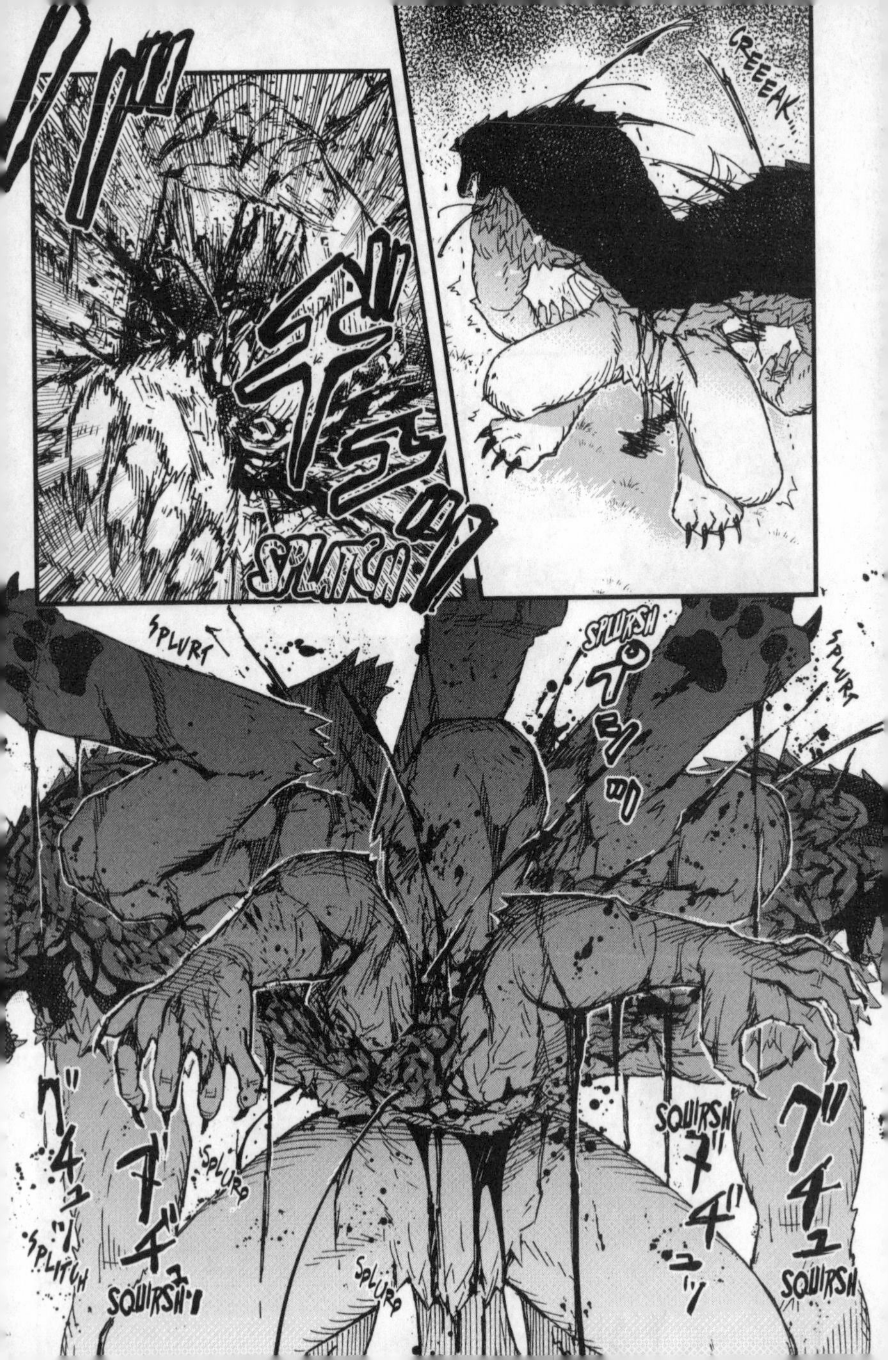
CREEEAK...
SPLATCH
SPLURT
SPLURSH
SPLURT
SQUIRSH
SQUIRSH
SPLURP
SPLURP
SQUIRSH
SPLITCH

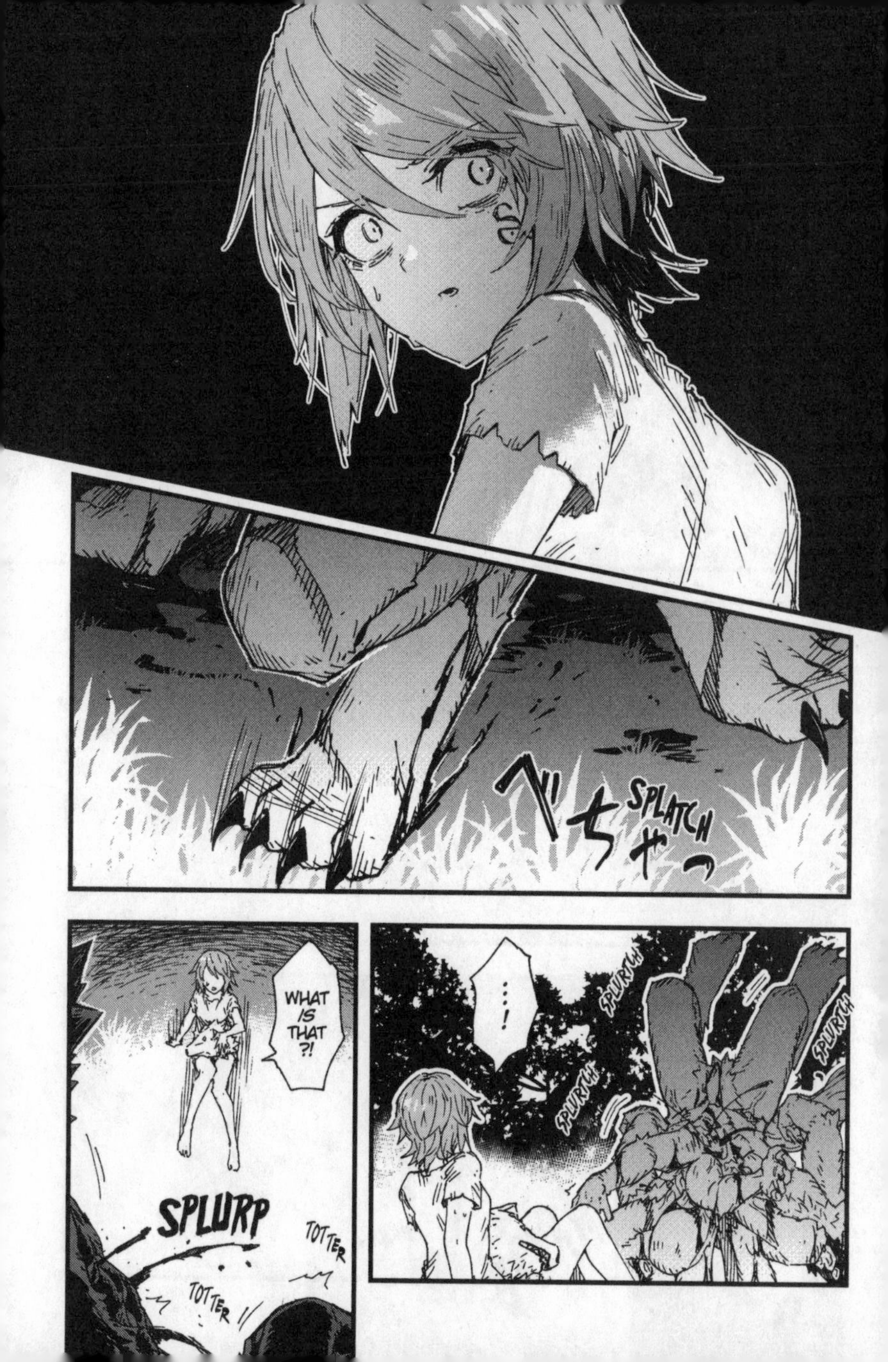
SPLATCH
べちゃっ
...!
SPLURTCH
SPLURTCH
SPLURTCH
WHAT IS THAT?!
SPLURP
TOTTER
TOTTER

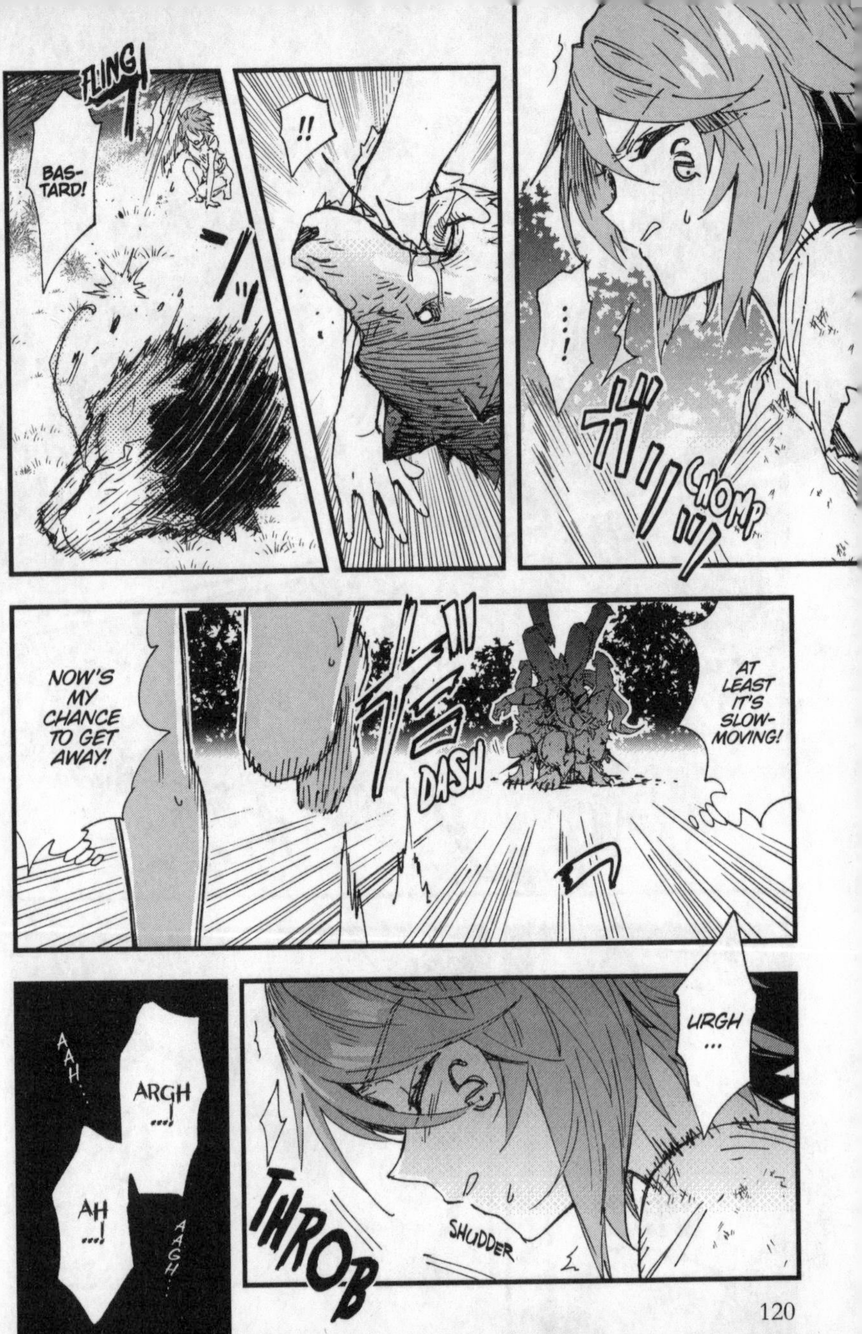
...!
ガリ
CHOMP
!!
FLING
BAS-TARD!
AT LEAST IT'S SLOW-MOVING!
DASH
NOW'S MY CHANCE TO GET AWAY!
URGH ...
SHUDDER
THROB
ARGH ...!
AAH...
AH ...!
AAGH...

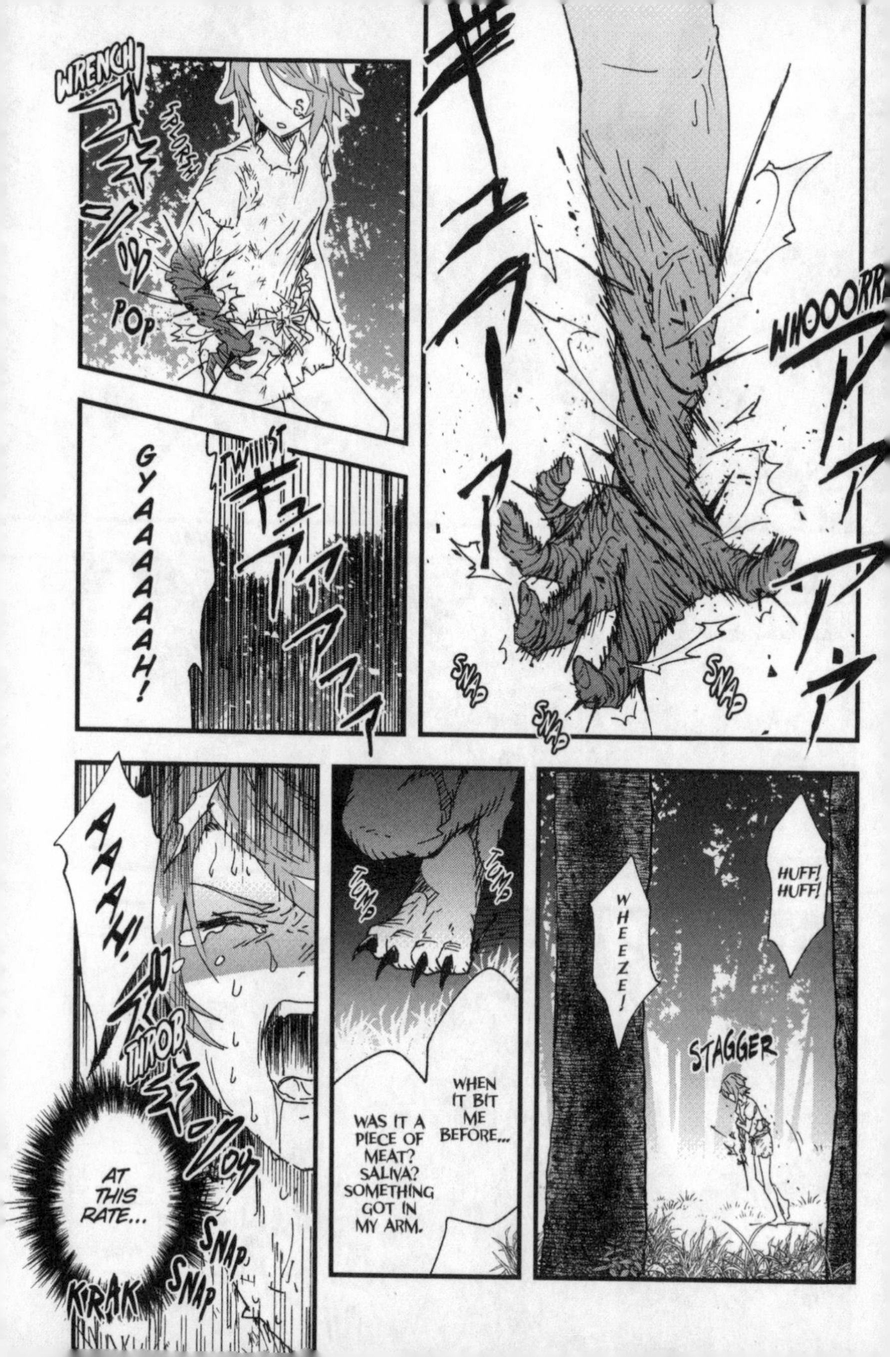
WHOOORR
SNAP
SNAP
SNAP
WRENCH
SPLORSH
POP
TWIIIIST
GYAAAAAAAH!
HUFF! HUFF!
WHEEZE!
STAGGER
TUMP
TUMP
WHEN IT BIT ME BEFORE...
WAS IT A PIECE OF MEAT? SALIVA? SOMETHING GOT IN MY ARM.
AAAH!
THROB
AT THIS RATE...
SNAP
SNAP
KRAK

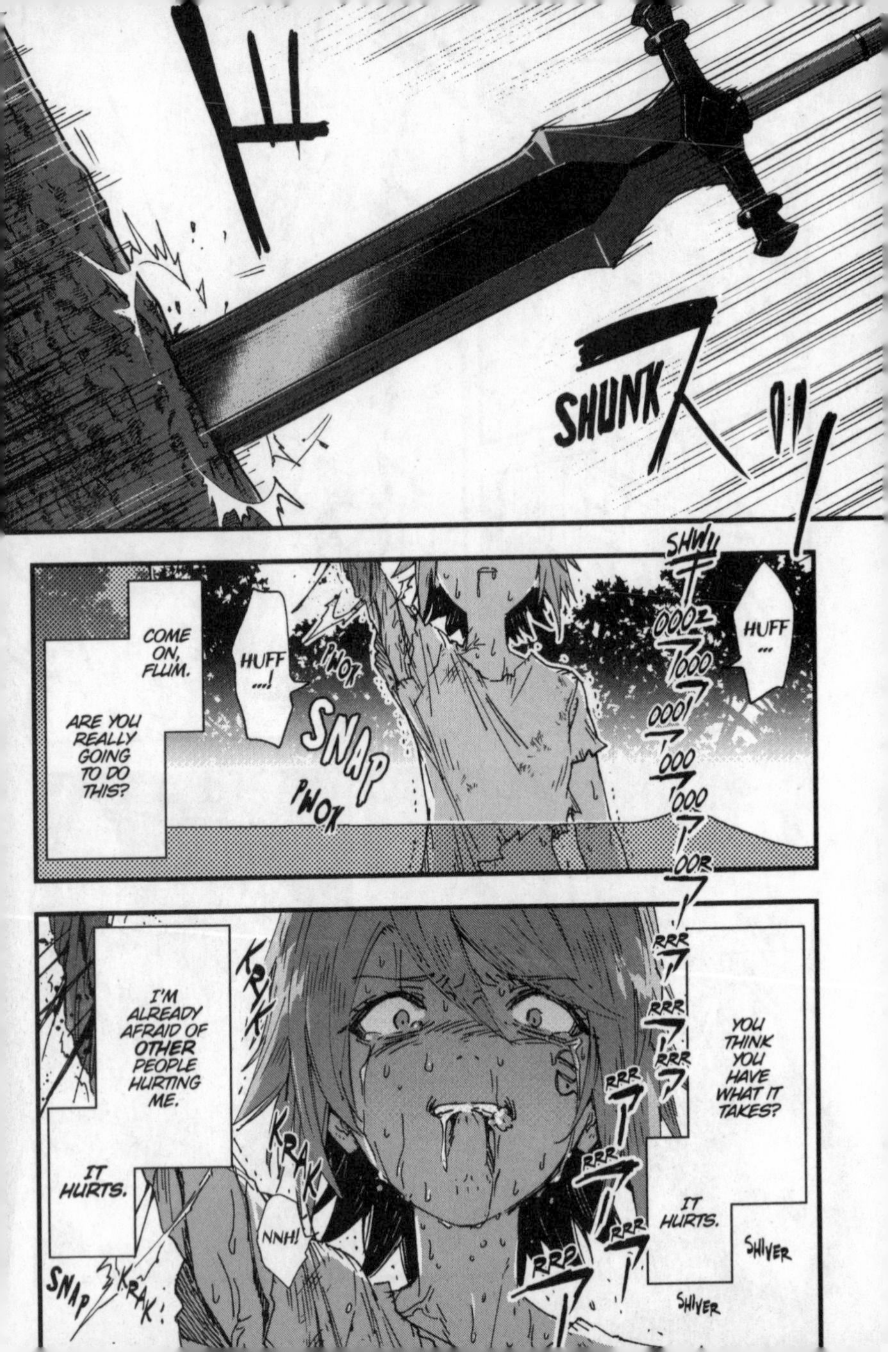
SHUNK
HUFF...
SHWOOOOOOOOOOOOOOOOOR
HUFF...!
PWOK
SNAP
PWOK
COME ON, FLUM.
ARE YOU REALLY GOING TO DO THIS?
RRR RRR RRR RRR RRR RRR RRR
YOU THINK YOU HAVE WHAT IT TAKES?
IT HURTS.
SHIVER
SHIVER
KRAK
KRAK
NNH!
I'M ALREADY AFRAID OF OTHER PEOPLE HURTING ME.
IT HURTS.
SNAP
KRAK

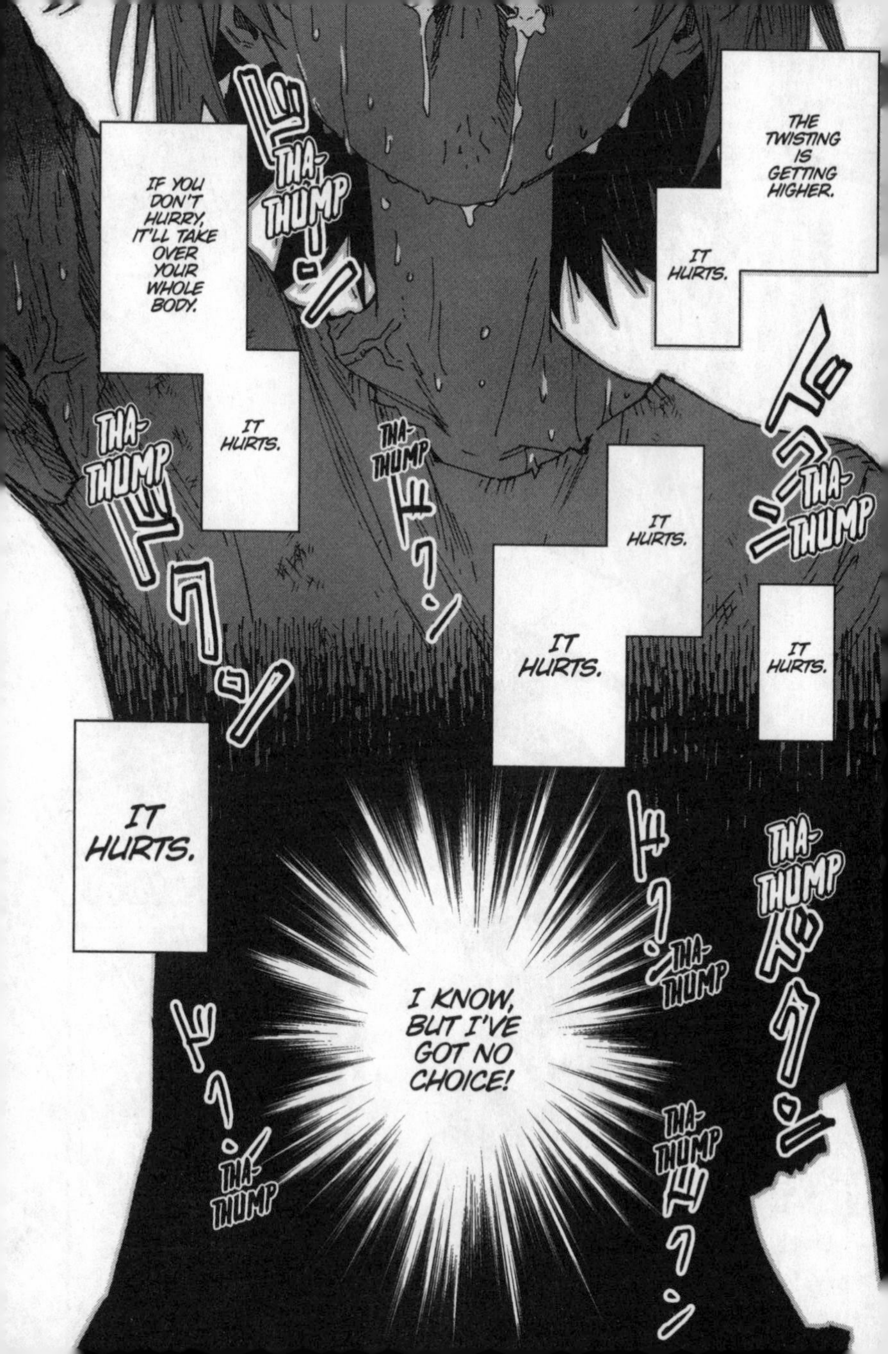
THE TWISTING IS GETTING HIGHER.
IT HURTS.
THA-THUMP
IF YOU DON'T HURRY, IT'LL TAKE OVER YOUR WHOLE BODY.
THA-THUMP
IT HURTS.
THA-THUMP
IT HURTS.
IT HURTS.
IT HURTS.
THA-THUMP
THA-THUMP
IT HURTS.
I KNOW, BUT I'VE GOT NO CHOICE!
THA-THUMP
THA-THUMP
THA-THUMP

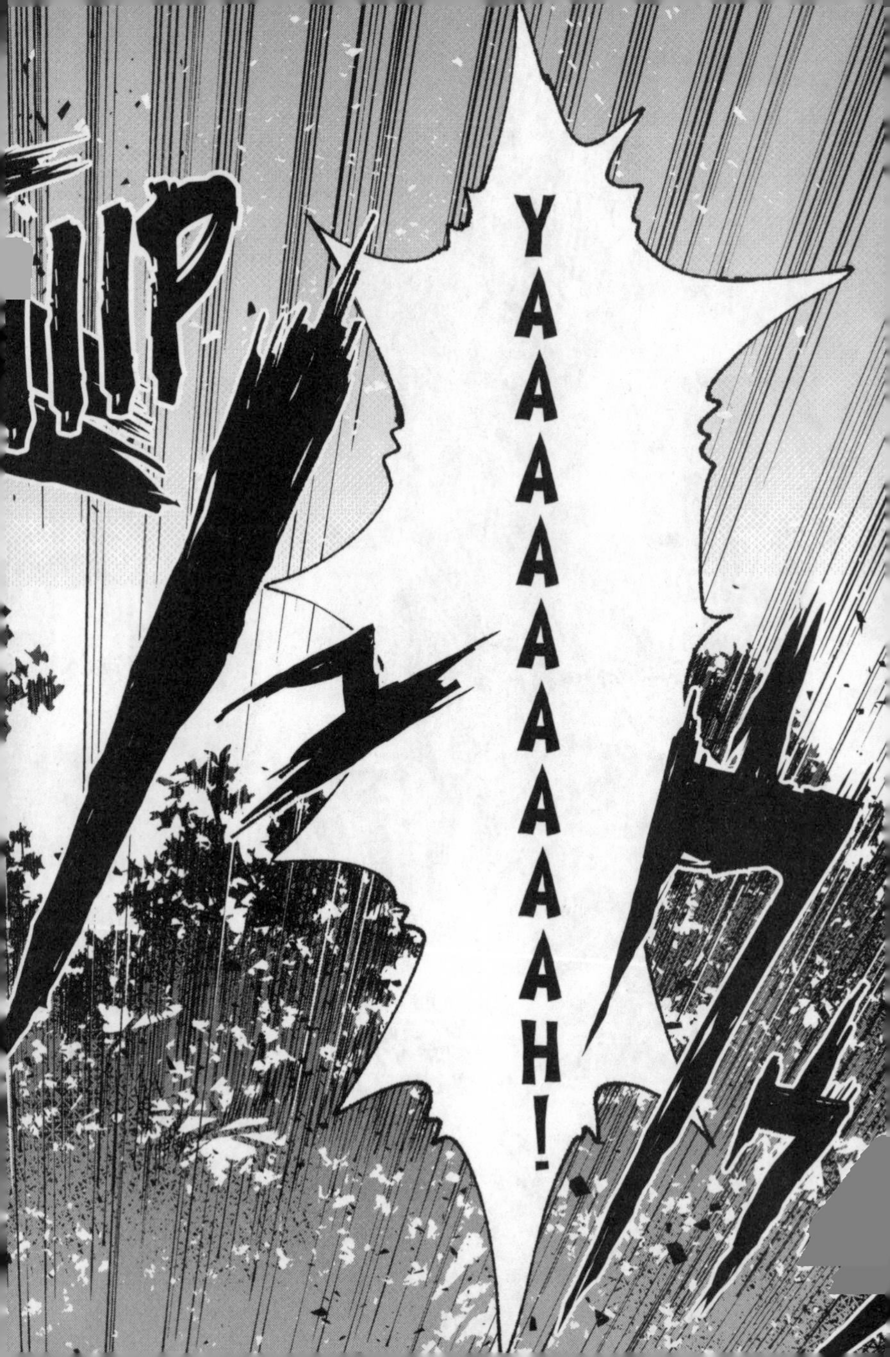
YAAAAAAAAAH!

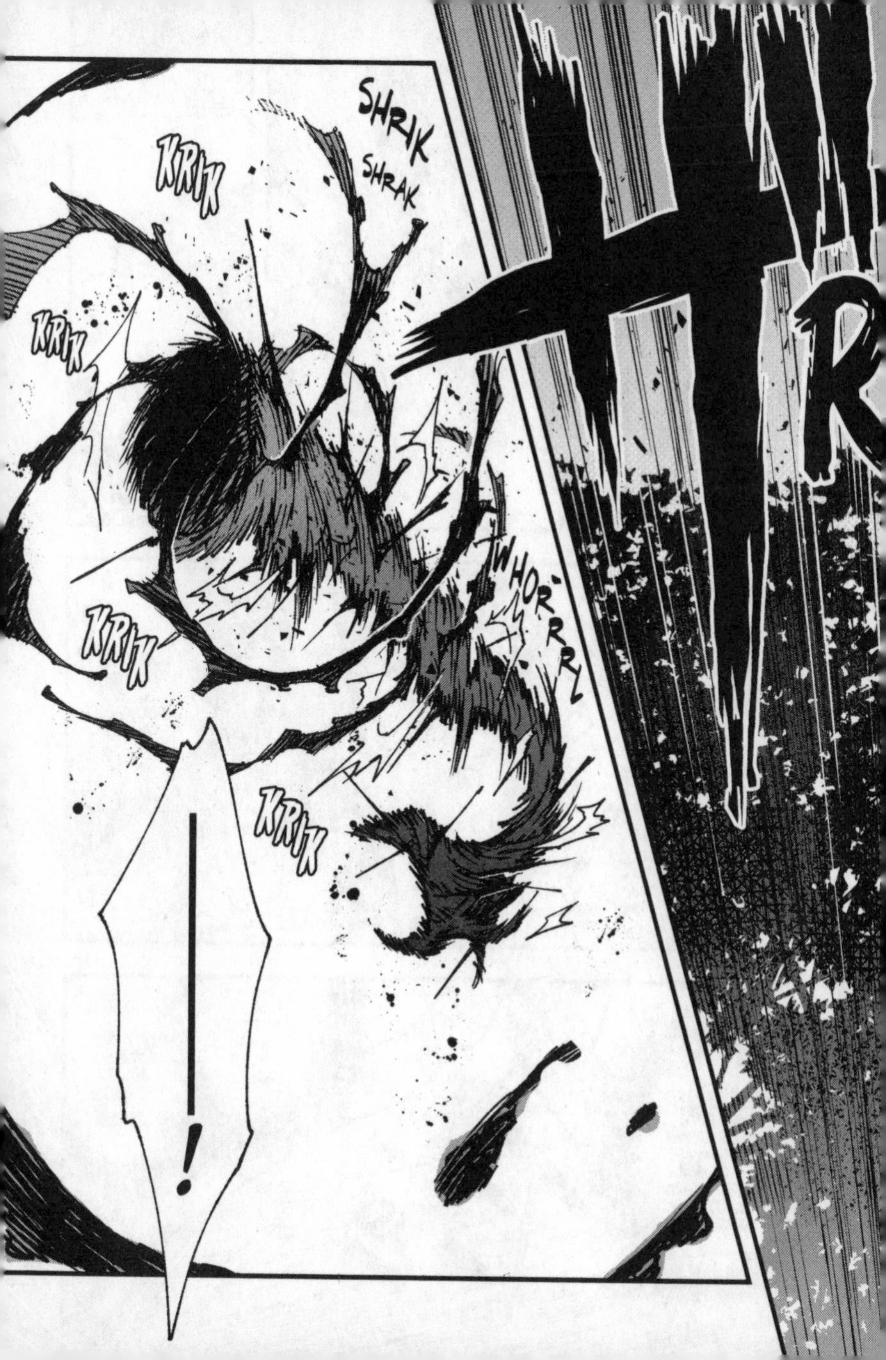
R
SHRIK
SHRAK
KRIK
KRIK
WHORRRRL
KRIK
KRIK
!

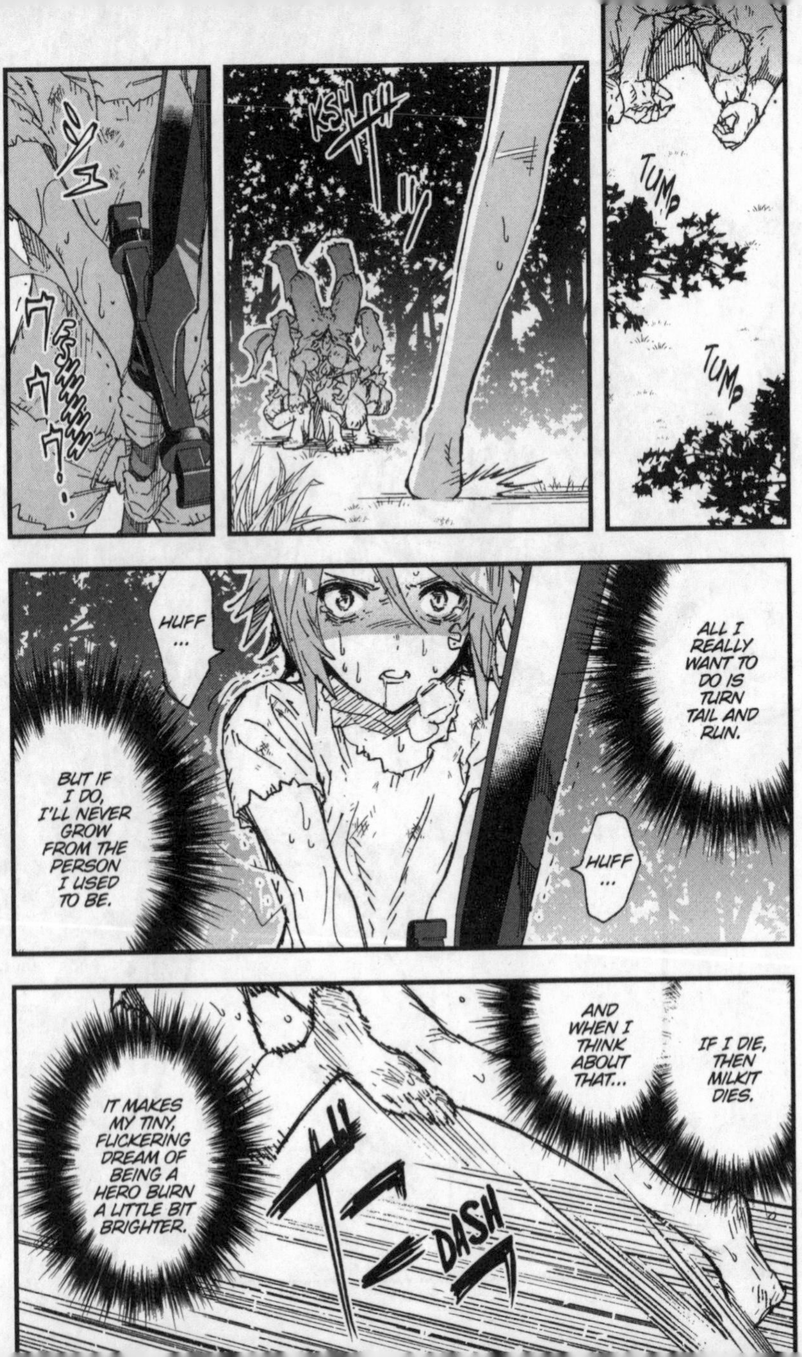
TUMP
TUMP
KSHHH
FSHHHHHH
ALL I REALLY WANT TO DO IS TURN TAIL AND RUN.
HUFF...
HUFF...
BUT IF I DO, I'LL NEVER GROW FROM THE PERSON I USED TO BE.
IF I DIE, THEN MILKIT DIES.
AND WHEN I THINK ABOUT THAT...
IT MAKES MY TINY, FLICKERING DREAM OF BEING A HERO BURN A LITTLE BIT BRIGHTER.
DASH

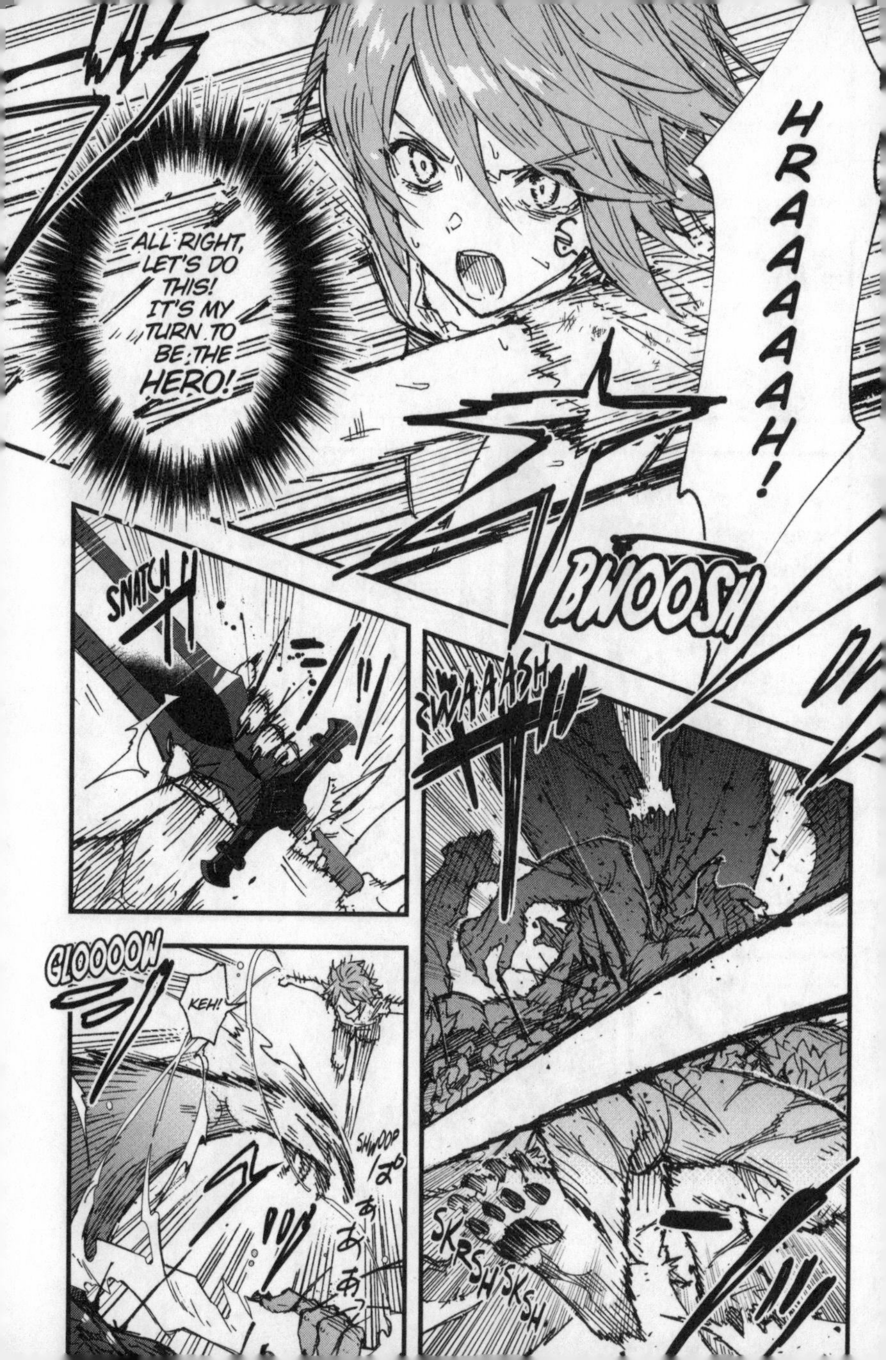
HRAAAAAAH!
ALL RIGHT, LET'S DO THIS! IT'S MY TURN TO BE THE HERO!
BWOOSH
WAAASH
SNATCH
SKRSH SKSH
CLOOOOW
KEH!
SHWOOP

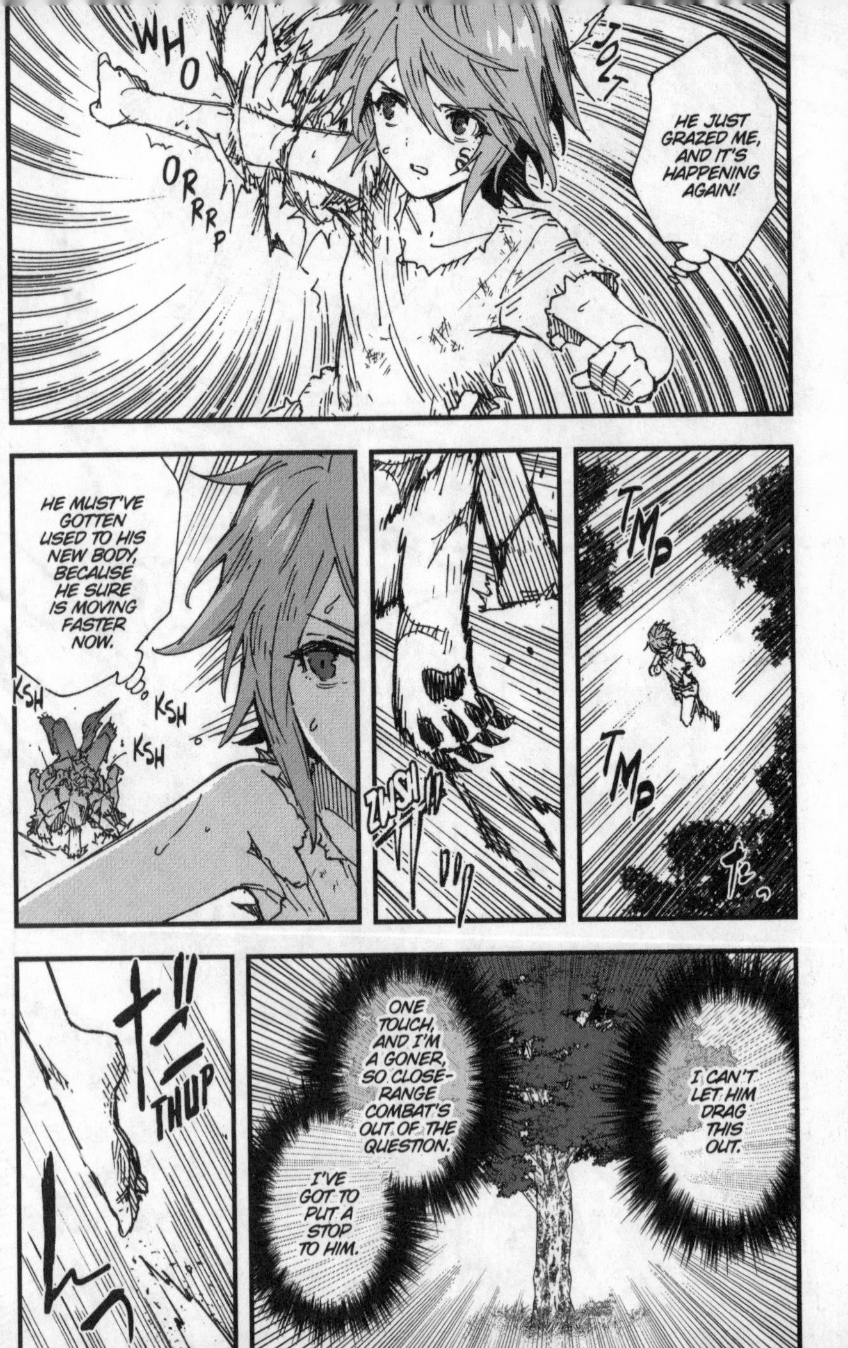
WHOORRRP
JOLT
HE JUST GRAZED ME, AND IT'S HAPPENING AGAIN!
TMP
TMP
ZWSH
HE MUST'VE GOTTEN USED TO HIS NEW BODY, BECAUSE HE SURE IS MOVING FASTER NOW.
KSH
KSH
KSH
I CAN'T LET HIM DRAG THIS OUT.
ONE TOUCH, AND I'M A GONER, SO CLOSE-RANGE COMBAT'S OUT OF THE QUESTION.
I'VE GOT TO PUT A STOP TO HIM.
THUP

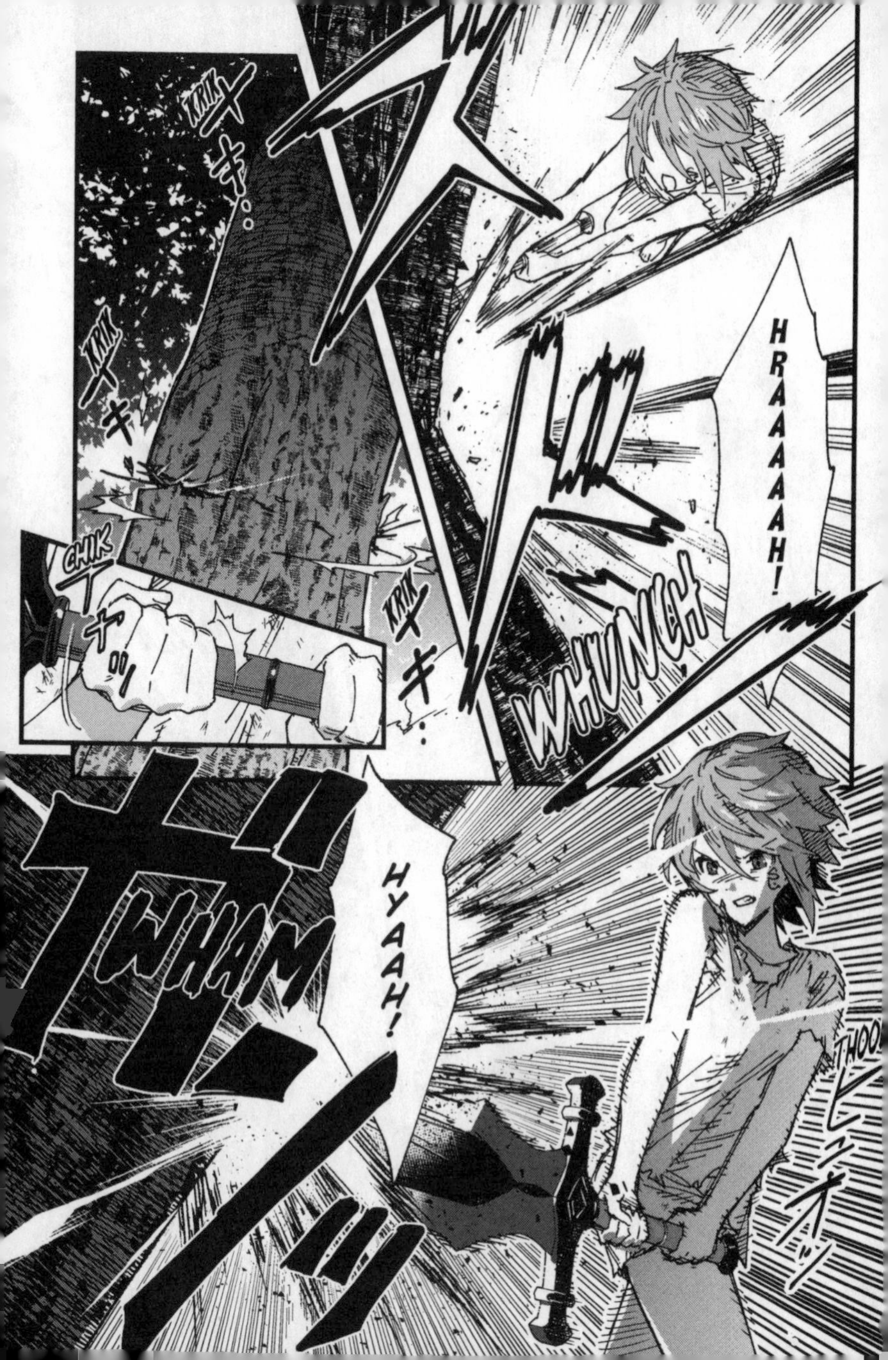
HRAAAAAAH!
WHUNCH
KRIK
KRIK
CHIK
KRIK
HYAAAH!
THOO
WHAM

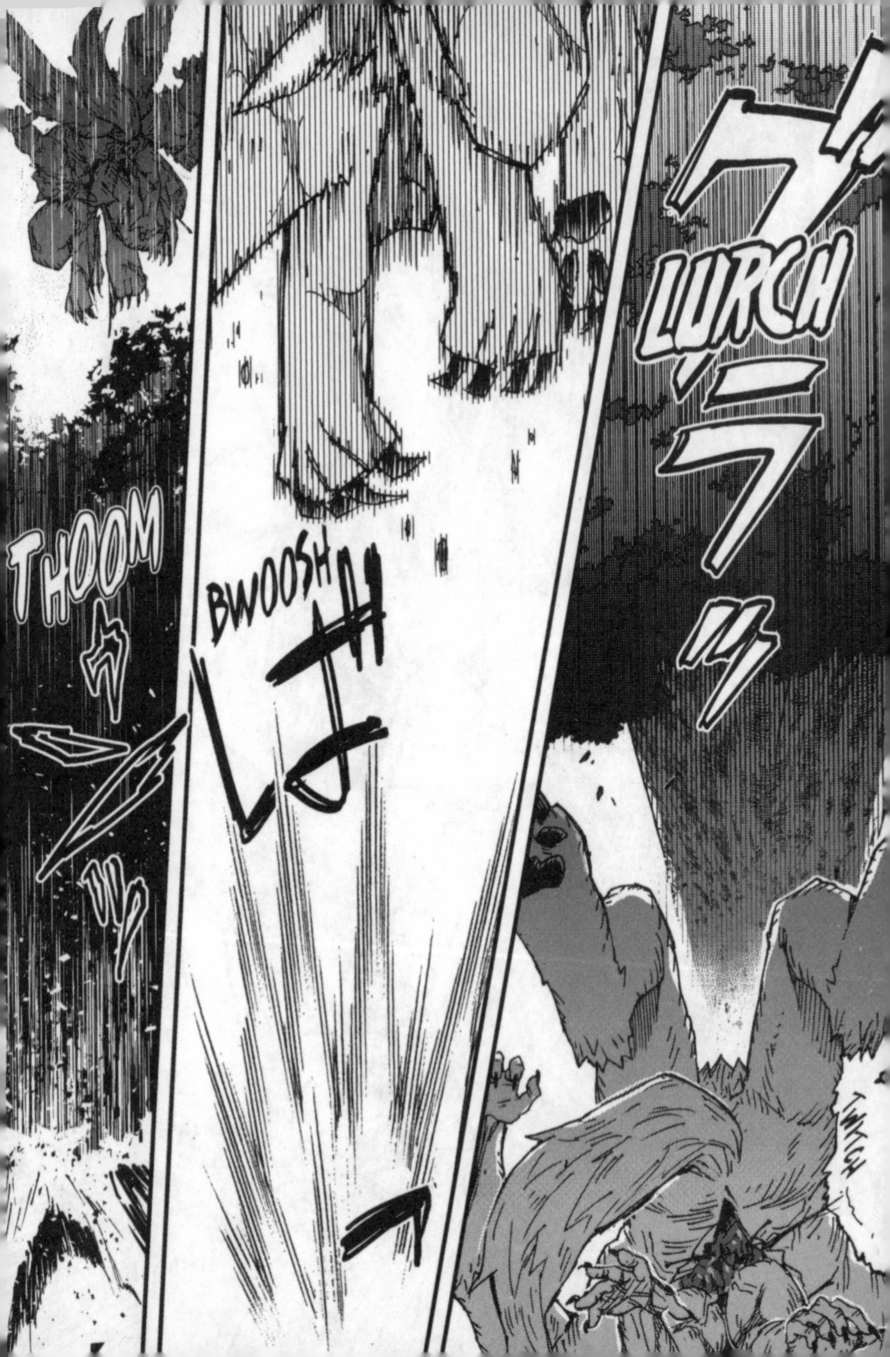

LURCH
TWITCH
BWOOSH
THOOM

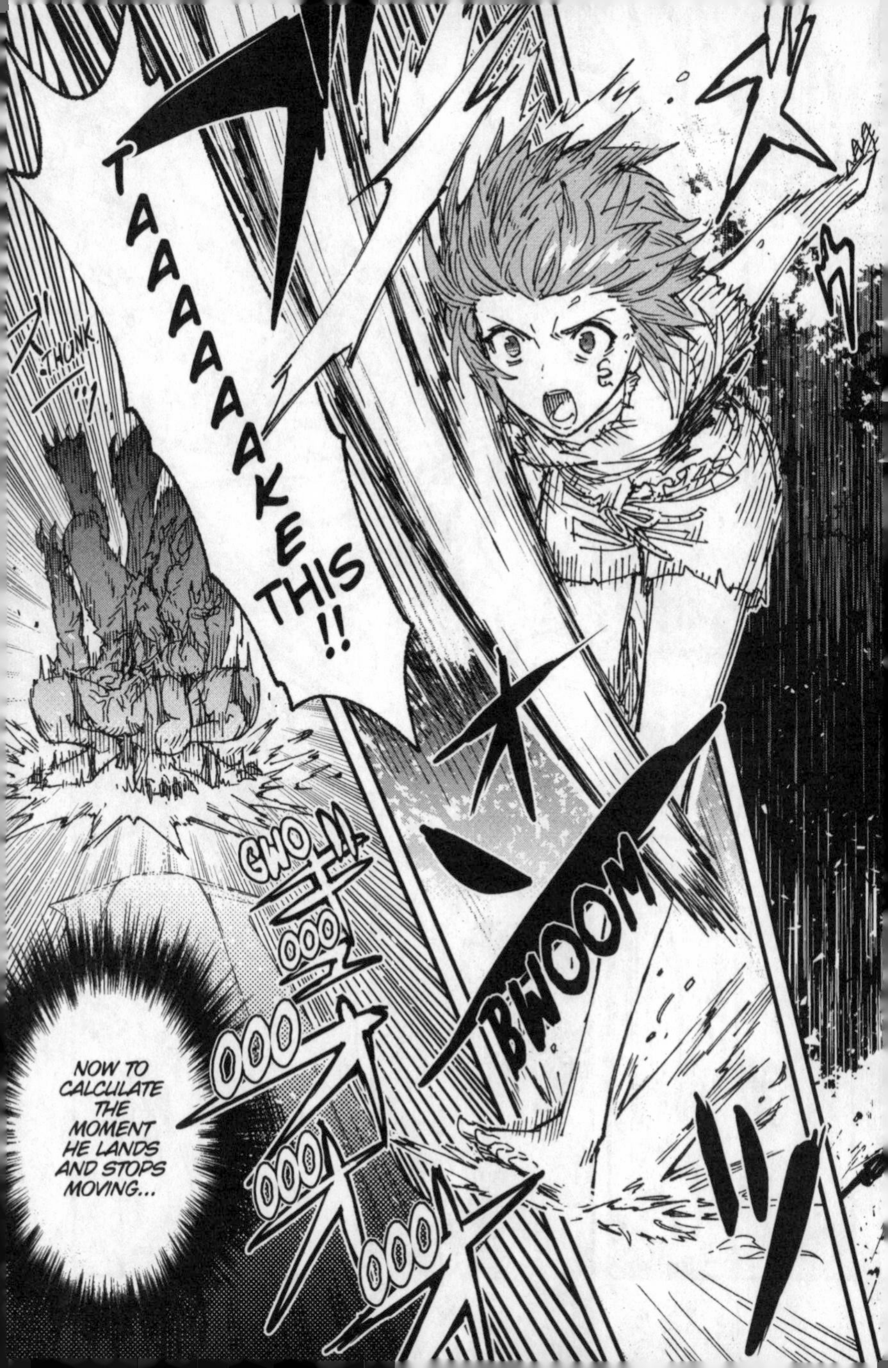

TAAAAAAKE THIS!!
THUNK
GWOOOOOOOOOOOOO
BWOOM
NOW TO CALCULATE THE MOMENT HE LANDS AND STOPS MOVING...

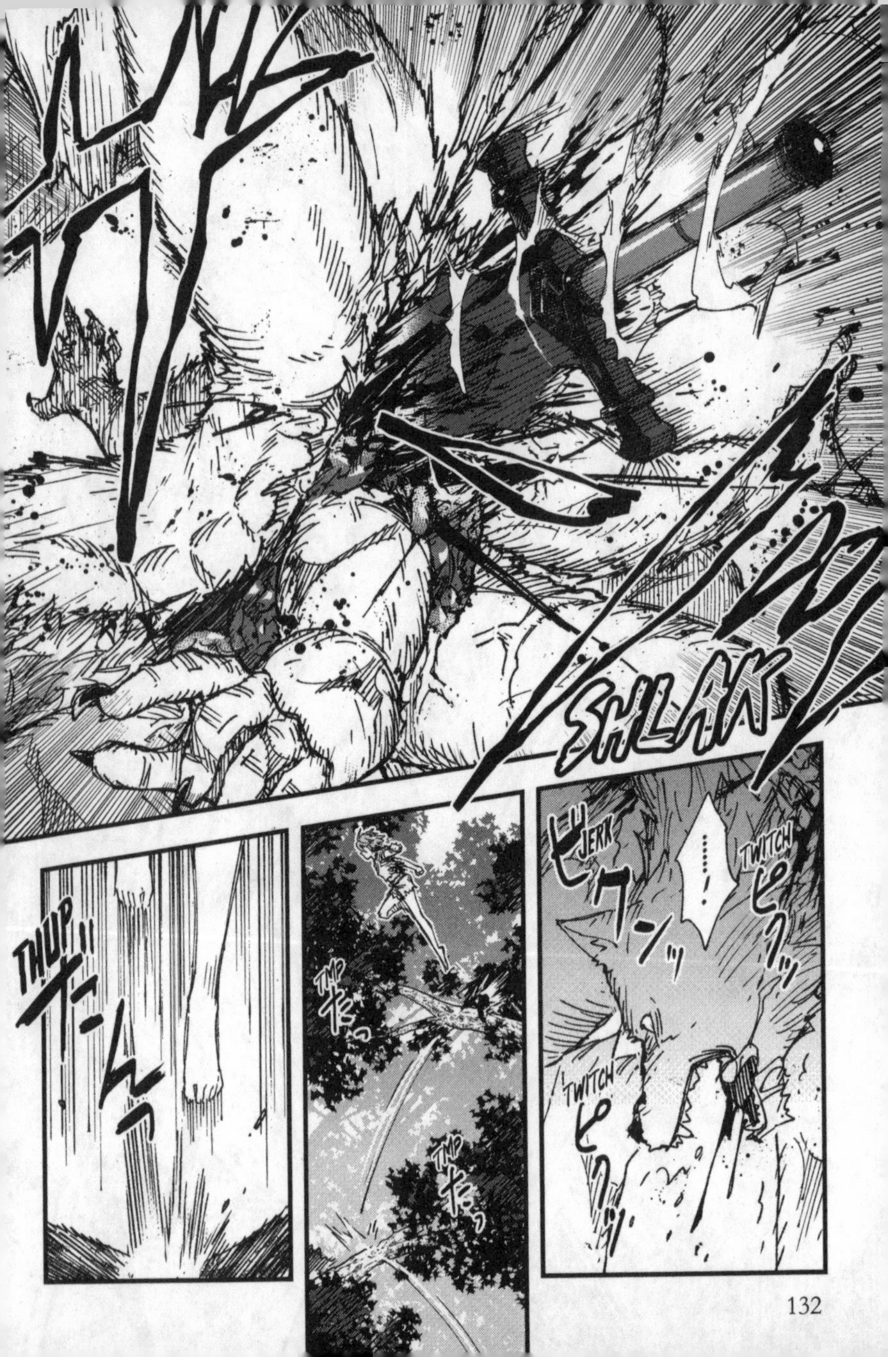
SHLAK
JERK
......!
TWITCH
TWITCH
TMP
TMP
THUP

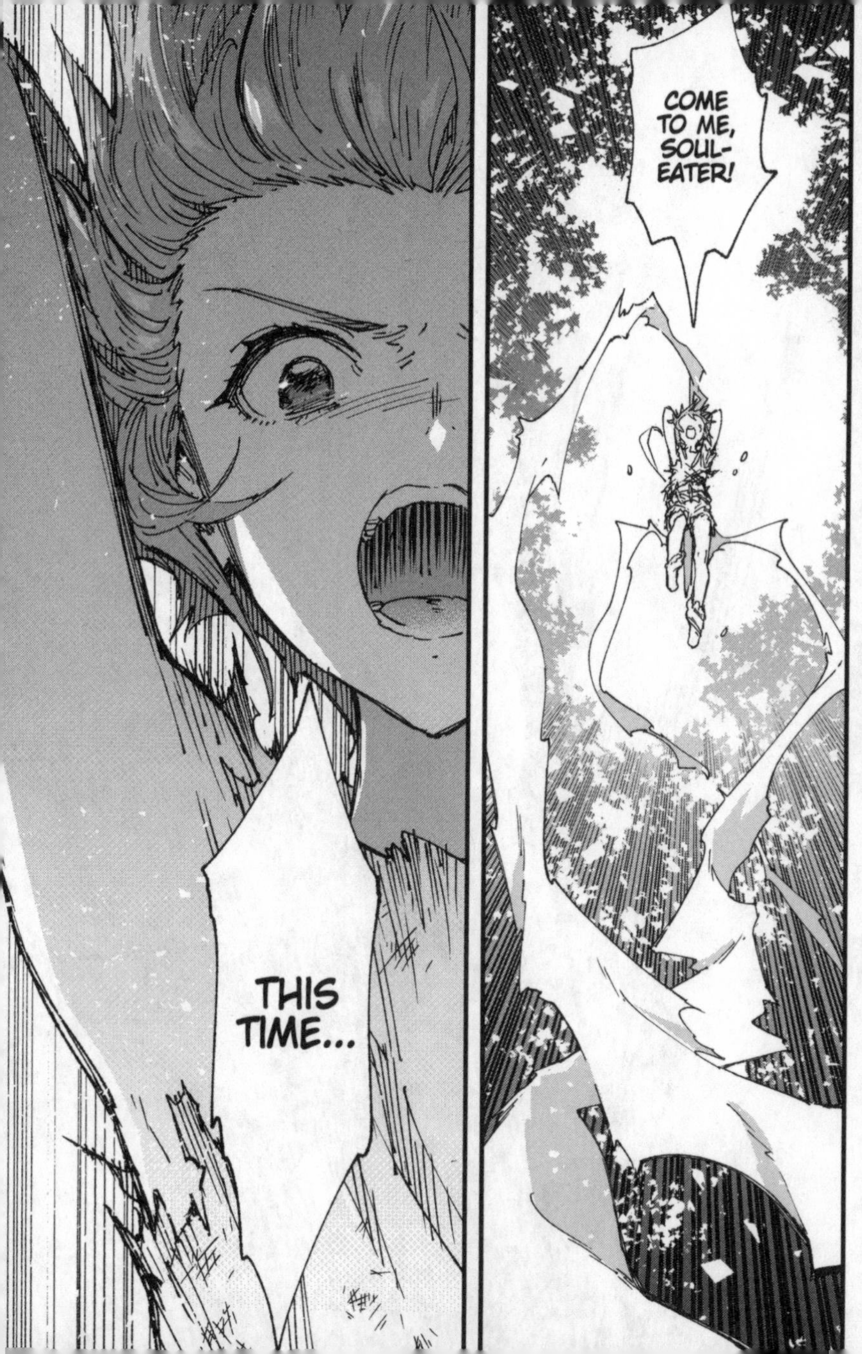
COME TO ME, SOUL-EATER!
THIS TIME...

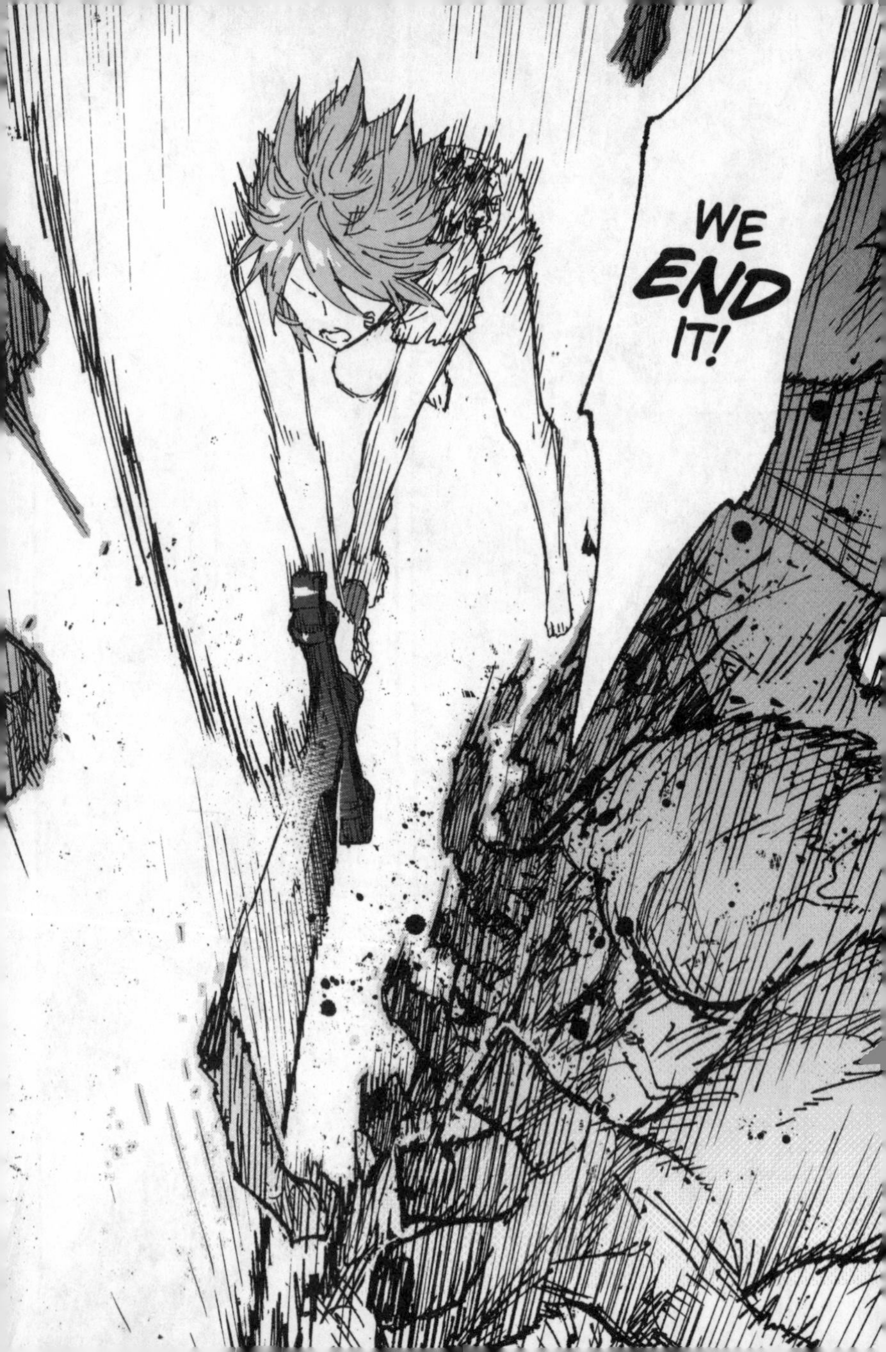
WE END IT!

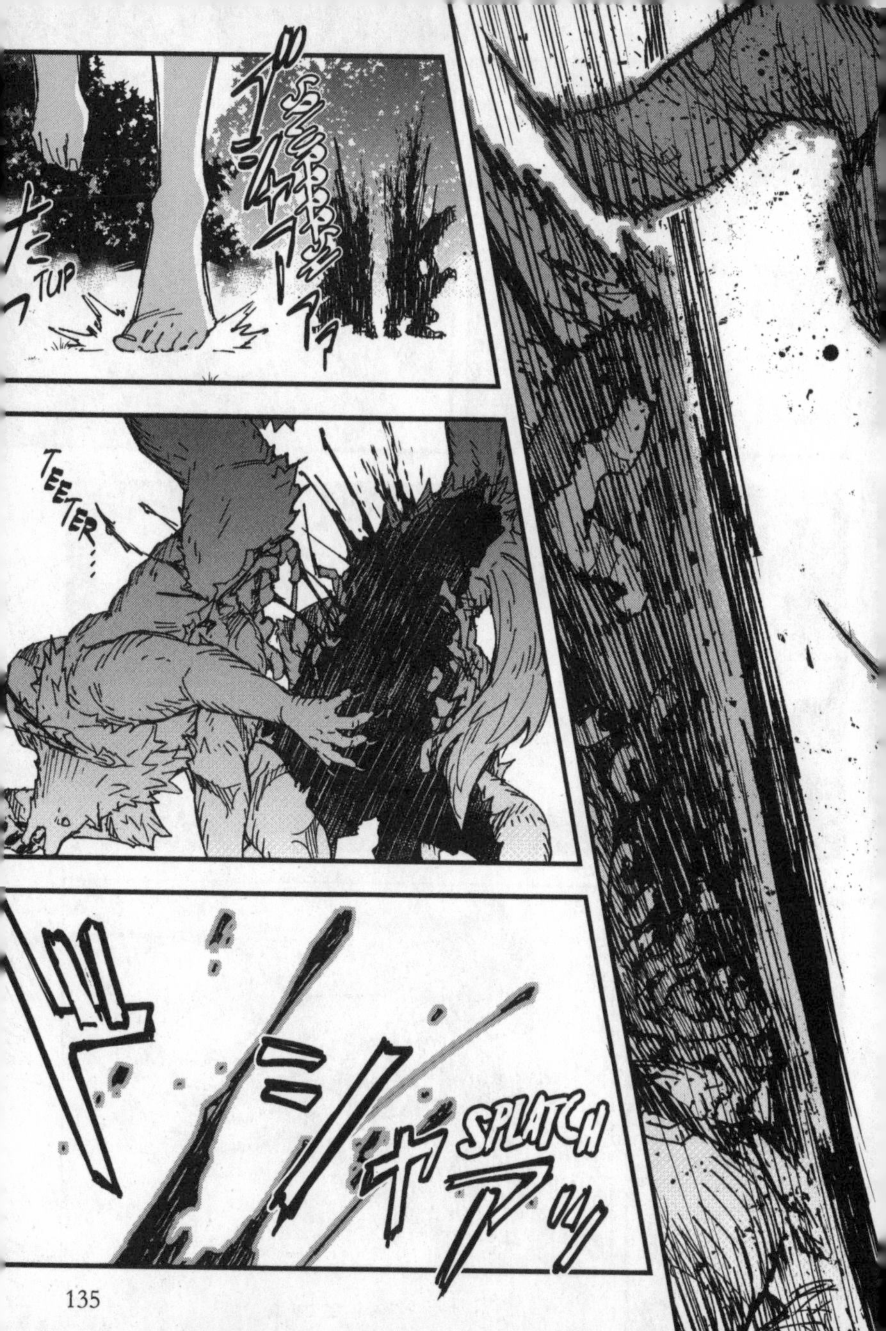
TUP
TEETER...
SPLATCH

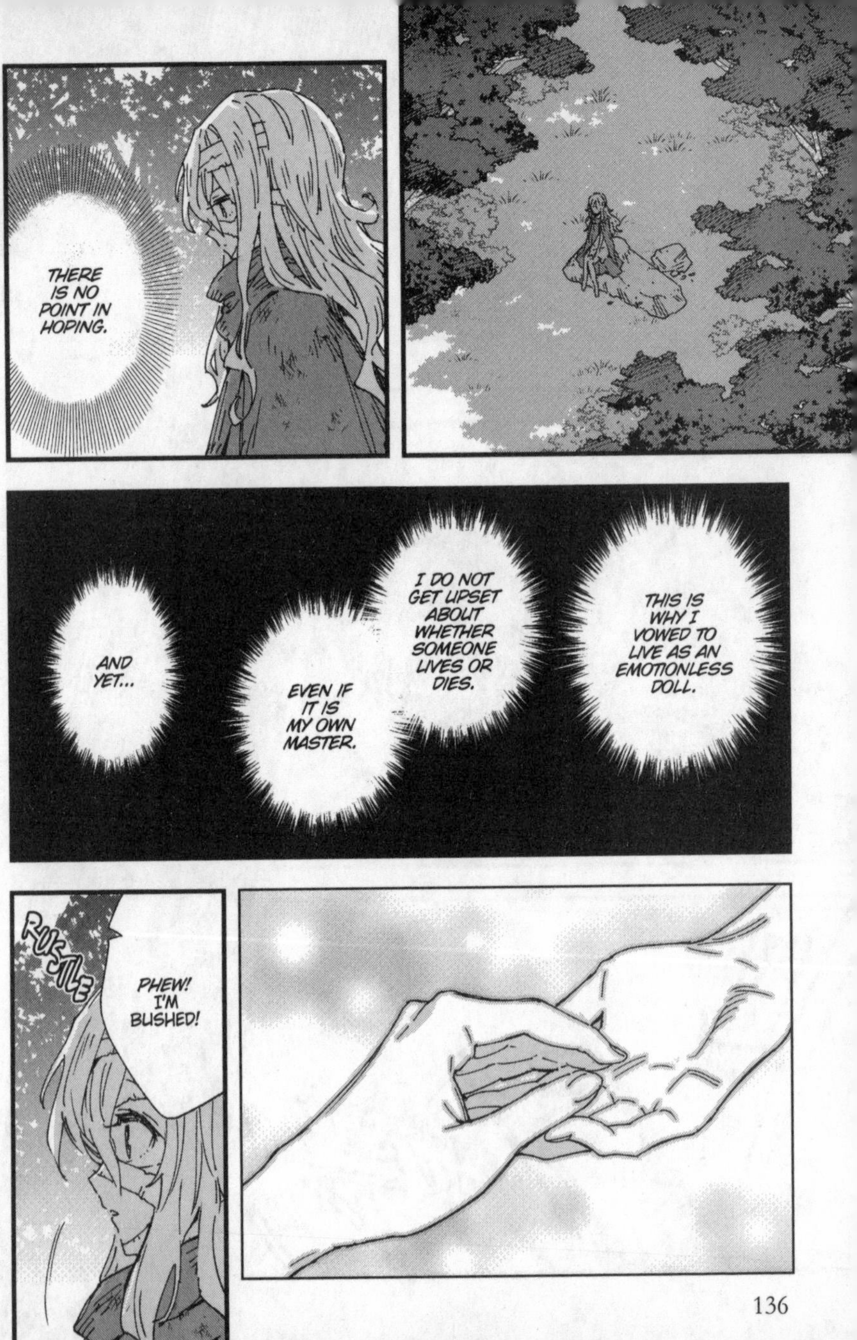
THERE IS NO POINT IN HOPING.
THIS IS WHY I VOWED TO LIVE AS AN EMOTIONLESS DOLL.
I DO NOT GET UPSET ABOUT WHETHER SOMEONE LIVES OR DIES.
EVEN IF IT IS MY OWN MASTER.
AND YET...
RUSTLE
PHEW! I'M BUSHED!

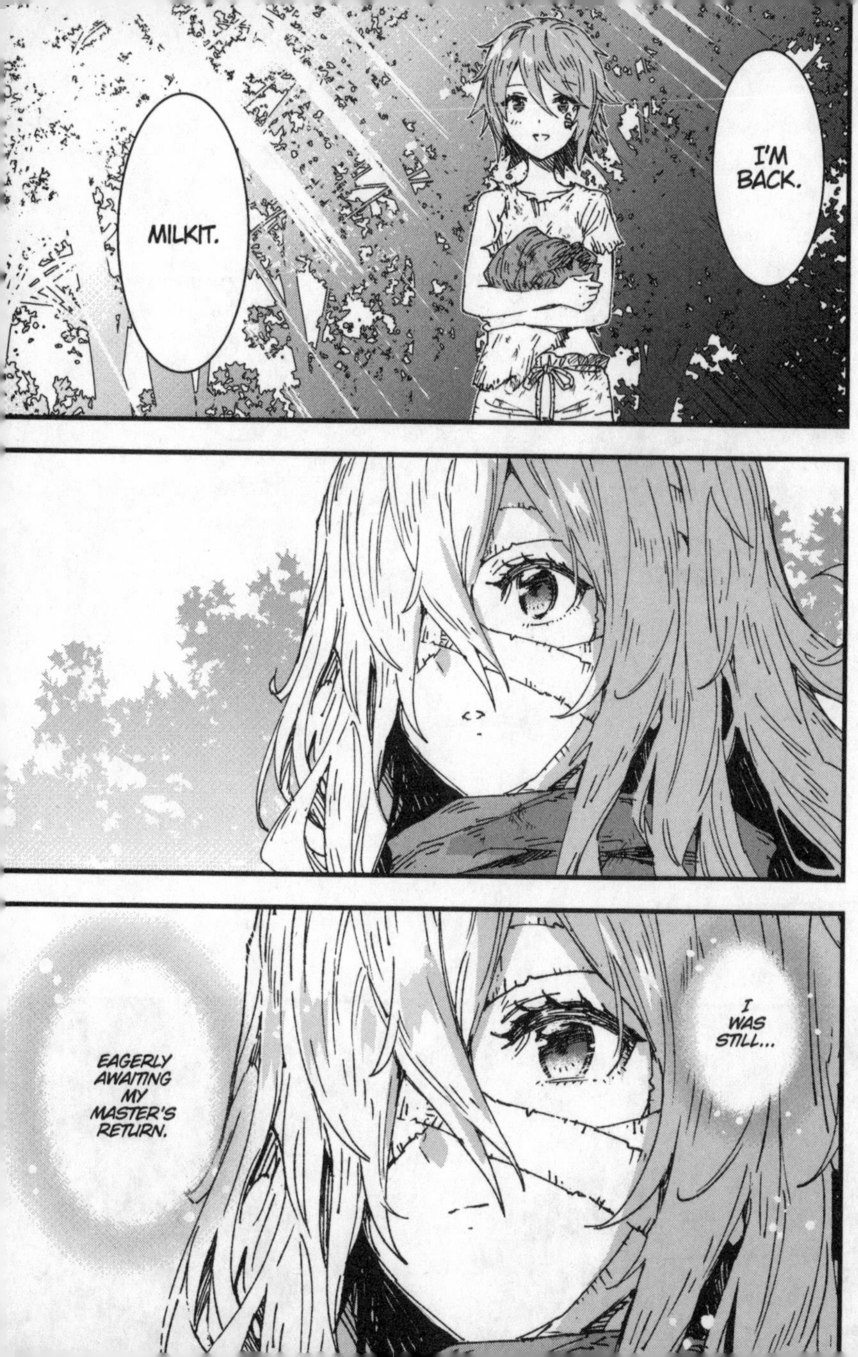
I'M BACK.
MILKIT.
I WAS STILL...
EAGERLY AWAITING MY MASTER'S RETURN.

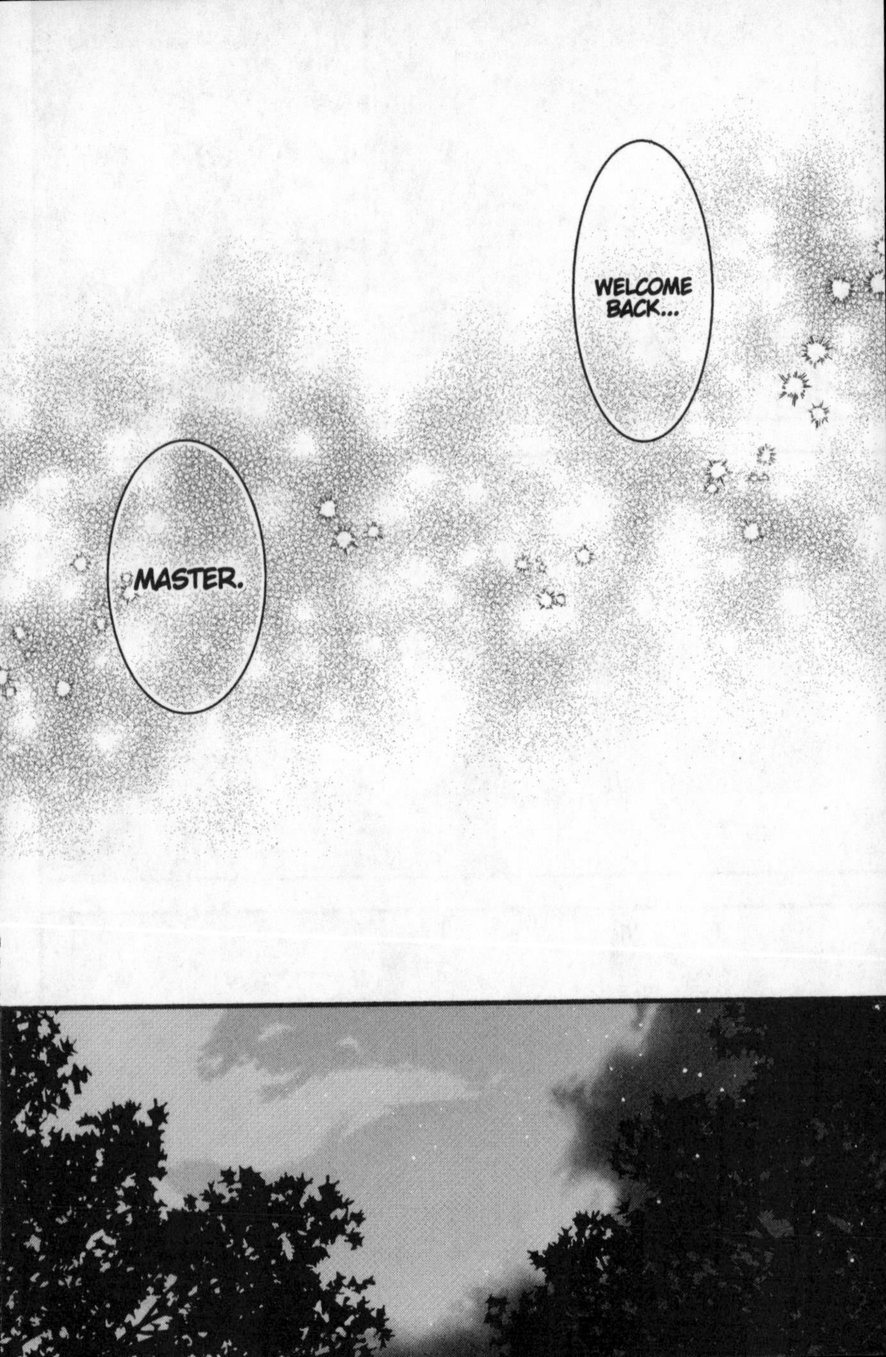
WELCOME BACK...
MASTER.

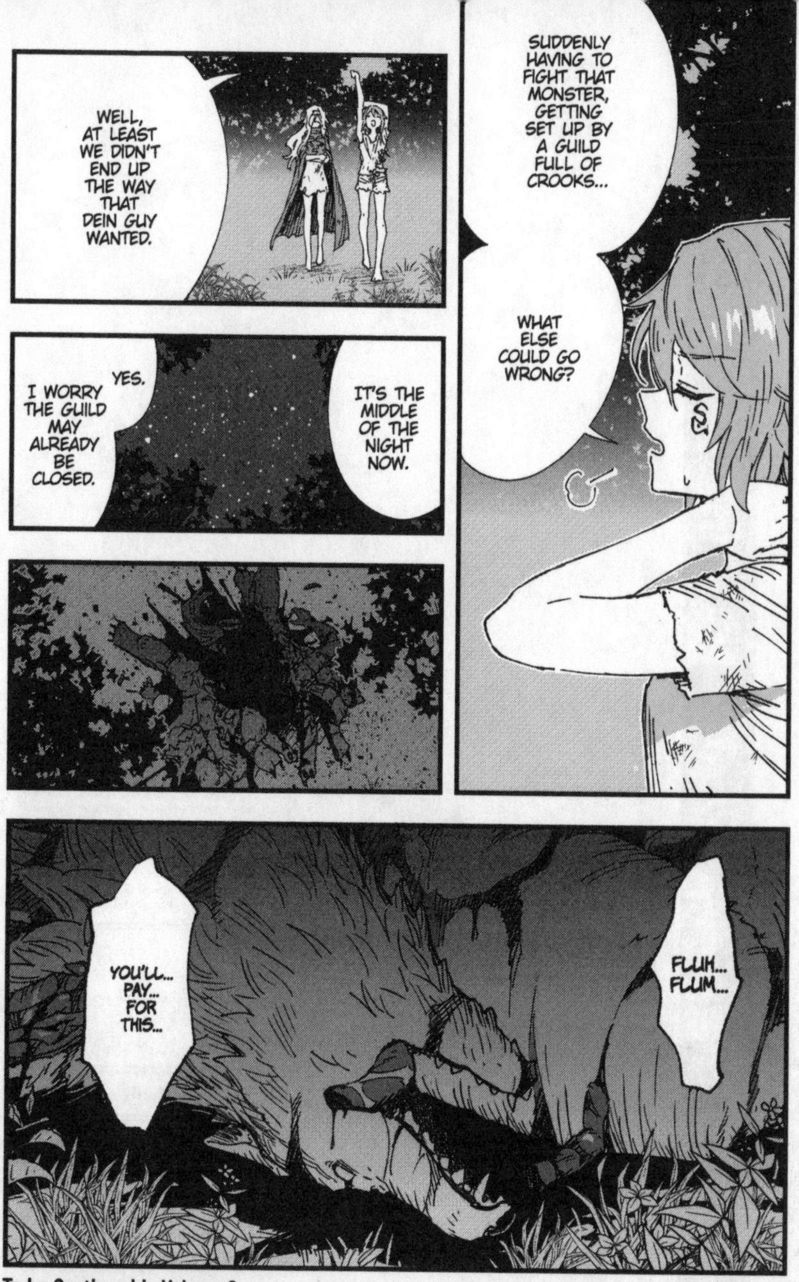
SUDDENLY HAVING TO FIGHT THAT MONSTER, GETTING SET UP BY A GUILD FULL OF CROOKS...
WHAT ELSE COULD GO WRONG?
WELL, AT LEAST WE DIDN'T END UP THE WAY THAT DEIN GUY WANTED.
IT'S THE MIDDLE OF THE NIGHT NOW.
YES. I WORRY THE GUILD MAY ALREADY BE CLOSED.
FLUH... FLUM...
YOU'LL... PAY... FOR THIS...

To be Continued in Volume 2

MATERIAL

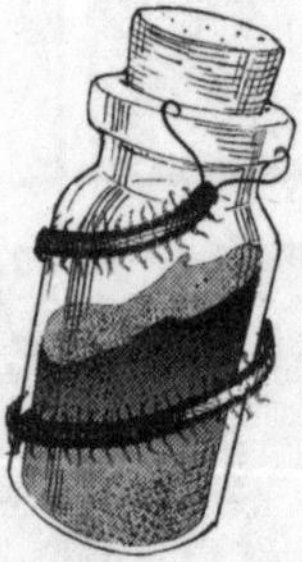

Mustard Poison

Insidiousness: ★★★★★★★★

A poison that inflames the skin. Even a small dose can cause symptoms. Rumor has it that a noblewoman once became jealous of a servant girl's beauty and mixed it into her meal, only to grow even more vexed when the disfigurement didn't change the beauty of the girl's soul.
It is curable using special medicinal herbs.

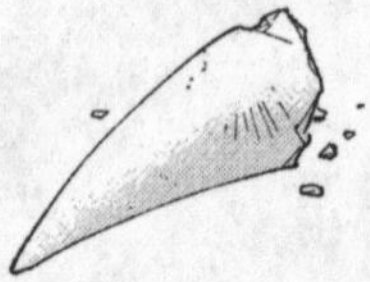

Werewolf's Fang

Rarity: ★★

A fang from the man-wolves who live in the forests throughout the kingdom.
It is often used as a material for weapons, shields, or good-luck charms. Although small, it is infused with Earth affinity magic, making it easy to Enchant one's stamina when used as a material.

It Didn't Start Off Like "That"

Written by kiki
Illustrated by Sunao Minakata

It happened about two months after the heroes first started out on their journey to defeat the Demon Lord, back when the party members were still getting along swimmingly.

Flum and Cyrill, each with an entire cake balanced on their plates, were just leaving the castle's galley. Grinning ear to ear, they walked down the red carpet of the palace corridor and entered Cyrill's personal quarters.

"I have to hand it to you, Flum. This cheesecake you made smells delicious."

"Not as much as your shortcake, Cyrill. It looks like it was done by a professional! Have you always baked?"

"Back when I used to live in Finats. What about you, Flum? Seeing as how you're always in charge of meal prep, it's no wonder it came out so well."

Flum chuckled. "You might have a point there. Oh,

shoot. I forgot to bring the forks and plates! I'll go grab them."

"I'll come with. I'd like to prepare some tea while I'm at it."

Placing their cakes on a table, the two hurried out of the room. Once they'd returned with their necessary cutlery and tea, they set them in front of their seats and sat down. Then, once a bit of time passed and they'd settled down, a startling realization hit them.

"Hey, Flum? Is it just me, or...are these a touch too large?"

True enough, the diameter of each of the cakes was larger than their heads.

They'd been enjoying baking too much to give any thought to the portion size. But now that they'd calmed down—well, even without being calmed down, the obvious truth was staring them in the face. Expecting the two of them (being the petite young ladies they were) to gobble down what was essentially a gigantic calorie bomb would require some serious sacrifices.

"I suppose it *is* a bit on the large side." Flum gave a pensive hum. "And with the party heading out tomorrow, it's not like we can just leave them behind."

"Maybe we could pack them with us for the trip."

"Jean will be furious!"

"Then a solid wallop to the face ought to shut him up."

"That'd only make things worse!"

It was then that a cunning plan formed in Flum's head.

"Then we'll just have to get someone else to eat it for us."
No sooner had the words left Flum's mouth when, almost
as if summoned by their cake conundrum, the sound of
footsteps came from just outside the room.

Moving with a swiftness befitting a warrior such as
herself, Cyrill burst forward and threw open the door.

"Whoa! You scared me!" It was none other than Eterna
Rinebow, who just happened to be passing by at that very
moment. By all appearances, she remained completely
undisturbed and emotionless, but the floating fish creature
that hovered by her shoulder reared back dramatically.

"Eterna, perfect timing. What do you say to some cake?"

"...You mean the ones on the table over there? What
for?"

"We baked them. You're always doing so much for
us, Eterna, won't you indulge in a bite with us?" Flum
wheedled, sidling up beside her. She was trying to frame the
whole thing as though they'd baked the cakes specifically as
a show of appreciation to her.

When worded that way, it was hard for Eterna to say no.
And besides, it wasn't like she had anything better to do, so
she had no reason to refuse.

"Fine. A young girl like me still has a sweet tooth. Being
a young girl and all." Insisting that she was indeed a young
girl, despite her being of indeterminate age, Eterna plopped
herself down on her seat.

And then there were three. Just as Flum was hoping they
could add at least one more to the group, she happened to

spy Maria through the open door. Their eyes met.

At that moment, Maria's face turned red as a tomato and she started blurting out apologies, her arms flailing in front of her. "Y-you've got the wrong idea! It wasn't that I was just looking around for a snack and was lured here by the smell of cake!"

"In other words, you were lured here by the smell of cake and came to find a snack, right?"

"No, Flum! I swear it!"

Seeming to sense that she was acting very much out of character, Maria immediately buried her face in her hands and shook her head with embarrassment. But her body betrayed her, and her stomach gave a low growl that even Eterna could hear as it echoed about the room. She sniffled back a tear. "And Linus had just told me a few hours ago 'Goodness, Maria, you certainly know how to eat.' It completely devastated me, and yet now look at me...!"

Apparently Maria still hadn't quite recovered from being out on a date with Linus.

Flum placed a sympathetic hand on Maria's shoulder and spoke to her gently. "Come have some cake. It will cheer you right up." She guided her inside.

Stomach empty, Maria couldn't refuse, and her head fell forward in agreement.

Extra sets of tableware and tea were brought for Eterna and Maria as they sat across from Flum and Cyrill, who both took their seats. The two cakes were then cut into slices and piled onto each person's plate, before the four women clasped their hands together and gave a quick word of thanks in unison.

It was their time-honored tradition to always do so before a meal.

Eterna began by sinking her fork into her cheesecake and putting a small portion of it in her mouth.

As the creator of the cake, Flum watched her face intently with bated breath.

Munching slowly, Eterna gave an approving little hum. The texture was on point, with a smooth mouthfeel. Compared to the average cheesecake, this cake's cheesy flavor was subtle and sweet, but the strong acidity of the apricot jam that frosted its surface struck a perfect balance.

"It's good."

Hearing Eterna's positive review, Flum put a hand to her heart and breathed a sigh of relief. "I'm so glad to hear that," she sighed. "This was actually my first attempt at cheesecake, but I guess it turned out well enough."

"If it was your first time, I'm even more impressed. I give it a perfect score of ten," Eterna said, showing her a thumbs-up.

"Thank you so much. With that kind of approval, I'll definitely be making it again!" Flum beamed with pride, and Eterna returned the smile with her own.

"And Cyrill, you made this shortcake, is that right?" Maria asked, with a spot of cream stuck to the corner of her mouth.

While Eterna was still enjoying her one mouthful, Maria

had already devoured more than half of her cake.

"Did you also make the cream, Cyrill?"

"Yes... I started on it yesterday, so it's from then. Does it taste funny?"

"Not at all. The milk really comes through, and I'm already a fan of the flavor. But it's nothing like the flavors from the bakeries around the capital, so I was curious."
It was something only someone who had a thorough understanding of the flavors of the cake shops throughout the capital could possibly say.

"Whatever happened to your vow as a nun to abstain from earthly pleasures?" Eterna muttered, and Maria's face turned bright red again as she shot back:

"Th-that's different! Plenty of people in the church love cake, and one of the girls in the Central District's church is like my own little sister!"

"No one's blaming you for liking to eat."

"Er...a-anyway," Maria stammered. "Cyrill, you're very good at baking cakes. I bet you could open up your own shop!"

"I bet if you called them Hero Cakes, they'd fly off the shelves."

"That's a great idea, Eterna. And maybe I could get hired on as an employee."

"It's just a hobby, you guys. You're making me blush when you say that..." Cyrill's cheeks had gone red at the lavish praise.

Like that, the four continued their idle chitchat as they

ate their cakes.

"Boy, am I stuffed!" Flum leaned back to stretch, patting the small bulge of her belly.

"Maybe I should try baking another kind of cake myself."

"Yeah! And maybe I'll try my hand at baking Cyrill's shortcake."

"Be sure to call me over when you do. I'll come with an empty stomach."

"And if there is a seat available, I would most appreciate your inviting me as well."

"No worries there. We'd never be able to finish them without you, Maria, so you can definitely expect to hear from us."

"Oh, Eterna, you're making me out to sound like some kind of a glutton!"

"That's rich coming from someone who ended up eating a whole cake."

"I did not eat the entire cake on my own!" she insisted, raising her voice. But in fact, she'd had about eighty percent, so there wasn't much point in denying it.

"But even on the journey, you've got one resilient appetite, Maria."

"I've always had a high metabolism. Using mace attacks and Light Attribute spells burns a lot of calories, I'll have you know."

"Either way, I'm impressed you can eat as much as you do and still maintain your figure. Does it all go to the same place?

"A-and just where are you looking?"

"Your boobs."

"Can't you at least talk about them more delicately?" Maria pouted and hid her chest with both hands. But the truth of the matter was she was without a doubt the most well-endowed among all the party's female members.

"Tell us the truth, Maria. What's it like? They must be heavy, huh?"

Maria's cheeks flushed slightly at Flum's innocent question as she answered, "I am accustomed to their weight, so I don't really notice. But during battle, it hurts when they swing around, so I sometimes bind them down more securely."

"Aren't you worried about getting stiff shoulders?" Cyrill asked, curious.

"Even if I get stiff shoulders, I'm able to heal them with spells."

"Oh, right. Regenerative spells. It'd be so useful if I could also use those easily."

"But if a warrior learned magic too, then what good would I be to the party?"

Cyrill was proud of her warrior's strength; it allowed her to handle almost anything all by herself when it came to battle. Still, there were times when it would be most convenient to be able to use Attribute-specific spells for her everyday life.

"Maria, I've got a favor to ask."

"What is it, Eterna?"

Eterna at first hesitated, but eventually giving in to her curiosity, she blurted out: "I want to lift your breasts."

"L-lift...them? Well, not that I mind, but it can't possibly be that entertaining to touch them, can it?"

"That's just what you'd say, Maria, because you're so used to them." Eterna retorted with a touch of bite in her words. Then, maneuvering herself behind Maria who was still seated in her chair, Eterna put her hands beneath her breasts and lifted.

Feeling Eterna's touch through the fabric of her robes, a startled little "oh" escaped her.

"See? Nothing special about it," Maria breathed, but as Eterna kept handling her breasts, more lewd gasps and surprised sounds of amazement slipped past her lips.

Naturally, Maria was growing more and more embarrassed, and although she didn't stop Eterna, her face was turning bright red again.

"U-um! May I give it a try?"

"Flum, not you, too! Well, I suppose it's all right."

Wasting no time at all, Flum took Eterna's spot. She put her hands beneath Maria's breasts and scooped them upward.

"Mmph!" At the touch of those hands, Maria let out a small moan.

"Oh, wow... They're really something..." Flum said in wonder.

Cyrill had only intended to observe, but after hearing

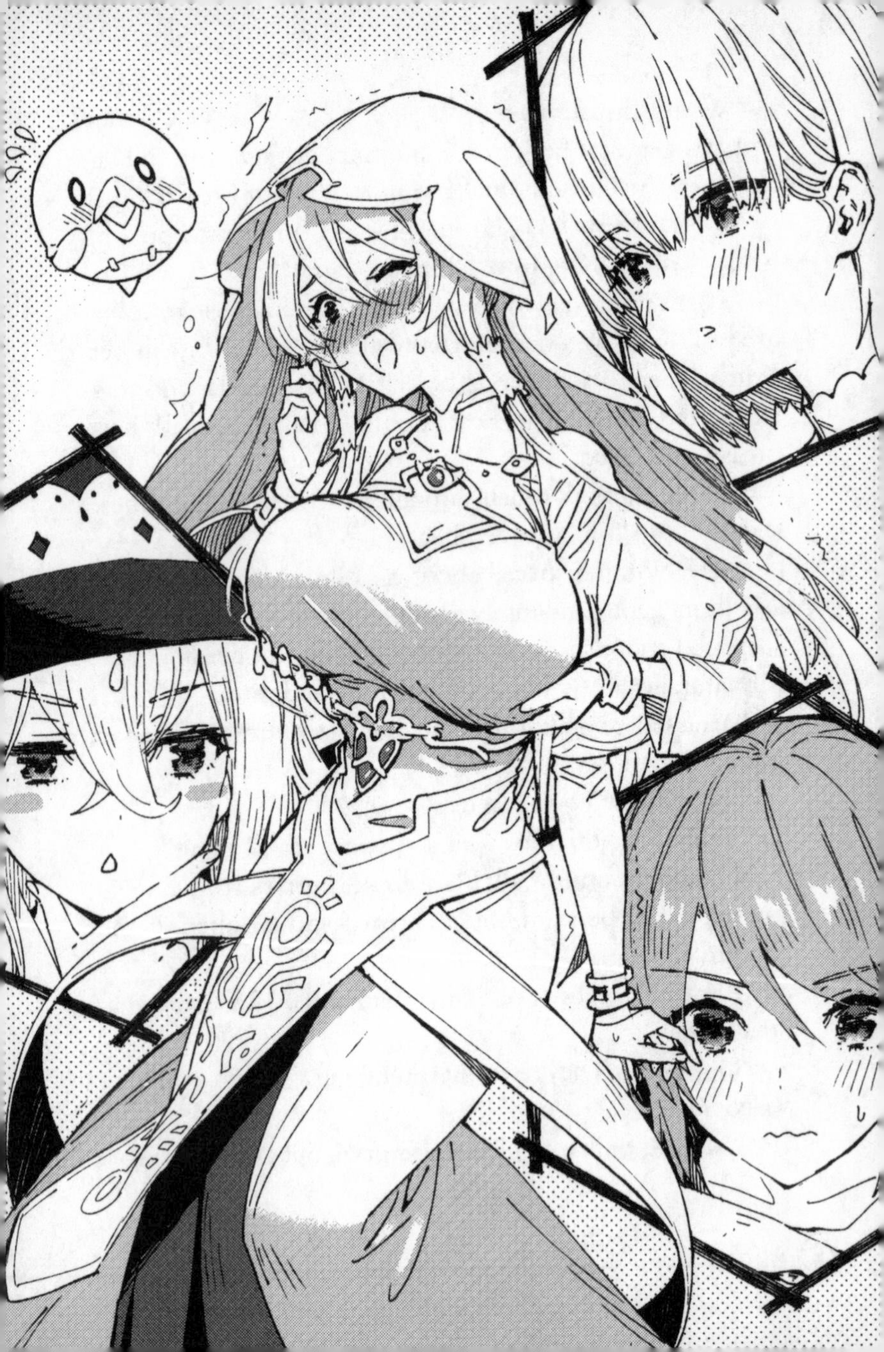

Flum's words of amazement, she could no longer sit and watch.

"Maria, I'd like to try. If I may," she said.

"If...you insist."

Perhaps all those long years without physical contact from those her age had finally caught up with her, because Maria looked not entirely displeased.

"Good grief. Did you really have to call us out here on our day off? Learn to take a vacation once in a while, Jean," Linus grumbled, walking along the castle corridor. By his side was a grim-faced Jean and next to him was the taciturn Gadhio.

"The journey may seem to be going just fine right now, but it's possible there will be an increase in disturbances from the demons. We're holding a strategy meeting to deal with it."

"Then why don't we just keep doing what we've been doing? See? Even Gadhio's pissed off about being dragged into this all of a sudden."

"I'm not pissed off."

"But didn't you have a dinner date with your wife and daughter?"

"They're not my wife and daughter. They're the wife and child of a deceased friend."

"Look, if you've been living with them for years,

it's about time you started calling them your wife and daughter..."

Reminded that his dinner plans had been interrupted, Gadhio really was pissed now. Not that Jean cared.

"You fools are too easygoing, whereas I am on constantly on alert, ready for action at a moment's notice."

"You just don't have any friends is all."

"H-how rude! With my genius intellect, I have no need to collude with so-called friends. There is strength in solitude!"

"Yeah, sure. Solitude."

"Linus. You, a *fool*, dare mock *me*, a *genius?*"

"Calm down, Jean. Here, we've reached Cyrill's room."

Before they're realized it, the three had arrived at their destination.

Jean gave a perturbed snort and put his hand on the doorknob.

"Whoa! What are you, stupid? You have to knock before you enter a girl's room!"

"So you *are* calling me a fool! I'm too much of a genius to be—" Jean had raised his voice as he opened the door, but it petered out at the sight that greeted him.

"N-no! Flum, not there! Ooh, not you too, Eterna! Eek! Please, Cyrill, I can't take any more... Ah!"

They'd come face-to-face with Flum, Cyrill, and Eterna all fondling Maria's breasts, while Maria herself was moaning obscenely and blushing.

For a moment, no one moved as the three men and four women stared at each other.

"Hold on. There's a perfectly good explanation," Cyrill started.

"Th-that's right! We weren't doing anything inappropriate. You could say we were just curious!"

"Flum," Eterna said flatly. "You're just digging your own grave with that kind of phrasing."

"Maybe so, but it was the best I could come up with on short notice, okay?!"

"Linus, please! There's a perfectly good excu—I mean, perfectly innocuous reason for this! Hey! Wait! Please don't close the door without even saying anything!"

As the girls practically tripped over themselves in a vain attempt to explain away what he'd just seen, Jean shut the door behind him.

With a face that said it all, Linus placed a hand on his shoulder. "I don't know about you, but I've gotten a bit peckish. What do you say we grab some grub?"

"Yes," Jean replied slowly. "Perhaps you're right. I suppose even a genius like me could stand to escort you simpletons on occasion."

"I'll come along too. Suddenly, I could use a drink."

With a strange feeling of solidarity in their chests, the three men left the room behind. From inside, they could still hear Maria and the other girls' plaintive cries echoing after them.

END

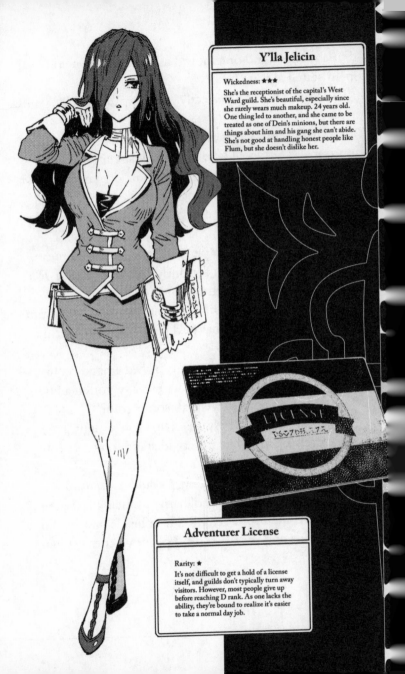

Y'lla Jelicin

Wickedness: ★★★

She's the receptionist of the capital's West Ward guild. She's beautiful, especially since she rarely wears much makeup. 24 years old. One thing led to another, and she came to be treated as one of Dein's minions, but there are things about him and his gang she can't abide. She's not good at handling honest people like Flum, but she doesn't dislike her.

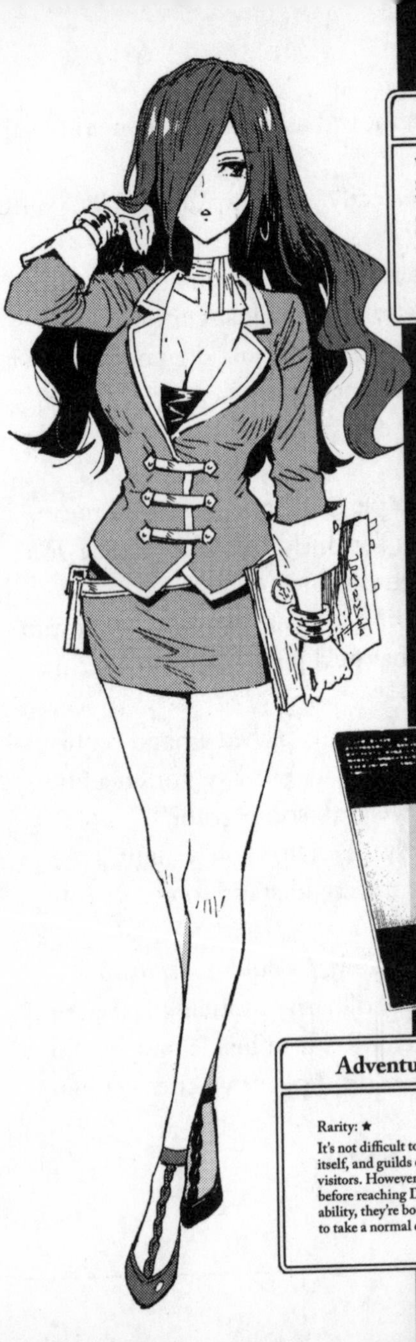

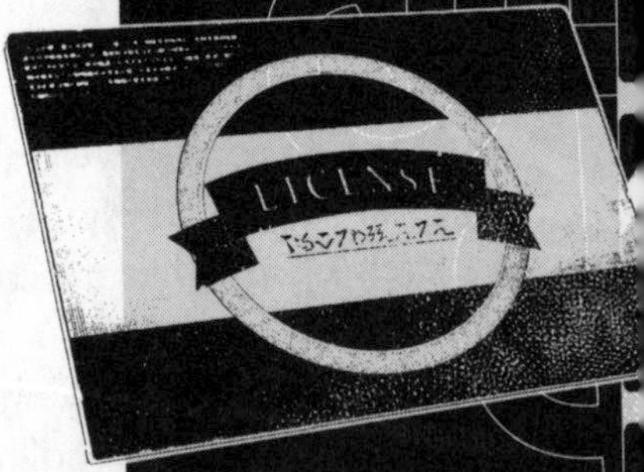
LICENSE

Adventurer License

Rarity: ★

It's not difficult to get a hold of a license itself, and guilds don't typically turn away visitors. However, most people give up before reaching D rank. As one lacks the ability, they're bound to realize it's easier to take a normal day job.

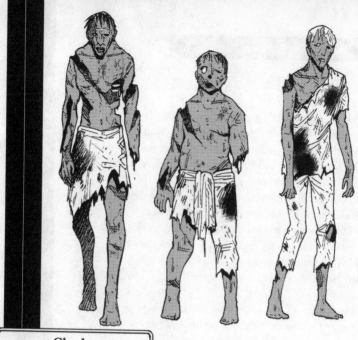

Ghoul

Danger Level: ★★

People who have become monsters due to magic stored in their corpses. It's easy for the dead to become ghouls if they are left unburied. Depending on the environment, it's possible to create them unintentionally. A connection to their past life may lead them to attack humans and eat them.

Werewolf

Danger Level: ★★★★

A bipedal wolf. Alone, they're not too strong, but because they move in packs, they have one of the higher danger levels among C-rank monsters. They're quite intelligent as well, so many beginner-level adventurers defeat them by ambushing them from behind and slicing their neck. On the flip side, some werewolves become emotionally attached to humans.

A Message from the Author

Thank you very much for purchasing Volume 1!
This is the author, kiki. How did you enjoy *Roll Over and Die*? We got to see some characters who don't appear in the novel version, so I had a lot of fun reading it, too. It's like a dream come true to have the talented Minakata turn my novel into a manga. All the drama, fear, and excitement of scenes I'd imagined were amplified many times over through Minakata's skill. And every time I think about how I'll get to see Flum and Milkit get up to so many things in the manga, I can't help but get excited as a reader!

...Okay, I'll lay off the enthusiasm for now. There must be many of you wondering, "What kind of story is this work? Isn't it supposed to be slice-of-life?" To put it simply, it's a dark fantasy. All hope for slice-of-life has died. Flum, who was sold into slavery, wishes to "live an ordinary life in the capital." She'll fight for her life to achieve that. She'll go up against some very tough enemies. Her weapons are "the power of Reversal" and "Regeneration," as well as the people she wants to protect. Flum may be beaten down each time, but she'll fight like a wild woman until the day where she can finally live that ordinary life.

And so, Flum's battle has just begun.
See you in Volume 2!

--kiki

AFTERWORD

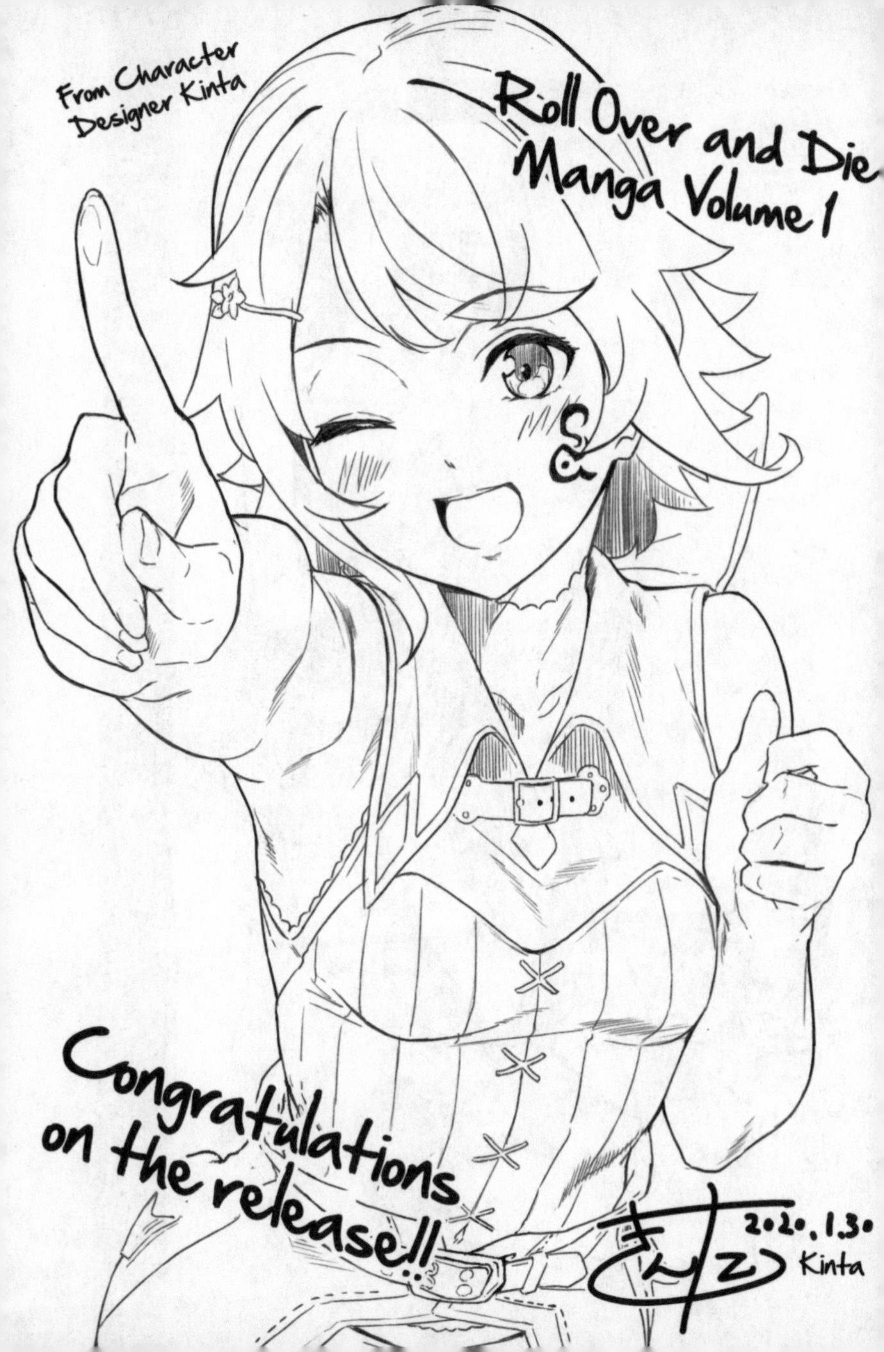
From Character Designer Kinta
Roll Over and Die Manga Volume 1
Congratulations on the release!!
2020.1.30
Kinta

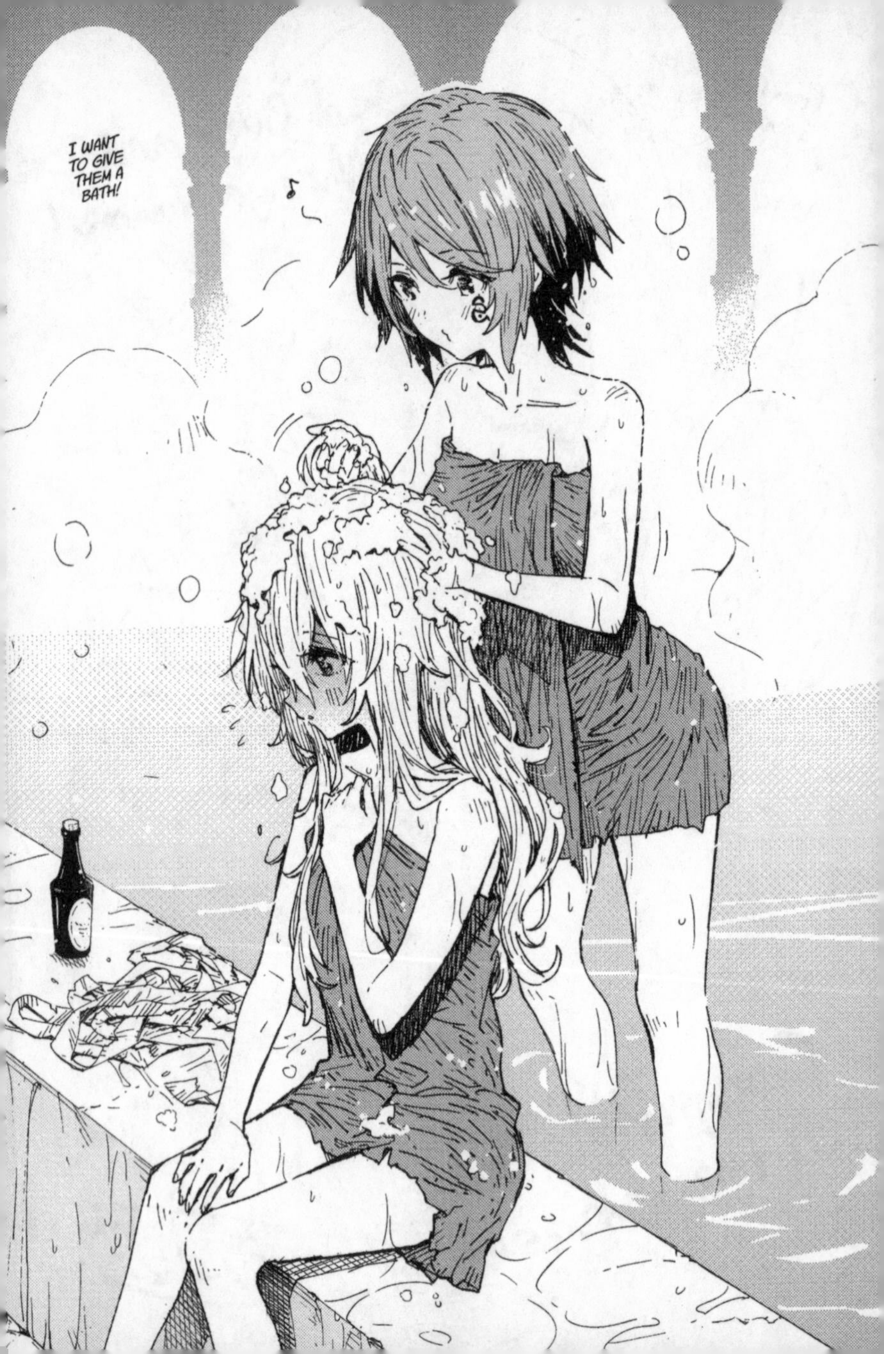
I WANT TO GIVE THEM A BATH!

SEVEN SEAS ENTERTAINMENT PRESENTS

ROLL OVER AND DIE

I Will Fight for an Ordinary Life with My Love and Cursed Sword!

VOLUME 1

story by **KIKI**   art by **SUNAO MINAKATA**   character design by **KINTA**

TRANSLATION
Christine Dashiell

LETTERING
Roland Amago
Bambi Eloriaga-Amago

LOGO DESIGN
George Panella

COVER DESIGN
Nicky Lim

PROOFREADER
Kurestin Armada

COPY EDITOR
Dawn Davis

EDITOR
J.P. Sullivan

PREPRESS TECHNICIAN
Rhiannon Rasmussen-Silverstein

PRODUCTION ASSISTANT
Christa Miesner

PRODUCTION MANAGER
Lissa Pattillo

MANAGING EDITOR
Julie Davis

ASSOCIATE PUBLISHER
Adam Arnold

PUBLISHER
Jason DeAngelis

「OMAEGOTOKI GA MAOU NI KATERUTO OMOUNA」TO YUUSHA PAATI WO
TSUIHOU SARETANODE OUTO DE KIMAMA NI KURASHITAI THE COMIC Vol. 1
©sunao minakata (Art) ©kiki (Original Story)
This edition originally published in Japan in 2020 by
MICRO MAGAZINE, INC., Tokyo.
English translation rights arranged with MICRO MAGAZINE, INC., Tokyo.

Seven Seas press and purchase enquiries can be sent to Marketing Manager Lianne
Sentar at press@gomanga.com. Information regarding the distribution and purchase of
digital editions is available from Digital Manager CK Russell at digital@gomanga.com.

Seven Seas and the Seven Seas logo are trademarks of
Seven Seas Entertainment. All rights reserved.

ISBN: 978-1-64827-071-0
Printed in Canada
First Printing: March 2021
10 9 8 7 6 5 4 3 2 1

//// READING DIRECTIONS ////

This book reads from *right to left*,
Japanese style. If this is your first time
reading manga, you start reading from
the top right panel on each page and
take it from there. If you get lost, just
follow the numbered diagram here.
It may seem backwards at first,
but you'll get the hang of it! Have fun!!

Follow us online: www.SevenSeasEntertainment.com